MASTERPIECES OF AMERICAN ROMANTIC LITERATURE

MASTERPIECES OF AMERICAN ROMANTIC LITERATURE

Melissa McFarland Pennell

Greenwood Introduces Literary Masterpieces

GREENWOOD PRESS
Westport, Connecticut • London

Library of Congress Cataloging-in-Publication Data

Pennell, Melissa McFarland.
    Masterpieces of American romantic literature / Melissa McFarland Pennell.
        p.   cm. — (Greenwood introduces literary masterpieces, ISSN 1545–6285)
    Includes bibliographical references (p.   ) and index.
    ISBN 0–313–33141–3 (alk. paper)
    1. American literature—19th century—History and criticism. 2. Romanticism—
United States. I. Title. II. Series.
PS217.R6P46 2006
810.9'145—dc22   2006007011

British Library Cataloguing in Publication Data is available.

Library of Congress Catalog Card Number: 2006007011
ISBN: 0–313–33141–3
ISSN: 1545–6285

First published in 2006

Greenwood Press, 88 Post Road West, Westport, CT 06881
An imprint of Greenwood Publishing Group, Inc.
www.greenwood.com

Printed in the United States of America

∞™

The paper used in this book complies with the
Permanent Paper Standard issued by the National
Information Standards Organization (Z39.48–1984).

10 9 8 7 6 5 4 3 2 1

For Sue
best sister ever

Contents

Preface

The chapters that follow provide critical introductions to works identified as masterpieces in the tradition of American Romanticism. These selections, including fiction, poetry, and nonfiction prose, reflect the range of views and interests that characterized the Romantic movement as a whole. The masterpieces under discussion include the novels *The Last of the Mohicans* (Cooper), *The Scarlet Letter* (Hawthorne), *Moby-Dick* (Melville), and *Uncle Tom's Cabin* (Stowe). Major poetic works include "The Raven" (Poe), *Evangeline* (Longfellow), and "Song of Myself" (Whitman), as well as a selection of lyrics by Dickinson. Three of Emerson's major essays and Thoreau's *Walden* present significant work shaped by the philosophy of Transcendentalism, while a selection of Poe's best-known tales represent his achievement in the gothic short story.

Each chapter offers an overview of the author's life and career, considering the biographical elements that had an impact on the writer's work as well as his or her connection to other writers associated with Romantic literature. It also contains explanations of the genre(s) in which the writer worked and his or her contributions to or innovations in that genre. Critical responses to the writer's work, both by contemporaries and by present-day critics, are incorporated into the discussion. The approach to the literary text itself features close reading. Those chapters that address fiction include analysis of setting and plot development; examination of major characters and the role of minor characters; and consideration of the themes that develop throughout the work. In the chapters that address poetry, attention is paid to form and style, diction and the use of figurative language, and the presence of allusions as means through which poets express their ideas and understanding. The chapters that focus on nonfiction prose address the arguments advanced within the texts and, in the case of *Walden*, the arrangement of chapters into a coherent whole. The bibliography includes biographical works and major critical commentaries on each of the writers addressed in this volume.

Acknowledgments

I wish to acknowledge the University of Massachusetts Lowell for support of my research. I thank my colleagues for their assistance and their patience as I worked to complete this project while assuming the duties of department chair. Thanks, as always, to my students, whose good questions help me to think more clearly about literature and why we read it. Thanks, too, to my family, whose support I appreciate. Lastly, I wish to express my deepest gratitude to my husband, Steve, whose unwavering encouragement, sense of humor, and generous understanding have made this and all things possible.

Introduction

Many discussions of the term Romanticism begin by explaining that the label is used to identify a broad movement encompassing art, literature, music, philosophy, politics, and cultural sensibilities in general. There is no simple definition of the term, and the debate continues over exactly what constitutes Romanticism and whether the term should still be used. There are, however, certain characteristics that most scholars agree were central to Romantic thinking: a focus on the individual, the subjective, and the spontaneous. This emphasis distinguished Romanticism from the Enlightenment outlook that preceded it. In fact, the various ideas that emerged as Romanticism took shape in the late eighteenth and early nineteenth centuries are sometimes referred to as constituting the Romantic rebellion or revolution, a rejection of the objectivity and empiricism that had defined intellectual understanding during the Age of Reason.

In the broader culture, ideas associated with Romanticism both instigated and grew out of the revolutionary movements that emerged in the United States and France as political philosophers argued that individuals could be self-governing. A primary impulse behind Romanticism was the desire to liberate the individual from that which limited self-realization and the exercise of individual thought, including oppressive government structures. Those who embraced the new sensibility of Romanticism also rejected the belief in human depravity and inherent sinfulness, endorsing instead the concept that humans were innately good. They also believed that emotion and intuition could provide avenues to truth. Many Romantic writers and artists as well as political and social critics embraced the idea of change, emphasizing flux and process, rather than accepting stasis or the perpetuation of the status quo.

In light of their interest in the individual, Romantics emphasized self-cultivation, a continual process of inner development, which allowed an individual to reach her or his full potential and, in the view of some, recognize the divinity within. They rejected the traditional concepts and practices of education, including the need to accept general truths and to learn by rote memorization. Instead they encouraged contemplation and self-awareness, direct contact with nature, and an exploration of inner feelings. Some, like the poet William Wordsworth, also encouraged adults to engage in recollections of childhood experiences, seeing in childhood the time when an individual enjoyed the most direct and unhampered relationship to nature and when the imagination was most active and alive. Many Romantics rejected the need to conform to social expectations or to behaviors and attributes identified as virtues by society. They argued that an individual lived best when he or she followed the dictates of his or her own vision and insight rather than externally imposed rules. Such thinking led to daring exploits on the part of some Romantics, whose dramatic lives, such as that of Lord Byron, often became as important as their art.

Authors and artists who are identified by the label Romantic attempted to find the extraordinary within the ordinary, to see the unique and individual within the common experiences of life. They emphasized intensity of feeling and experience instead of the moderation and restraint preferred by their predecessors. Rather than studying tradition and the representative type, writers and artists in the Romantic era viewed imagination and the original as appropriate sources and subjects of creative work. They also sought to free themselves from rules of composition and style that they saw as inhibitions to artistic expression and the work of genius. Many had mixed feelings about the past, some wishing to break from it, to undermine its influence in order to find the new and innovative. Others looked to the distant past as a source of inspiration.

INFLUENCE OF BRITISH LITERARY ROMANTICISM

Although the term Romanticism was first applied to literary work by the German poet Friedrich Schlegel, it was soon taken up in France and England as well. When it was initially used by some critics, however, it carried a derogatory connotation, so that many of the poets and artists first labeled Romantic rejected the term.

Many of the traits and trends associated with Romanticism did not suddenly burst upon the literary and artistic scene, but grew out of ideas and techniques that had been evolving in the late eighteenth century and are sometimes called proto-Romantic. These include the emergence of the gothic novel and the novel of sentiment, as well as the interest in primitivism and the sublime. Both the gothic novel and the sentimental novel focused on human emotion, although the gothic relied on terror, while the sentimental emphasized sympathy. The gothic novel explored the irrational and unexplained, allowing authors to challenge reason and the scientific method as the sole sources of truth. The sentimental novel, on the other hand, treated the bonds of human affection and innate benevolence that allowed an individual to respond to the pain of others. Those interested in primitivism drew on arguments that humans were corrupted by social institutions and operations of civilization advanced by philosophers like Rousseau. Through their examination of "uncivilized" or "primitive" cultures, those who embraced primitivism found evidence of innocence and inherent human goodness, revealed especially in a simple and direct relationship to nature. Interest in nature also influenced the concept of the sublime, which explored the strong emotions, including awe and terror, inspired by scenes of natural wonder and vastness.

Although debate exists over the official start of the Romantic period, the year 1798, in which appeared the first edition of Lyrical Ballads by William Wordsworth and Samuel Taylor Coleridge, tends to be used in many literary histories. This volume of poetry celebrated the personal lyric poem, with its expression of a subjective vision, as a literary form worthy of as much respect as the more public forms of epic and satire. In his poems especially, Wordsworth looked to country life as a source of subject matter for verse, seeing in it simplicity and a closer relationship to nature than urban dwellers experienced. He did not wish to create idealized pastorals written in elevated poetic diction, instead arguing that common language was appropriate for verse. He emphasized the value of everyday life as a fit subject for poetry and saw in nature a moral influence that could be apprehended through feeling. He rejected an intellectual approach to poetry that denied the value of human feeling. The second edition of Lyrical Ballads included a preface in which Wordsworth defended his approach to poetry, arguing that nature could inspire powerful feelings that were later recollected by the poet and expressed in the form of poems.

The poems that Coleridge contributed to Lyrical Ballads were strikingly different from those of Wordsworth. For Coleridge, imagination was crucial to the composition of poetry, and he saw imagination in its purest form as the source of original ideas. Interested in dream-visions and the unconscious, Coleridge infused his poems with complex symbolism and the workings of the supernatural. His best-known poem from the collection, "The Rime of the Ancient Mariner," explores the fate of its narrator, who recounts his violation of the relationship with the natural world through his killing of an albatross and the fate that then befalls him. His redemption comes through his recognition of the interconnectedness of all creation, a lesson he must share with all who listen. Coleridge's interest in the supernatural, the effects of terror and strong emotion, and his own experience of drug-induced visions also link him to what is sometimes labeled dark Romanticism, an aspect of the overall movement that is more pessimistic about human nature and that acknowledges the presence of evil and the effects of unrestrained impulses. Coleridge was interested in the philosophical arguments that shaped romanticism, and his prose work, especially the *Biographia Literaria* (1817) influenced the thinking of later writers, especially on the topics of imagination and creativity.

As the movement labeled Romanticism continued to unfold, other British poets, including John Keats, Percy Bysshe Shelley, and Lord Byron, also influenced the thinking of their contemporaries. In his poems, Keats focused on the apprehension of beauty and the ways that works of art resisted the ravages of time. Shelley's personal sensitivity and commitment to nonconformity, as well as his explorations of beauty and the power of the imagination in his lyric poems, made him a major voice within the Romantic movement. Byron's creation of the daring, mysterious, and darkly passionate rebel (a role he played in his own life) who came to be known as the "Byronic hero" was a lasting contribution to the tradition. Prose writers, including novelists, also had an influence, particularly Walter Scott, whose establishment of the historical novel as both a serious and popular mode of fiction inspired imitators both in Britain and America. Mary Shelley's *Frankenstein*, which combined gothic elements with an interrogation of Romantic beliefs and ideologies, contributed to the vein of dark Romanticism.

AMERICAN CONTEXTS

Although some debate exists over the exact dating of the period marked by the flourishing of American Romanticism, the years 1820 to 1865 are generally agreed to be the core of the era. American authors and poets embraced the revolution in consciousness associated with Romanticism and looked to the work of their British antecedents as starting points for their own creative endeavors. They were, however, also committed to producing a national literature that would be distinctly American rather than imitative of their British counterparts. For some, this meant focusing on the American landscape as a setting, while others looked to America's colonial past as a source of history that was uniquely American. Still others believed that by advancing a democratic aesthetic in their work, one that challenged concepts of hierarchy and privilege, they would be true to the principles articulated in the Declaration of Independence and the Constitution. A variety of factors in the U.S. political, economic, and social environment during the first half of the nineteenth century also influenced the work of American writers. Among them were the emergence of Jacksonian democracy, the rise of industrialization and market capitalism, the interest in social reform, and the belief in progress.

In the 1820s, support for the increased participation of the common man in U.S. politics grew, as pressures were brought to bear to extend suffrage to all white men of legal age, regardless of their status as landholders. This had the effect of altering the political and social landscape, as individuals who had previously been excluded from government found opportunities not only to vote, but through their political participation to secure government employment as part of the patronage or "spoils" system that President Andrew Jackson instituted. Jackson, conditioned by the Western frontier, was viewed by many of his supporters as a figure whose background reflected their own interests and experiences in contrast to politicians from the settled Eastern seaboard who were often resistant to change and concerned with preserving their own economic and social advantages. Supporters of Jacksonian democracy were committed to the continuation of westward expansion until the United States stretched from the Atlantic to the Pacific, an idea that came to be known as Manifest Destiny.

While political changes were underway, America also saw profound changes take place in its economy and in its basic understanding of work. In the first two decades of the nineteenth century, many projects were undertaken to expand the nation's transportation infrastructure, including the construction of canals and bridges. By the late 1830s, the railroad also made the transportation of people and goods easier and faster. The Industrial Revolution, which began in the Northeast in the early decades of the century, changed the landscape and the social consciousness of the North. Mechanization began to affect many types of manufacture, and factories enabled mass production of consumer goods such as textiles, shoes, and household items. Individuals who were used to living on farms or in small villages and whose rhythm of life had followed the cycle of the seasons moved to factory towns and growing cities, where their days were governed by the clock and the factory bell. Some individuals praised the Industrial Revolution as a sign of progress, predicting that it would allow for greater human freedom, while others saw it as introducing "wage" slavery, which they thought was little better than the chattel slavery of the South. Critics of the system also questioned the idea of market capitalism, in which individuals made money by investing, rather than by their own direct labor.

Inspired to realize what they believed were the ideals of America, including the possibility of what the Constitution calls "a more perfect Union," Americans throughout the nineteenth century embraced reform movements, some aimed at individuals and others aimed at the culture as a whole. Some of these reforms were influenced by changes in religious sensibility, as evangelical sects, particularly the Methodists working in frontier encampments, began to preach that individuals could change their lives and work to prepare for salvation. This stood in sharp contrast to the doctrines that had been preached in colonial New England, the concepts of election and predestination, that had placed salvation solely at God's discretion. Other liberalizing trends in religion, particularly the rise of Unitarianism and later Transcendentalism, focused on concepts of self-cultivation and the ability of every individual to achieve his or her full intellectual and creative potential. Reformers who focused on the individual believed that society itself would improve when its members had changed their lives. Other popular reforms directed at the individual included temperance, diet, and hygiene.

Reform movements also focused on change at the societal level, particularly reforms concerned with liberty and equality. Two of the most important reform movements to emerge in the first half of the nineteenth century were anti-slavery (its more radical branch called abolition) and women's rights. These two movements were closely intertwined. Women who dedicated themselves to the anti-slavery cause and gained experience in the public sphere through their activities gradually embraced the ideal of full political and social equality for women as well. Those Americans who supported the anti-slavery cause saw slavery as a moral wrong and an institution that made a mockery of the principles articulated in the Declaration of Independence and the Constitution. Throughout the period identified with American Romanticism, the crisis over slavery deepened, resulting in the eruption of the Civil War in 1861. Although the campaign for women's rights did not divide the country in quite the same way, it provoked strong resistance from those who feared that changes in the roles and rights of women would threaten the foundation of social order.

The popularity of reform movements reflected the belief in progress, the possibility of continual change that would lead to better lives for all

Americans. This idea both grew out of and sustained Romantic thinking in America. It emphasized optimism about the future, about the limitless potential inherent within the United States as a nation, and about the ways that America could turn aside from the burden of the past. A number of the authors associated with Romanticism in America embraced this concept of progress; others critiqued it, seeing human potential as more limited and social relations as more complex.

Within this context of social, political, and economic change, the writers discussed in the chapters that follow embraced tenets of Romanticism that had been formulated in England and on the Continent but modified them in accordance with American outlooks and experience. The dynamic artistic and intellectual activity of the period encouraged experimentation and inspired works of originality and brilliance that defined an American tradition in literature.

1

James Fenimore Cooper
The Last of the Mohicans
1826

During his career, James Fenimore Cooper was at times referred to as the American Walter Scott, a comparison to the successful British writer of historical romances that he came to resent. His historical romances, including the Leatherstocking Tales, echoed many of the themes and techniques used by Sir Walter Scott, author of such popular works as *Waverly* and *Ivanhoe*. Like Scott, Cooper explored conflicts between competing cultures, often setting his fictions during times of war or rebellion. Cooper also explored codes of conduct that governed individual behavior, adapting Scott's treatment of chivalry to life on the American frontier, and emphasizing distinctions of class and race among his characters. Although the association with Scott and the tradition of romance earned him the scorn of realist writers like Mark Twain in the post–Civil War era, Cooper enjoyed a successful career, producing 32 novels. He was among the first American authors to earn a substantial living from his writing career. He was also one of the first American authors to find a wide audience in Europe; his detailed descriptions of the American setting drew praise from reviewers and authors, such as the French novelists Honore de Balzac and Victor Hugo.

In his Leatherstocking Tales, Cooper explored America's past and its frontier as a means of discerning the roots of the culture that defined the American character. He created a mythic woodsman, Natty Bumppo, who appears in all five novels and is known by various names, including Deerslayer, Pathfinder, and Hawk-eye. Bumppo embodies a way of life that is free from the constraints of civilization, yet he follows a strict code of conduct and reveres the wilderness, which he often interprets as expressive of truths about human nature. Among the Leatherstocking Tales, *The Last of the Mohicans*, with its action-filled narrative of adventure and pursuit, has remained the most popular. A play based upon the novel was produced as early as 1831, and it has also been adapted as an opera and a ballet. Twenty-four films based on the novel have been produced, from the first in 1909 directed by D. W. Griffith to the 1992 version by Michael Mann.

BIOGRAPHICAL CONTEXT

Usually associated with Cooperstown, the community in upstate New York that bears his family name, James Cooper was born in Burlington, New Jersey, in 1789, the twelfth child of William and Elizabeth (Fenimore) Cooper. When Cooper was still an infant, his family moved to Lake Otsego, northeast of present day Oneonta, and his father established a settlement in what was still a frontier region. James and some of his brothers attended public school in Cooperstown; he later enrolled in Yale College in 1803. A less-than-diligent student, James was dismissed from the college at the age of 16, after a series of destructive pranks provoked school authorities. He returned to Cooperstown, where he studied with a private tutor and began to prepare for his future.

Like many young men, he entertained romantic notions of the adventurous life to be had at sea, so he signed on to the merchant vessel, the *Stirling*, in 1806–1807, visiting England and Spain. His father secured a commission for him in the U.S. Navy as midshipman in 1808. He was stationed at Fort Oswego, an outpost on Lake Ontario, where he saw firsthand more of the frontier environment that was to figure so prominently in his novels. Cooper's experiences at sea and his later financial interest in the whaler *The Union* provided him with material for the many successful sea novels that he produced. The plans Cooper had for his life changed in 1809 when his father died. Cooper inherited a cash legacy and a share in his father's estate. He requested a leave from the Navy and returned to Cooperstown to help settle family affairs. Cooper resigned his naval commission and married Susanna De Lancey, the daughter of a wealthy Westchester County family, on New Year's Day 1811. The couple initially settled at one of her family properties in Mamaroneck, New York, but during the first few years of marriage moved back and forth between Cooperstown and Westchester County. During this period, Cooper lived as a gentleman farmer but struggled financially.

According to family legend, in 1819 Cooper was reading a recently published novel to his wife and, finding it so poorly done, cast it aside and claimed he could do better. His wife laughed at his declaration, but Cooper began work on a manuscript that became his first novel, *Precaution*, published in 1820. This novel of manners met with little success, but Cooper fared much better with his second novel, *The Spy* (1821), a historical novel set during the American Revolution. One of the reviewers of *The Spy* criticized Cooper for his lack of specificity in describing the American landscape. In his next novel, *The Pioneers* (1823), for which he drew on his own experiences growing up in a frontier settlement, Cooper demonstrated his ability to capture the natural scene through descriptive detail. *The Pioneers* launched the Leatherstocking Tales, a series of novels that have been among Cooper's most enduring contributions to American literature. In the early 1820s, he moved his family to New York City, where he had more opportunity to interact with painters, poets, and other professionals.

Energized by his success, Cooper embarked on a remarkable period of productivity, writing two sea novels, *The Pilot* (1824) and *The Red Rover* (1827), another historical romance, *Lionel Lincoln* (1825), and two more Leatherstocking Tales, *The Last of the Mohicans* (1826) and *The Prairie* (1827). Responses to these works varied. Some reviewers praised Cooper's interest in America's historical past; others criticized his lack of fidelity to historical detail and his improbable plots. Most reviews commented on the importance of Cooper's having demonstrated that American subjects and settings were suitable for romance, but many felt that his narratives tended to be repetitious, with a certain predictability of character and event. Despite these criticisms, Cooper's works sold well, and the reading public, including that of Europe, welcomed new works by him.

In the midst of this period of intense activity, the Coopers moved to Europe in 1826, stopping first in England and then settling in France. In 1828, Cooper returned to England to finish and see into publication *Notions of the Americans* (1828), a book designed to dispel mistaken impressions about American customs, ideas, and characters held by Europeans, especially the English. The book irritated many English reviewers, who found it to be full of bragging and hyperbole on American virtues, but Cooper was intent on delineating the separation of American culture from that of the Old World. While in Europe, he completed his next historical novel, *The Wept of Wish-ton-Wish* (1829), set during King Philip's War, and *The Water-Witch* (1830), a sea tale.

In the fall of 1833, the Coopers returned to America, a country that had changed since their departure seven years earlier. Cooper was dissatisfied by the America that he saw, and he expressed his views in *A Letter to His Countrymen* (1834). The book alienated many Americans, who felt that Cooper, a professed republican, was expressing anti-republican views. Cooper returned to Cooperstown, where he purchased the original family home, Otsego Hall. During this time, he was also busy producing political articles and travel writings, although his fiction had declined in popularity in America. By 1837, he and his family were living in Cooperstown, where Cooper became entangled in legal battles over property rights with some of his neighbors. Attacked in the newspapers, Cooper filed libel suits, which again cost him popularity and reputation. During this time he published *Homeward Bound* (1838) and *Home as Found* (1838), novels that expressed his critical views of American culture.

In 1839, Cooper resumed work on the Leatherstocking Tales, writing *The Pathfinder* (1840) and then *The Deerslayer* (1841), which is chronologically the earliest of the Natty Bumppo narratives. Cooper continued writing throughout the 1840s, producing naval histories, biographies, and fiction. By 1850, his health was failing, but he continued to write until he became too weak to hold a pen in the summer of 1851. James Fenimore Cooper died on September 14, 1851, one day shy of his 62nd birthday. He was buried in the family graveyard at Cooperstown.

GENRE

The genre of the historical novel/romance developed in the late eighteenth and early nineteenth century, as writers attempted to explore and celebrate national origins and identities by looking at the past. They particularly examined moments in time when two cultures were in conflict—one experiencing decline and failure, the other ascendancy and success. Fictional characters as well as historical figures participate in the events of the historical moment, reflecting the impact of these events not only in the past but as a legacy to the future. In early nineteenth-century America, writers were attempting to define a unique American identity that corresponded to the ideals of the new nation. To distinguish their work from that of their European counterparts, American authors turned their attention to a setting and a cultural opponent specific to the American experience: the frontier and the American Indian.

A subgenre of the historical romance is the frontier romance, which takes place between space defined and regulated by civilization and space demarcated as wilderness. In this borderland, characters from both spaces meet and interact, and their competing interests, values, and drives generate the conflicts that shape the plot. For some American authors in the nineteenth century, the frontier romance also served as a means of justifying America's westward expansion as part of the inevitable progress of history. They saw the culture of white Protestant America as being in a period of ascendancy, while that of the American Indian was fated to disappear. In *Mohicans*, Cooper uses conversations between Hawk-eye and Chingachgook to raise questions about the relationship between whites and Indians, especially in terms of the taking of Indian lands and the settlers' desecration of the wilderness.

The frontier romance, especially in its treatment of Native Americans, blends elements from captivity narratives and from the romantic ideal of the "noble savage." Captivity narratives, published in the seventeenth and eighteenth centuries, recounted the experiences of white settlers who were captured by Indians and carried away to live in Indian villages. The narratives recounted harsh travels through wilderness, and many depicted cruelty and lack of compassion on the part of Indian captors. These narratives also underscored the idea of two peoples competing for possession and control of the continent, emphasizing the cultural otherness of the Indians and therefore their expendability in the process of conquest. The romantic ideal of the noble savage complicates the treatment of Native Americans in the frontier romance. It asserts that those who are products of the primitive and untamed wilderness are untainted by the evils of civilization and retain an original innocence and virtue that their civilized counterparts lack. Thus, in Cooper's fiction and in many other frontier romances, the Indians are divided between "good" figures, such as Chingachgook and Uncas, and "bad," such as Magua and his Huron brethren. Ultimately, this distinction makes no difference, for the "good" as well as the "bad" are destined to disappear.

THE LAST OF THE MOHICANS

In *The Last of the Mohicans*, Cooper is keenly aware of the cultural shift occurring in his own day, as Americans participated in westward expansion and moved further away from the settled Eastern seaboard to the frontier and the "unknown" lands of the west. He sets *The Last of the Mohicans* at the frontier and in the wilderness of eighteenth-century New York. This allows him to consider questions that pertain not only to America's past, but to his own time, including the process of history and the ideology of empire that entails the triumph of one nation and people at the expense of another.

Setting and Plot Development

In *Mohicans*, two significant elements of setting are at work: the historical events of 1757 and the natural landscape of upstate New York. Cooper addresses the period of the French and Indian War (1754–1763), specifically the massacre at Fort William Henry (1757). The French and Indian War was a culmination of the rivalry between England and France for control of the North American continent. Three earlier wars had been fought between these opposing forces, but the French and Indian War encompassed a greater sweep of territory, focusing initially on control of the Ohio Valley but soon extending into New York and Canada. In addition to the regular armies and colonial militias, both European powers cultivated alliances with Native American tribes in the region, including the powerful Iroquois or Six Nations. Initially the French prevailed, but Britain eventually won the war. This conflict of cultures shapes the first half of *Mohicans*, as Cooper treats the presence of Montcalm and the actions that take place at Fort William Henry as a microcosm of the larger contest between French and English influences on what will become the American identity.

Writing his fiction during the era when the Hudson River School of American painters was active, Cooper shared their interest in capturing the American landscape as a fit subject of art and celebrating its evocative powers. In *Mohicans*, the natural landscape of upstate New York, especially the region surrounding Lake George, which Cooper calls by its Indian name, Horican, plays a dominant role. This territory is divided into two parts in the novel: the relatively known environment that lies between Fort Edward and Fort William Henry, through which the characters travel in the first half of the novel, and the unknown environment of the Adirondack wilderness that frames the second half of the novel. Cooper develops both of these environments in great detail. Lakes and waterways are particularly important, often serving as reflective surfaces that magnify the beauty of the woods that surround them, and through their own clarity and purity suggesting the undefiled state of the wilderness. However, in chapter 18, following the massacre at William Henry, the condition of the Horican underscores the defilement of nature through human warfare as "the green and angry waters lashed the shores, as if indignantly casting back its impurities to the polluted strand" (678).

Within the natural setting, Cooper develops his narrative around the quest motif, creating two separate quests, each of which shapes half the novel. The quest motif appeals to writers of romance, for it entails a narrative of adventure that ultimately results in either self-knowledge or cultural validation. In traditional quests, a hero must follow a dangerous path to achieve some purpose. He faces trials and challenges along the way that will test his worthiness or suitableness for the quest. In *Mohicans*, Cooper modifies this motif to suit his purposes, not only by creating two separate quests that involve largely the same characters, but by shifting the main performer of the quest from Duncan Heyward in the first half of the novel to Uncas in the second half.

In *The Last of the Mohicans*, the first quest is shaped by the conflict between British and French forces, as Duncan Heyward has been commissioned to deliver the Munro sisters, Cora and Alice, to their father's keeping at Fort William Henry. Ultimately, this quest is successful, but not through Heyward's agency alone. Heyward proves to be an ill-prepared hero whose knowledge of military procedure does him little good once he departs the safety of Fort Edward and enters the forest, which is governed by a different set of rules. A small band of travelers, including Heyward, the Munro sisters, and their Indian guide Magua, departs from Fort Edward along with troops that General Webb has dispatched to Fort William Henry to prepare for Montcalm's attack. Magua, whom Heyward assumes is reliable because he has served British forces, claims that he can deliver the party more quickly to Fort William Henry via a shortcut through the forest. This deviation from the main path not only forces the travelers to make a more difficult passage, but places Heyward in an environment that he does not understand, increasing his dependence upon Magua. The travelers are joined unexpectedly by David Gamut, whose own ignorance of the wilderness adds to the danger they face. Cooper shapes this situation as a disaster waiting to happen, and, if Magua has his way, it will.

Fortunately for Heyward's party, Natty Bumppo, known as Hawk-eye, and his friends Chingachgook and Uncas are traveling in the same wilderness. They are surprised to find the small party of travelers in the woods, and Hawk-eye quickly discerns that Heyward does not understand the peril in which they have placed themselves. Heyward attempts to behave by the rules of military conduct and hierarchy, but Hawk-eye explains, "Whoever comes into the woods to deal with the natives, must use Indian fashions, if he would wish to prosper in his undertakings" (514). This becomes one of the challenges that Heyward faces on both quests: can he adapt to the new circumstances of the frontier rather than rely upon the civilized world's book-knowledge that Natty Bumppo so disdains? Initially Heyward demonstrates his inability to grasp what Hawk-eye is telling him. He disregards Hawk-eye's instructions, allowing Magua to escape into the forest. This becomes a pattern in the characters' interactions with Magua, also known as *le Renard Subtil* or the Sly Fox. Magua adeptly reads his opponents' intentions and, until the end of the novel, makes his moves before others can act.

Knowing that they cannot travel at night because of the Indian warriors roaming the forest, Hawk-eye decides to conceal the travelers at Glenn's (now Glen's Falls) in a secluded cavern known only to Hawk-eye and his companions. Reaching a place of relative safety, the travelers view their rescuers through the lenses of class and race prejudice. They see Hawk-eye's "rude equipments" and "blunt address" (528) as signs that he is not their social peer, and they question whether Uncas's nobility of face and form can be indicative of virtue, given that he is a "savage" (529). Once in the cave, the men attempt to create an approximation of domestic space for the comfort of the women. Through this scene, Cooper introduces the tension between the wilderness and the domestic, for the domestic is associated with the taming of the frontier and settlement. Their efforts are disrupted by a wild screech, the sound of their terrified horses, reminding them that such a domestication has yet to happen.

The dawn attack by Magua's confederates reasserts the danger that awaits in the forest. Through the activity that follows, Cooper brings the first quest to a close. In scenes of intense activity, the small band fends off the first and second of Magua's assaults, but they discover that their remaining ammunition has been stolen, leaving them defenseless. Cora convinces Hawk-eye to go with Chingachgook and Uncas to get help from her father. The Hurons return and take the party, left in Heyward's care, into captivity. For a brief period, Magua asserts his power, offering to free all but Cora, whom he wishes to take as his wife. He plans to use her as an instrument of revenge against her father who had humiliated Magua by whipping him in front of the garrison. Hawk-eye returns and, with the help of Chingachgook and Uncas, frees the captives. The journey to Fort William Henry resumes, still under the threat of danger posed by the French forces that surrounded the fort. Heyward's knowledge of French allows the party to pass unmolested, and after a final trial of finding their way in the fog, the sisters are delivered, almost literally, into their father's arms.

Cooper separates the two quests with the interlude at Fort William Henry in chapters 15 and 16. This interlude provides a period of stasis in the narrative, despite the fact that the fort remains under siege by the French. Cooper uses his powers of description to convey the tranquility and beauty of the landscape, emphasizing its romantic aspects visible when the two opponents have declared a truce and "everything wore the appearance of a day of pleasure" (640). In light of the cessation of hostile action, the Munro family enjoys a moment of domestic peace, as father and daughters find relief in "the security of the moment" (650). Heyward also discusses domestic matters with Munro, professing his love for and desire to marry one of Munro's daughters. Mistaking Heyward's intentions, Munro is surprised to learn that Heyward's choice is Alice. Cooper takes this opportunity to let Munro tell his family's history, in which he reveals Cora's mixed race background. Munro confronts Heyward about his "southern" mindset in which "these unfortunate beings are considered of a race inferior to your own" (653). Heyward denies that he holds her lineage against Cora, but his embarrassment reveals otherwise. Heyward is relieved to hear the story of Munro's second marriage, which confirms Alice's "white" identity, making her in Heyward's eyes a suitable partner for him.

In the state of warfare, the domestic interlude cannot last. Munro relies on Heyward to conduct negotiations for the fort's surrender. Montcalm promises that the surrender will occur in honorable fashion, but chapter 17 details the bloody massacre that ensues as the defeated English leave the fort and its surrounding encampment. French troops do not fire, but their Indian allies, led by Magua, rain terror down upon the British. Cooper presents in detail some of the horrors that occur and depicts the Indians as bloodthirsty, "many among them kneeled to the earth, and drank freely, exultingly, hellishly, of the crimson tide" (672), echoing the language and attitude found in captivity narratives. The massacre brings to a close the "historical" portion of the narrative. Cora and Alice are again carried into captivity, and to effect their rescue, their male protectors must enter into wilderness controlled by the Indians.

The captivity sets in motion the second quest within the narrative, this time to be undertaken by Uncas, who, in answer to Munro's plea, "Give me my child!" replies, "Uncas will try" (682). In the second quest, Uncas emerges as a tragic figure who demonstrates his perfection in wilderness skills but who ultimately fails in his quest. Cooper reveals through this failure that even though Uncas has perfected the ways of the Indian world, that environment is changing through the presence of whites. Uncas's skills and the culture they represent will give way before the pattern of conquest and settlement that Major Heyward and Alice Munro represent. The second quest takes place in the sphere of action where Indian laws still rule, and Magua can use his rhetorical skill in the Indian language to motivate others to obey him. Magua emerges as a powerful enemy in the second quest, but he, too, cannot stop what Cooper sees as the progress of history, the eventual domination of the wilderness by white American culture. The second quest is more complex, and through it Cooper raises the problematic elements of his narrative, including the destruction of the Native American peoples and his views on the impossibility of achieving a multiracial American identity.

The second quest also focuses on the immersion of white characters in an alien world. In order to move through that world, some characters don disguises that temporarily alter their identities. To enter the Huron village, Heyward disguises himself as a madman and passes himself off as a French healer. When he is questioned by the Hurons about his appearance, Heyward answers, "My brothers have given me paint, and I wear it" (742), claiming an identification with the Indians that he does not feel. Heyward never loses sight of his true purpose—to free Alice and return her to the safety of civilization—nor his true identity as a white man shaped by the values of the "civilized" world. During this same episode, Hawk-eye steals the bear costume of a shaman and wears it to make his own safe passage through the village.

While in the Huron camp, Heyward witnesses the delivery of Uncas, who has been captured by a war party. Cooper uses the scene that follows as an opportunity to intensify the personal enmity between Uncas and Magua, for Uncas provokes Magua through slurs against the Hurons' courage. Magua responds by demonstrating his power as an orator, ultimately demanding the death of Uncas. To create suspense over Uncas's fate, Cooper shifts the focus back to Heyward and his effort to rescue Alice in what may be one of the most improbable episodes in the novel. Hawk-eye, attired in the bear costume, subdues Magua, and Heyward carries Alice to safety while Hawk-eye returns to free Uncas. Suffering embarrassment at his enemies' successful escape, Magua's wrath is further provoked. He again uses his powers of rhetoric to stir up the Hurons and motivate them to seek revenge, while seeking cooperation of the Delawares in the return of his hostages.

The Delawares agree that a formal assembly of the nation must decide the question, and this requires the presence of Tamenund, the wisest of the elders and a venerated chief. This assembly serves two purposes: it impedes the forward momentum of the narrative, and it allows for the revelation of Uncas's true identity. Ironically, Magua contributes to this process by making a speech before the assembly, in which he praises the origins of the Delawares before he asks for his prisoners. Tamenund consents to Magua's request, but Cora steps forward to make an impassioned plea for Uncas to be heard. In this appearance before the assembled nation, Uncas reveals the turtle tattooed upon his breast, the sign that he is a descendant of the original Uncas and a line of chiefs who have upheld the Delaware nation. Uncas convinces Tamenund to release the prisoners, except for Cora, who, under Indian law, is justly claimed by Magua. Uncas has no intention of allowing Magua to keep Cora and prepares the Delawares for war through a ritual dance, chanting a war song and claiming his rightful place as their leader.

Through the novel's climax, Cooper attempts to eradicate the problematic issue of racial mixing as he brings the second quest to its close. Cooper infuses the final battle scene with symbolic elements to heighten its importance to his major themes. In pursuit of Magua, Uncas ascends the mountain until he is above his opponent, signifying his rise to power and his superiority, but he must lower himself literally and figuratively to battle his enemy and attempt to save Cora. Magua has brought Cora with him up the mountain, stopping on a ledge when she refuses to go farther. Forcing the moment of crisis, Magua unsheathes his knife, a symbolically sexual action, and bids Cora choose between his wigwam and death. As he is about to stab Cora, Magua is startled by the piercing cry of Uncas, who leaps down to challenge him. One of Magua's warriors fatally stabs Cora. Magua, angered by this action and by the appearance of Uncas, buries his tomahawk in Uncas's back, "a dastardly deed" (862). Mortally wounded, Uncas again demonstrates his superiority, killing the warrior who stabbed Cora to avenge her death, then facing Magua to receive his deathblow with utter disdain for his Huron enemy. Magua, confident that he will escape once again, misses the precipice he seeks and, shot by Hawk-eye, plunges to his death.

The last chapter records the Indian funeral rites for Uncas and Cora, during which references are made to the possibility of their reunion in the afterlife. Hawk-eye rejects this, seeing "the error of their simple creed" and later informing the Indian women who have attended to Cora's burial that "the spirit of the pale-face has no need of food or raiment—their gifts being accorded to the heaven of their colour" (873). When Munro raises the possibility of all assembling before the throne of God "without distinction of sex, or rank, or colour" (874), Hawk-eye again rejects this as something that controverts the natural order. Hawk-eye can profess his own friendship with Chingachgook, through which he offers consolation for the loss of Uncas, because it respects differences and does not confuse "natural" boundaries. In the elegiac close of the novel, Tamenund announces that the "pale-faces are masters of the earth" (877), and the death of the "last warrior of the wise race of the Mohicans" (878) foreshadows the passing of an entire Indian nation.

Major Characters

Cooper's contemporary reviewers and critics ever since have noted his lack of skill for creating convincing characters. Many of Cooper's characters are flat types, representing certain races or social classes but failing to develop as individual beings. Cooper often asserts that one's gifts and actions are determined by "blood," one's racial background, so his characters are limited in what they can be and do. This aspect of Cooper's thinking disturbs modern readers whose understanding of human development incorporates the significance of environment and culture in the shaping of an individual. One of the ways that Cooper attempts to enhance character development involves pairing or doubling so that one character serves at times as a foil or an alter ego to another, bringing out important traits in each. This pattern of doubling complements the use of the dual quests in *Mohicans* to advance Cooper's themes and outlook. In *Mohicans*, Cooper also uses his characters' responses to the wilderness in which they travel as a means of revealing more about them.

As the figure who links the five Leatherstocking Tales, Natty Bumppo exists as the center of the novel. In his 1831 introduction, Cooper describes Natty Bumppo as "a man of native goodness, removed from the temptations of civilized life, though not entirely forgetful of its prejudices and lessons" (475). Modeled in part on Daniel Boone (1734–1820), whose legendary skills as a frontiersman contributed to the process of westward expansion, Hawk-eye, as Bumppo is known in *Mohicans*, has lived in the wilderness and has become as adept as his Indian friends in reading that wilderness and in responding to its demands. He is self-disciplined and self-reliant, keeping his relationships with others, even his good friend Chingachgook, formal. He resists intimacy with women and the limitations such intimacy would impose on him. Hawk-eye serves as an intermediary figure between the settlements and the wilderness. He sees the impulses of settlement bringing destruction to the world he loves, and yet he is also tied to those forces by his role as a scout for the military. Ultimately a solitary figure, despite his friendship with Chingachgook, he becomes a prototype for numerous figures in American literature, including Twain's Huckleberry Finn and Hemingway's Nick Adams.

Natty Bumppo's ability to keep his emotions in check allows him to maintain his "stern and unyielding morality" (555). He also ties morality to race. He excuses Chingachgook's killing of the French scout as being in his "nature" when it would have been wrong for a white man, and he explains his decision not to kill Magua while he is powerless in the cave by claiming that it would have been expected from an Indian but not a white. He carries the conviction that what God or Providence wills cannot be changed, that "what is to happen will happen" (526). This, too, affects his ideas on race, for he believes that the separation of people into distinct racial groups, each with its own gifts and attributes, is part of a foreordained plan for the order of the world. Bumppo repeatedly notes that, despite his wilderness skills and his upbringing by Indians, he is "a man without a cross," white in his identity and his "gifts." He is particularly troubled by the possibility of racial mixing, for he sees in it the potential for social disorder when what he believes are fixed distinctions become blurred.

In contrast to Hawk-eye, Duncan Heyward has been shaped by the traditions and expectations of the civilized world. He often expresses a sense of superiority toward those around him, although he lacks wilderness survival skills and depends on those of others. He believes he is a subtle and gifted negotiator, but both Magua and Montcalm outsmart him. Heyward's time on the frontier and in the wilderness is a period of education based on direct experience. On the frontier and in the wilderness, Heyward's ideas are undermined by the lay of the land and the conduct of opponents. Heyward himself thinks "the foresters had some secret means of intelligence, which had escaped the vigilance of his own faculties" (696). In the final battle between the Delawares and the Hurons, Hawk-eye wants Heyward to learn how to behave in the wilderness and how to anticipate the actions of his enemies. Hawk-eye perceives that Heyward will be part of the force of conquest that will eventually subdue the wilderness and make it suitable for settlement and the spread of civilization. He also appears to be preparing Heyward, as a proto-American, for the kind of war the colonial forces will wage against the British regulars during the American Revolution.

While Heyward discovers the need to think in different ways in the wilderness, he does not shed his ingrained prejudices and assumptions. With women, Heyward conforms to a chivalric code that regulates his conduct and defines appropriate gender roles. When Alice greets Heyward as a "recreant knight" (641), she underscores their shared awareness of how that code defines him as well as herself. Because Alice conforms to the role of passive damsel in distress, Heyward can demonstrate his worthiness and manliness by rescuing her, albeit with help from others. For Heyward, race is a more problematic area, affecting not only his view of Cora when he learns her background, but also his relationship with Uncas. After Uncas saves his life in an early skirmish, they shake hands, and "the two young men exchanged looks of intelligence, which caused Duncan to forget the character and condition of his wild associate" (553). But for Heyward, this forgetting is temporary. Ultimately, he is a man of tradition and civilization, "gladly throwing himself into the saddle" (875) to return to the known world "within the posts of the British army" (875).

The handshake exchanged between Duncan Heyward and Uncas establishes their position as doubles within the narrative, and Cooper takes advantage of the juxtaposition of these two characters to contrast two cultures' values. Uncas and Heyward each embodies his culture's ideals of young manhood, and each engages in a quest that tests those ideals in a changing environment. Always a more physical presence in the novel than Heyward, Uncas's "graceful and unrestrained . . . attitudes and movements of nature"(528) and his "beautiful proportions" (790) suggest his rightness for the environment he inhabits, while his "fearless eye" and "noble head"

(529) identify him as distinctive, even before his true identity is revealed. In the wilderness, Uncas is clearly Heyward's superior. Whereas Heyward assumes he knows the answers to problems and acts often to the detriment of the situation, Uncas consults with his father and Hawk-eye, respectful of their experience and wisdom. Like Heyward, Uncas conveys his feelings of superiority over others, but his feelings are merited, based upon skill, not just social rank.

In many ways, Uncas points up Heyward's shortcomings and appears to be the natural protagonist for a wilderness narrative, for even when he is taken captive, he stands "firm and erect, prepared to meet his fate like a hero" (744). But the changes wrought by the presence of whites in the wilderness and Uncas's growing attraction to Cora undermine this position. Uncas begins to adopt the chivalrous conduct of Heyward, for "denying his habits, we had almost said his nature, [he] flew with instinctive delicacy . . . to the assistance of the females" (601). While separated from Cora during the Fort William Henry interlude, Uncas does not lose his interest in her. When the second quest begins, Uncas discovers the piece of Cora's veil that points them on the right track, and he continues to look for signs of her that serve as goads to his desire. As this desire becomes a motivating force, Uncas loses some of his self-discipline, and Hawk-eye rebukes him, saying "you are as impatient as a man in the settlements" (683). This change does not bode well for Uncas, who, caught up in the heat of pursuit in the final battle, acts on impulse rather than strategy, making himself vulnerable to his arch foe, Magua.

Just as Cooper pairs Uncas and Heyward to develop aspects of their characters through contrast, Cooper also pairs Uncas and Magua, setting up the classic dichotomy of the "good" and "bad" Indian. In contrast to Uncas's physical perfection, Magua initially has an "air of neglect about his person," but his eye "glistened like a fiery star" (487), signaling his inner drive. Skilled at reading what his opponents intend, Magua uses his knowledge of the wilderness and of human behavior to his advantage. When he reappears to take hostages during the first quest, his "malignant, fierce and savage features" (570) identify him as a force associated with evil. Cooper, however, gives reasons for Magua's actions, rooted in both his humiliation at the hands of Munro and his expulsion from his own tribe. Hawk-eye attempts to denigrate Magua, calling him "a lying and deceitful varlet" (601), but, upon his return to the Huron encampment, the narrative labels him the "artful and dreaded chief" (755). His powerful use of rhetoric to rouse others to his cause, his "dangerous and artful eloquence" (759), recalls the persuasive abilities of Satan in Milton's *Paradise Lost* and makes Magua a formidable enemy. He, like Uncas, has natural leadership abilities and is willing to vie with Uncas for power and authority. In his confrontation with Uncas in the Huron camp, they stand side by side, divided by their loyalties and their personal ambitions, but serving as mirror images of each other as well.

The figure who undergoes the greatest transformation in the novel is David Gamut, a young man who has been shaped by the bookish world of New England to such a degree that he has no realistic conceptions of what life on the frontier will demand. He begins the novel as a comic figure, with his odd dress and peculiar habits, his need for glasses emphasizing his lack of perception. During the first quest, his inexperience in the wilderness and his lack of skills make him vulnerable. Gamut often expresses himself in figurative language that at times obscures his meaning. He also finds his orthodox views of election and salvation rejected by Hawk-eye, who sees them as disproved by experience in the wilderness. During the second quest, Gamut undergoes more noticeable change, at one point assuming an alternate identity by trading clothes with Hawk-eye. This change of attire suggests that Gamut is being affected by his wilderness experience, that he is beginning to see from a different perspective and respond to his environment in more appropriate ways. In the battle between the Delawares and Hurons, he even takes up arms, relying upon a slingshot, in imitation of his Biblical namesake, to contribute to the effort to save Cora and return both women to their father.

While Cooper's male characters undergo some development over the course of the narrative, his female characters remain types who represent sets of values. Cooper frequently pairs female characters, presenting one whose coloring and manner identify her as the pure, naïve, and innocent white heroine and another, whose darker and more vivid coloring connotes sexuality and forbidden knowledge. In *Mohicans*, this division exists between the Munro sisters. Alice, with her "fair golden hair, and bright blue eyes" (488) conveys childlike innocence and ingenuousness, while Cora, with her "dark eye" and "shining and black" hair (488), expresses an undercurrent of sensuality and experience. Alice's weakness, timidity, and need for protection are frequently mentioned, and both Cora and Heyward attempt to shelter her from the unsettling truths of their experiences in the wilderness. Alice's "infantile dependency" (593) and her meekness underscore her suitability as a woman of the settlements who depends upon male protection and guidance. In contrast, Cora manifests a steadiness and "self-command" (589) so that she does not draw back from encounters with danger, exemplified in her calm exchange with Magua the first time she is taken hostage. She also perceives things in the wilderness that neither Alice nor Heyward do; she is more aware of her environment and the actors who define it.

Cooper complicates Cora's circumstances by placing her at the center of a love triangle between two Indians, a situation that in Cooper's view and in that of many of his contemporaries cannot end happily. While Magua initially pursues Cora as a means of punishing her father, he comes to admire and desire her. Cora's "rich, speaking countenance" (533) attracts Uncas from the start. Cora exerts power over both Uncas and Magua, and she is willing to use this power over Uncas to secure his cooperation. However, when Magua looks at her with "wavering glances," Cora feels shame at encountering "an expression that no chaste female might endure" (590), her sexual attractiveness contributing to her potential entrapment. Cora, too, has prejudices based on race and finds Magua's demand that she become his wife a "degradation" (834). One wonders how she would have responded to Uncas's attentions had they both lived. Some of Cooper's contemporaries offered different interpretations of Indian-white relationships, including Catharine Sedgwick in her novel *Hope Leslie* and Lydia Maria Child in *Hobomok*.

Minor Characters

Two pairs of minor characters stand out in *The Last of the Mohicans*. The first, Colonel Munro and General de Montcalm, are part of the historical record of the French and Indian War. They represent two types of military men with conflicting ideas about honor and responsibility. The second pair, Chingachgook and Tamenund, represent chiefs of Native American tribes who have witnessed the destruction of their peoples and the loss of their lands to the encroaching white populations.

Munro is a product of the civilized world, and, although he has been commander of a fort on the edge of the frontier, he retains the values and expectations of this training. The surrender of Fort William Henry and the destruction of the British during the retreat deal a blow to his psyche, one intensified by the captivity of his daughters. He loses the ability to function as a military man and is too old to develop the skills that would make him suitable for action in the wilderness. In light of this, Cooper hides him away for most of the second half of the novel, placing him in Chingachgook's care in an abandoned beaver lodge. Munro stands in contrast to Montcalm, for Montcalm seems to shake off his inability to prevent the destruction of his opponents. A skilled soldier and a sophisticated negotiator, Montcalm uses his knowledge of multiple languages to his advantage in manipulating others. He prides himself on his chivalrous conduct, but Cooper presents him as a man of questionable character. The massacres at Oswego and William

Henry that occur on his watch suggest his willingness to take advantage of the "uncontrollable" nature of his Indian allies to gain ground in the battle for North America.

Chingachgook, also known as Sagamore, appears in a number of the Leatherstocking Tales, although in *Mohicans* he plays a lesser role, especially while tending Munro. A skilled warrior and wise chief, he clearly loves his son and takes great pride in him. He talks to Uncas in the "soft and playful tones of affection" (701) when they are not engaged in battle and with pride tells Uncas of battles that he has fought. Chingachgook often has a melancholy outlook, for he anticipates that his tribe's displacement and decline prefigures what will befall the native peoples as a whole. This knowledge compounds his grief at Uncas's death, for Chingachgook sees himself as a "blazed pine, in a clearing of the pale-faces" (877), a marked and solitary figure, despite Hawk-eye's profession of friendship. The great chief Tamenund, who appears only briefly in the novel, reinforces Chingachgook's view of what appears to be inevitable loss for the native tribes. Tamenund, a very old man, had been alive when the English settlers first established themselves, so he bears witness to all that has befallen his people. He weighs Cora's reference to one act of mercy shown by her father against the rapacious greed of the settlers and critiques the racism that underpins their actions. His voice closes the novel, as he bemoans the cycle of history that has allowed him to witness the destruction of the best of his peoples.

Themes

Cooper perceived within the story of the frontier experience the potential for exploring two cultures in conflict, that of the white European immigrant and the indigenous American Indian. Within this larger pattern of cultural conflict, Cooper also considered other issues, including the tension between wilderness and civilization, the issue of race as a determinant of identity, and the definition of gender roles. All of these themes support Cooper's exploration of the nature of an American self and an American nation.

In Cooper's vision, the frontier exists as a middle ground between wilderness and civilization, much as Natty Bumppo serves as a mediating figure between the two. The wilderness, with its lack of definition and structure, represents complete freedom from the laws and customs of civilization and from the restrictions an individual experiences when he or she lives in society. In the wilderness, an individual is subject only to the laws of nature but is confronted by a harsh and primitive physical existence that demands self-sufficiency. Civilization, on the other hand, entails order and hierarchy that limit individual freedom, but it offers the benefits of communal endeavors, including the advancement of learning and the production of both culture and material comforts. On the frontier, these two entities collide as civilization, represented by pioneers and early settlers, encroaches on the wilderness and changes it. As Hawk-eye observes, "natur [sic] is sadly abused by man, when once he gets the mastery" (609). Achieving this mastery demands the exercise of brute force over the natural world and violent encounters with indigenous people. Literary characters on the American frontier, such as Heyward and Gamut, often experience what Richard Slotkin calls "regeneration through violence," the emergence of a new and better self out of the trials they experience (473). This creation or formation of a new self in a new land forms the basis of a central tenet of the myth of American identity, a myth critiqued by feminist critics such as Annette Kolodny.

In *The Last of the Mohicans*, American identity is complicated by the issue of race. Throughout the novel, characters make observations that address race and racial identity, particularly the attitudes of whites toward those they identify as other. Hawk-eye's repeated comments on racial "natures" and "gifts" reveal that he perceives each race as a distinctive group that must remain separate. Other characters, such as Tamenund, confront the racist superiority inherent in white attitudes toward American Indians, particularly through white rejection of intermarriage. Munro twice in the novel addresses the issue of race, taking a more liberal position than any other character. Having been married to a woman of mixed race background, he challenges the notions of racial hierarchy and of racial separation, but his views are regarded as naïve by Natty Bumppo. By including these alternative views in his novel, Cooper offers a critique of prevailing American assumptions, but the story's ending seems to underscore the need for racial separation and legitimate the elimination of an Indian presence within the American nation.

While race functions as an obvious determiner of identity in the novel, Cooper also explores issues of gender roles and appropriate traits. Ideals of masculinity are important in both the white and Indian worlds, while women and the feminine are seen as subordinate in both. In both cultures, men who fail to perform according to the ideals of masculinity are criticized by being labeled womanish, implying weakness and inferiority. In contrast, strong men who have resisted feminizing influences, such as Hawk-eye and Chingachgook, are permitted to shed tears, an act that would be perceived as weakness in any other male character. The male characters also have definite ideas about woman's place, as Heyward reveals during the first Indian attack, when he directs Alice and Cora to remain in the cave and "bestow a care suited to your gentle natures" on the wounded David Gamut (546). Cora's desire to be more directly involved and her willingness to take action make her problematic. Hawk-eye admires her courage, but when she exclaims, "We are equal! . . . on such an errand we will follow to any danger" (633), she crosses the boundary of what is acceptable for a woman to claim. Clearly in Cooper's world, the creation of a new self on the frontier is an option open to men but seldom to women.

2

Ralph Waldo Emerson
Selected Essays

A descendent of New England ministers, Ralph Waldo Emerson anticipated that he would follow in their footsteps. Not long after his ordination, however, his life took a different turn. Instead of serving the needs of a congregation, Emerson left his church pulpit to become a public intellectual and lecturer who shaped American values and sensibilities. Early in his career, he was a definer of and spokesperson for what came to be known as Transcendentalism, a philosophy that asserts the presence of divinity within nature and within humans. Transcendentalists encouraged individuals to study nature and themselves to discover truths about the Creator's intentions and their own creative powers. As his career continued, Emerson addressed a wide range of topics but always grounded his ideas in his own evolving understanding of the principles that emerged in his early work.

No author exercised more influence on the shape of American Romanticism than did Emerson, whether by inspiring other writers and thinkers who agreed with him or by provoking dispute and rebuttal from those who did not. Philosopher, essayist, poet, and lecturer, Emerson gave voice to Romantic ideals within an American context. To challenge American values and understanding, he drew upon ideas expressed by European thinkers such as the philosophers Rousseau and Kant as well as the work of British Romantic poets and apologists such as Coleridge and Carlyle. He saw Romanticism's emphasis on the individual and its focus on nature as avenues toward liberation from the strictures of the past and from the materialism of the day. He believed that by cultivating the self, trusting intuition, and living in the present moment, individuals could unleash their creative potential and more fully apprehend the divinity within themselves.

BIOGRAPHICAL CONTEXT

Although he spent much of his life in Concord, Massachusetts, and his presence there made Concord a site of pilgrimage for many intellectuals and aspiring writers, Ralph Waldo Emerson was born in Boston on May 25, 1803. His father, William Emerson, was then pastor of First Church in Boston, the oldest congregation in the city, which by the 1790s had embraced Unitarian concepts and a more liberal theology. Ruth (Haskins) Emerson, Ralph's mother, also came from a family of clergymen, but her own father was a successful distiller. Emerson's parents took their responsibilities for rearing their children seriously and strove to instill virtue and discipline in their natures. When William Emerson died from tuberculosis in 1811, he left his wife with six children and few resources. Education, however, was important to her, and Ralph attended the Boston Latin School, where he prepared for entrance into Harvard College. During these formative years, Emerson's aunt, Mary Moody Emerson, lived with the family and had a profound influence on Ralph's understanding of his family history as well as issues in theology.

In 1817, Emerson entered Harvard as the youngest member of his class. He studied classical and modern languages as well as history. He wrote poetry and submitted essays to various competitions, and won prizes for a few. Upon completing his degree, he began teaching in his older brother William's school. While teaching, Emerson continued to write, publishing his first essay, "Thoughts on the Religion of the Middle Ages," in the *Christian Disciple* in 1822. During this period, Emerson resolved to prepare for the ministry and dedicate himself to the church, gaining entrance to Harvard Divinity School in 1824. His studies were interrupted by health problems, and for a period of time he returned to teaching. In 1826, he was licensed to preach by the Unitarian church. Emerson preached from various pulpits in 1827, and, at a service in Concord, New Hampshire, on Christmas Day of that year, he met Ellen Tucker, who would become his wife in 1829.

Ordained a minister in the Unitarian Church in the spring of 1829, Emerson was called to the Second Church in Boston as an associate pastor, where he preached and engaged in various pastoral duties. He married Ellen Tucker in September, knowing that her health was fragile and that she suffered from tuberculosis, which plagued both their families. Ellen died in 1831, after only 17 months of marriage, leaving Emerson heartbroken. To shield himself from such pain in the future, he resolved not to let anyone else become so deeply entwined in his affections. Prior to his relationship with Ellen, he had often lamented his emotional coldness, and her early death brought the return of his reserve. Emerson continued in his ministerial work, but he began to question the validity of church traditions and customs and therefore grew uncomfortable in this role. In 1832, he asked to be excused from conducting the communion service, and later in the year he resigned.

In the winter of 1833, he arrived in Europe, traveling through Italy and France before going to England, where he met William Wordsworth and Samuel Taylor Coleridge, leading figures in the Romantic movement. In Scotland he met Thomas Carlyle, another Romantic writer, who became a lasting friend. Upon his return to New England, Emerson continued to preach and began to lecture as well, defining a new career for himself. He received a legacy from Ellen's estate that provided him with some financial security, and he moved to Concord in 1834. In 1835–1836, Emerson devoted more of his time and energy to lecture series in Boston and Salem. He also married Lidian (Lydia) Jackson from Plymouth, Massachusetts, but saw his second marriage as based on practicality rather than romantic love.

As he became more fully immersed in new intellectual pursuits, Emerson became friends with various individuals who were also engaging in philosophical and spiritual inquiry, including Bronson Alcott and Margaret Fuller. He also began to study more extensively the works of the German Romantic Goethe. Emerson's first book *Nature* appeared in 1836, a volume in which he redefined the relationship between humans and the natural world and between humans and God. That year, Emerson also formed the Hedge Club, sometimes known as the Transcendental Club, which met periodically at his house in Concord. These gatherings allowed him to engage in dialogue with like-minded contemporaries, including George Ripley, Fuller, Alcott, and Elizabeth Peabody.

The year 1837 marked the beginning of a highly productive period for Emerson. That year, he delivered one of his best known addresses, "The American Scholar," in which he called for intellectual independence and original thinking. He also became friends with Henry David Thoreau. He continued to deliver secular lectures in various communities, and finally resigned from all preaching duties. His 1838 "Divinity School Address," in fact, encouraged his auditors to abandon the traditions of the past that had become simply hollow ritual without spiritual connection. It scandalized leading figures in the religious community, and Emerson was not invited back to Harvard for nearly 30 years. In 1840 he worked with Margaret Fuller to publish the first issue of *The Dial*, the journal that for four years was a major vehicle for the publication of Transcendentalist essays and poems.

By 1841, he had his own *Essays* ready for publication. This volume included "Self-Reliance," the essay that defined Emerson's concepts of individualism, intuition, and self-cultivation. Throughout this period, Emerson also did what he could to assist various friends and associates, providing hospitality to many, securing work for some, and helping others see their work into print. Having mourned the deaths of many family members of his own generation, Emerson was particularly distraught by the death of his young son Waldo in 1842. Although he continued to lecture and took over editorship of *The Dial*, the impact of this loss remained with Emerson, evident in the tone and subject of his essay "Experience," published in his *Essays: Second Series* (1844).

Throughout the 1840s and 1850s, Emerson remained active as a lecturer, traveling more widely in the United States to deliver presentations and accepting invitations to lecture in England. He addressed public issues of his day, especially the injustice of slavery. He also supported arguments for women's rights and addressed one of the Women's Rights conventions. His intellectual interests continued to expand as he acquired translations of Asian and Indian philosophers and poets. In 1846 he published *Poems* and in 1850 *Representative Men*, a collection based on a series of lectures he had delivered at home and abroad on figures such as Plato, Shakespeare, and Napoleon. By 1856, Emerson had in print another collection, *English Traits*, a volume in which he assessed English culture and nineteenth-century England for both good and ill. Emerson valued many qualities that he found in the English, but he was critical of England's colonial rule and materialism.

In the late 1850s, as arguments over slavery grew more intense, Emerson continued his support for abolition, moved, as many were in Concord, by a speech delivered there by the radical abolitionist John Brown. During this period, Emerson devoted more of his time to poetry, publishing verse in the new *Atlantic Monthly*. He continued to travel farther afield in the United States as his lecture tours took him to Chicago and other Midwestern cities. He published another volume, *The Conduct of Life*, in 1860, based upon lectures on topics such as power, wealth, and behavior; it proved to be one of his best-selling volumes.

During the Civil War and especially in the years immediately following it, Emerson was in high demand on the lecture circuit, maintaining a grueling schedule of personal appearances and serving as an informal instructor at Harvard. He published *Society and Solitude* in 1870, a volume that contained essays based on his lectures, still urging his readers to look within and to look critically at the directions being taken by the society around them. The toll of his journeys on the lecture circuit had started to appear as early as 1867, when his eyesight began to trouble him. By the early 1870s, Emerson found he could no longer manage extensive working tours, although he continued to enjoy leisure travel within the United States and abroad. In his last years, his memory began to fail, and he spent his time more quietly, working with his daughter Ellen to prepare additional manuscripts for publication. He continued to make a few public appearances but depended upon her help to do so. In 1882 he contracted pneumonia and died on April 27. He was buried in Sleepy Hollow Cemetery in Concord, along what is known as Author's Ridge, where his neighbors Henry Thoreau and Nathaniel Hawthorne had already been laid to rest.

EMERSON AND TRANSCENDENTALISM

The challenge of defining Transcendentalism has been compared by Myerson in *Transcendentalism* to "grasping mercury: both are fluid and hard to pin down" (xxv). The explanations and definitions offered by its proponents were seldom in complete agreement, their personal intuitions and perspectives affecting which elements of the philosophy and movement were most important to them. American Transcendentalists were influenced by many streams of thought. They embraced ideas articulated by Emmanuel Kant on the division between the ideal and the physical world and on the existence of types of knowledge that are innate or a priori. They rejected the empiricist philosopher John Locke's concept that individuals are born blank slates, or tabula rasa, upon which observations and sense impressions inscribe knowledge. The Transcendentalists were also drawn to ideas voiced by the German philosopher Friedrich Schelling, who defined nature as a spiritual entity, an outward manifestation of the divine. The works of English Romantics were also important to the Transcendentalists, especially the poetry of William Wordsworth and the critical writings of Samuel Taylor Coleridge.

Developments that occurred in American culture also affected the responses of the Transcendentalists. Most began as members of the Unitarian Church, which had broken away from the Calvinist orthodoxy that had shaped New England. The Puritans and later Calvinists had preached a stern religious code based upon concepts of human depravity or sinfulness, dependence on the grace of God for salvation, and election, by which only those randomly chosen by God would be saved. Those who broke away to form Unitarianism rejected the idea of God as embodied in a trinity and asserted that Jesus was not divine, but an exemplary man. They argued for a more liberal theology in which an individual's life conduct had an effect on salvation and believed that humanity was inherently good. They believed that individual conscience, rather than church doctrine and dogma, was a sound guide to belief and action. Many welcomed the principle put forth by William Ellery Channing, a major voice in Unitarianism, that divine elements existed within humans, that humans bore what he termed a likeness to God. Those who eventually broke from Unitarianism felt that it, too, began to place form and doctrine above the liberation of the individual soul. Emerson, especially, accused his former church of engaging in false prayer and upholding outworn creeds.

In their efforts to define a philosophy and spirituality that would encourage what they saw as the full development of humans, the Transcendentalists focused on certain principles. They began to conceptualize the divine in nonpersonified terms, referring to an "over-soul," a force or energy that pervaded all of creation, even though some continued to use the term God in their writings. They also emphasized a particular form of individualism based on the role of intuition and the process of self-cultivation, that they believed would foster the potential for creativity and self-improvement in all humankind. Accepting the philosopher Jean Jacques Rousseau's assertion that human beings are innately good and are corrupted by society, some Transcendentalists believed that if individuals cultivated the good within themselves, they could resist the negative influences of society. In many of his writings, Emerson encouraged readers to embrace nonconformity and act upon their own insights rather than accept the dictates of their social environment. Their belief in the value of self-cultivation also affected how the Transcendentalists viewed education. They believed education was a lifelong process that should encourage thinking and promote self-expression, rejecting the common practice of rote memorization that accepted the value of received knowledge. In addition to experimental schools, many Transcendentalists, including Emerson, saw the lecture circuit as an opportunity to promote education and lifelong learning.

EMERSON AS POET

Many people associated Emerson with his essays and addresses, but he was interested in poetry from his youth and devoted significant time and energy to the composition of verse and to theorizing on the role of the poet. In his essay "The Poet," Emerson claimed that "it is not metres, but a metre-making argument, that makes a poem" (*Essays and Lectures* 450). This statement opened the way for the types of experimentation that appear in the poetry of Walt Whitman, but as a poet Emerson stayed closer to the traditional forms of English verse. Many of his poems address Transcendentalist themes, focusing especially on nature and how the natural world manifests both beauty and truth. He often explores the integration of the elements of nature into a unified whole and how humans relate to nature in both positive and negative ways.

An early poem, "Each and All," addresses Emerson's understanding of the "perfect whole" that nature embodies, even though it may not be immediately perceived. The poem is composed in rhyming couplets, which emphasize the concept of pairing and of elements working together toward expression. Constructed in three related sections, the poem develops the concept that "All are needed by each one; / Nothing is fair or good alone" (*Collected Poems* 9). The speaker begins by mentioning a series of figures and actions about whose impact another seems unaware. The speaker suggests, however, that this lack of awareness or intention does not undermine the place each figure or action holds in the scene before him. Although each element seems discrete, there is an underlying unity that binds them together.

In the second section, he recalls moments in which he found something of beauty in nature and attempted to take it home, but discovered that once separated from its natural context, the song of the sparrow or the delicate color of the seashells no longer retained its beauty. Instead, the shells "Had left their beauty on the shore, / With the sun and sand, and the wild uproar" (*Collected Poems* 9). The speaker realizes that it is not the single object that contains nature's beauty, but the object's relationship to the other elements of its natural context that awakens in the speaker an awareness of beauty. The speaker extends these examples by considering how a lover views his beloved before she is his. While in the company of other maidens, the "virgin train," a young woman who is the object of desire seems to have a magical grace. Once she is separated from this context of innocence, which Emerson compares in a simile to the caging of a woodland bird, she loses some element of her beauty, for "The gay enchantment was undone, / A gentle wife, but fairy none" (*Collected Poems* 9).

In the last section of the poem, the speaker decides that he desires only truth and assumes it is something set apart from beauty. He goes so far as to suggest that beauty is something that appeals to the immature, that seekers of truth must "leave it behind with the games of youth" (*Collected Poems* 10). He thinks this while standing in a forest and soon discovers that all the elements of nature that surround him—the ground pine, the scent of violets, the oaks and firs, the rolling river, the song of birds—in their perfect relation to each other inspire his reawakening to beauty's role. He admits that "Beauty through my sense stole; / I yielded myself to the perfect whole" (*Collected Poems* 10). It is beauty that allows him to perceive the underlying unity, the truth of the perfect whole, of which he too is a part.

In some poems, such as "Hamatreya," Emerson takes a critical look at the relationship most individuals have with the natural world, one defined by the concept of ownership that treats nature, or at least some portion of it, as a commodity. The poem is divided into two sections, the first written in blank verse, the second in more compressed stanzas. He begins the poem with a list of family surnames associated with the town of Concord, each of which identifies a farmer who "owned" the land he worked. The speaker imagines the farmer walking his land and using the possessive pronouns "mine" and "my" to describe all he sees, suggesting the farmer's belief that a kind of permanence can be claimed through possession. Yet, the speaker then asks, "Where are these men?" (*Collected Poems* 28), acknowledging that all have died, their lands passed into others' hands. The earth sees the farmers as "boastful boys": each has assumed that in transforming the land as he saw fit, he gained control over it and time, but the speaker notes, "the hot owner sees not Death, who adds / Him to his land" (*Collected Poems* 28).

In contrast to the farmers' short-sighted ideas, "Earth-Song" gives voice to a deeper wisdom born of the fact that humans are mortal while "Earth endures" (*Collected Poems* 28). Earth chants the long age of nature to which no human life span compares, then remarks on the human customs of deeds, wills, and inheritance, all attempts to define and control ownership of the land. Earth remarks on the longevity of the natural world that stands in contrast to the fleeting existence of humans and their contrivances and asks the paradoxical question, "How am I theirs, / If they cannot hold me, / But I hold them?" (*Collected Poems* 29). Rather than respond directly to this question, the speaker concludes the poem, implying that his own relationship to the land has changed, that his "avarice" or desire to possess it has "cooled" or lost its intensity, "Like lust in the chill of the grave" (*Collected Poems* 29). This final simile creates a complex closure that reintroduces the fact of human mortality and suggests that the earth in fact already lays claim to the speaker as one that the earth will eventually hold.

Later poems, such as "Days," reveal Emerson's awareness of the passage of time and of lost opportunities. In this tightly constructed poem, Emerson uses personification, diction, and imagery to construct an allegory that invites readers to contemplate the effect of each day's passing. The first six lines focus on the actions of the personified days, to which the speaker responds in the last five. Emerson opens the poem by referring to days as "Daughters of Time" whom he envisions "marching single in an endless file" (*Collected Poems* 178). Through this personification, he makes the abstract idea of time tangible, but then complicates the figure by referring to the days as *hypocritic*, a word that in its Greek origins describes actors or performers, but in its more modern usage means deceivers. Emerson plays with this dual possibility by describing the figures as "Muffled and dumb like barefoot dervishes," making the days veiled and silent, suggesting secrecy.

The word *dervishes* refers both to members of a Muslim sect who use body movements within devotional exercises to induce trances and to individuals who whirl or dance with wild abandon. He goes on to say that the days bring both "diadems" (crowns) and "fagots" (bundles of sticks), again playing up dual possibilities or a sense of alternatives. He then introduces the human element into his consideration, that "To each they offer gifts after his will" (*Collected Poems* 178), suggesting that an individual's own inclinations and intentions affect what the days bring.

The second half of the poem focuses on the I persona's response to this vision of Days. The speaker stands in his "pleached" garden (one that is fenced with or sheltered by intertwining boughs), suggesting a space that is contained and regulated. He watches this imaginary procession, which distracts him so that he forgets his "morning wishes," his own intentions for the day, harvesting only a "few herbs and apples," a mundane gathering. He discovers that "the Day / Turned and departed silent" (*Collected Poems* 178). The day, or the time it represents, proves to be something that slips away, that eludes the speaker's control. He remarks "I, too late, / Under her solemn fillet saw the scorn" (*Collected Poems* 178), suggesting that time or the day respects no person. Even though the measurement of time is a human construct, it is something that also remains outside human control.

EMERSON'S ESSAYS AND ADDRESSES

In his addresses and essays, Emerson articulates many of the ideas that emerge from his philosophical inquiries. Influenced by his Transcendentalist beliefs, many of his essays express the possibilities for liberation from the weight of the past, for the fuller realization of human potential. When composing his essays, Emerson drew on material from his journals and his letters as well as from the public lectures he had delivered. At times within the essays he leaps from one point of his argument to the next, but this is intentional, for he wants readers (or listeners) to engage in the thought process, to work out the connections that are implied but not spelled out. For Emerson, this thought process was more important than the written product, although he took great care in shaping his essays. Emerson was always concerned with what he called "Man Thinking," the active engagement of the mind in the act of discovery and realization. Although Emerson's essays inspire a degree of optimism about the human condition, some critics thought that he failed to deal adequately with the problem of evil. Others saw a certain coldness in Emerson's philosophy, a lack of charitable feeling toward those in less fortunate life circumstances. More recent critics have called into question

Emerson's analysis and rejection of his social and economic world, seeing in his writings representations of middle class values and aspirations.

"The American Scholar"

Sometimes referred to as America's intellectual Declaration of Independence, "The American Scholar" was delivered by Emerson as an address to the Phi Beta Kappa Society at Harvard in 1837. As he considers the process of intellectual activity, Emerson encourages the audience to break with the past, turn away from the influence of Europe, trust their own insights, and engage in self-cultivation. He also turns a critical eye toward what he sees as America's lack of dedication to arts and letters, rebuking the "sluggard intellect of this continent" (*Essays and Lectures* 53). He reprimands the scholar who is content to repeat others' thoughts rather than devoting his energies to coming to know his own. He also paints a bleak picture of the human condition in a society in which individuals have been trapped by routine and materialism so that they are objectified into things.

Emerson argues, however, that this bleak situation does not have to prevail, that individuals, especially those engaged with the life of the mind, can break free of these social influences. Emerson considers three main factors that work upon the individual's capacity to be a thinker: nature, books, and action. He credits nature with being a mirror of the soul that allows those who study nature to perceive the underlying connections that reveal the order of both mind and matter. He claims that "study nature" and "know thyself" are one in the same maxim (*Essays and Lectures* 56). Emerson then considers the role of books, asserting that each age must write its own. He does not disparage books in and of themselves, but he quarrels with the way books tend to be used. He thinks that readers tend to view books as sacred rather than the thought process that led to their creation. In this way, people slip into the habit of worshipping the past and its ideas, allowing the past to limit what can be thought and created in the present. Instead, Emerson argues that readers must use books as inspiration for coming to know their own thoughts, then must express those thoughts through their own acts of creation. He also calls upon the individual to engage with the world, to take advantage of what can be learned through experience, even though the meaning of particular experiences may not be apparent until some time in the future.

Once he establishes this pattern of the proper education of the scholar, he turns to the issue of the scholar's duties. Here Emerson emphasizes a principle that runs throughout his writings, the concept of self-trust. He admits that there are many barriers that keep individuals from accepting and acting on this principle. The temptation to conform to popular opinion or to the ideas of the past keeps individuals from discovering what is true for themselves and for their age. He argues that what one discovers is true for the self is in some way true for all. It is in discovering this truth and expressing it so that others may grasp it that the scholar performs the highest duty. In this section of the address, Emerson draws a gendered definition of the scholar as masculine. He claims that the scholar should reject the notion that, "like children and women, his is a protected class"; that instead the scholar must be "manlike" in standing up to ignorance and the fear it instigates. At the time he delivered this address, only men belonged to Phi Beta Kappa. In linking the work of the scholar to manliness, however, Emerson also echoes the nineteenth-century concept of separate spheres for men and women to argue for the scholar's place in the public arena. According to Emerson, the scholar can transform his society by awakening individuals to an awareness of a higher good than the material wealth to which most aspire.

The last portion of "The American Scholar" looks specifically at the role of the scholar in America and expresses some of the ideas that reflect Emerson's own democratic ideals. He celebrates the fact that literature in his day has found value in "the near, the low, the common" (*Essays and Lectures* 68), for in coming to see the "spiritual cause" present in the everyday, the writer discovers "but one design unites and animates the farthest pinnacle and the lowest trench" (*Essays and Lectures* 69). In addition to articulating this sense of equality between the highest and the lowest, Emerson also praises the individual and the power that lies within a single person. He encourages his audience to reject "the courtly muses of Europe," which by implication are associated with aristocracy and hierarchy. Instead, he wishes them to embrace "the spirit of the American freeman" and to claim the creative power that will allow the individual "to yield that peculiar fruit which each man was created to bear" (*Essays and Lectures* 71).

"Self-Reliance"

In his essay "Self-Reliance," Emerson continues to explore some of the principles he articulated in "The American Scholar," especially the importance of self-trust and of nonconformity. This essay examines two interrelated concepts in some detail: the value of self-cultivation and the resulting possibilities for self-realization. This essay also refers more extensively to the idea of genius, the unique intellectual and creative gifts within a single individual that generate new ideas and new forms of artistic expression. This idea, linked to that of originality, was an important aspect of the Romantic interest in the individual. For Emerson, it was evidence of the presence of the divine within the human, confirmed by the individual's ability to engage in creative acts.

Emerson begins with the idea of an inner light, that intuitive sense that allows an individual to perceive truths. He claims that most individuals ignore this potential within themselves, for they do not trust their own insights and have become dependent upon the ideas and insights of others. But he cautions that "imitation is suicide," that to live by another's views and habits is to deny and, in effect, kill the self (*Essays and Lectures* 259). He then states "that though the wide universe is full of good, no kernel of nourishing corn can come to [the individual] but through his toil bestowed on that plot of ground which is given to him to till" (*Essays and Lectures* 259). This metaphor that compares the nurturing of the inner self to farming suggests that self-cultivation is work that requires an investment of energy and resources. By engaging in self-cultivation and acquiring self-knowledge, the individual reaps the benefit of discovering his or her own originality or genius. Thus he or she can respond to Emerson's dictum, "Trust thyself" (*Essays and Lectures* 260).

Urging readers to live in the present moment, Emerson also encourages them to be nonconformists. He argues that an individual must respond to his or her own inner wisdom and not simply accept what society claims is right, good, or true. He explains that everything must be questioned and examined to determine which precepts and principles are worth accepting and which are merely the baggage of the past. To conform to tradition and social expectations dissipates the vital energy that should be invested in self-cultivation. Emerson warns, however, that acting according one's own insights is not easy, that "for nonconformity the world whips you with its displeasure" (*Essays and Lectures* 264), because the nonconformist threatens the security of those who live by external dictates. He cautions as well against placing too much value on consistency, for the process of self-cultivation is dynamic and brings about change.

According to Emerson, self-reliance "works a revolution" in the relationships and actions in which an individual engages (*Essays and Lectures* 275). He claims that the relationship with the divine changes, for when one is self-reliant and recognizes the presence of the divine within the self, then prayer becomes an act of relationship and not of begging. He also suggests that all action that is taken in light of self-knowledge becomes a form of prayer because it celebrates the connection between the divine, nature, and the individual. A self-reliant individual is content at home and sees around him- or herself a world of meaning, so that travel no longer serves as a means of obtaining culture or of escaping the boredom that plagues modern individuals. Likewise, a self-reliant individual does not need to imitate others, to copy the manners or styles of other cultures. To Emerson, self-reliance will free American artists and writers to express new and truly American thoughts and ideals. Because he believes that the individual's inner self is the source of change, Emerson also rejects reform movements, for he sees them as working upon individuals from outside, so that they may bring about superficial alterations rather than lasting improvements.

Throughout the essay, Emerson enumerates the faults that arise from a lack of self-reliance, from the slavish imitation of others to timidity in the conduct of life. As in "The American Scholar," he draws upon gendered ideas of manhood that include courage and fortitude to inspire readers to claim their true identities and live by the promptings of their inner selves. He rejects conventional attitudes toward morality and virtue, but argues that the person who seeks the truth will live by a natural morality that recognizes the good. He also urges readers to reject the materialism of the age, to measure themselves and others by their character and not by what they own. Emerson suggests that the individual who knows the self will have a kind of "living property" (*Essays and Lectures* 281) that spares him or her from the vagaries of economic life and the transitory nature of things. In many instances, he echoes attitudes held by his Puritan forebears, but turns them toward a new purpose. He encourages readers to let their actions reveal their inner beliefs and to live in the world but to resist its temptations that lead one away from true being.

"The Poet"

Published in *Essays: Second Series*, "The Poet" extends Emerson's principles from "Self-Reliance" to explore how they affect the work of creativity. He sees the poet as a figure who is immersed in the search for spiritual truth and who expresses that truth in the poetry he or she composes. As he does in many essays, Emerson begins by pointing out what is wrong—in this case, with the state of poetry and the work of poets. He claims that too much emphasis is placed on taste and form, leading to superficial verse that fails to express ideas or truths. Emerson believes that when viewed the right way, nature and the material world reveal meaning that the poet perceives and articulates, making the argument or premise of a poem more important than its shape or design. His ideas about poetry and the role of the poet opened the way for innovations in American verse and influenced the work of many American writers, among them Walt Whitman and Emily Dickinson.

To Emerson, the poet functions as a representative figure who discovers truth and then reveals it to others who do not see as deeply or as clearly as the poet but who are receptive to the poet's vision. The poet is an interpreter who recognizes through his or her own experiences the universalities that apply to all. The poet also perceives beauty to a greater degree than the average person and finds beauty present in things that are often regarded as vulgar or low. Emerson argues that "thought makes everything fit for use," freeing the poet to explore and incorporate those experiences of life and images that have been "excluded from polite conversation" (*Essays and Lectures* 454). In order for the poet to do this, he or she must possess a purity of soul as well as genius and be self-reliant enough to use them to uncover the truths that reveal the interconnectedness of all things. Thus, the true poet follows the principles of Transcendentalism. When the poet expresses the truths that he or she perceives, the poet becomes a liberator who frees others to seek spiritual heights.

In "Nature," Emerson discussed the way nature and language are interrelated, that "words are signs of natural facts" and that "particular natural facts are symbols of particular spiritual facts" (*Essays and Lectures* 20). He asserts that to "read" nature rightly and deeply is to read truth. Fascinated by the ways in which symbols convey meaning, Emerson returns to this concept in "The Poet," highlighting how individuals use symbols. The poet, however, grasps the implications in symbols that ordinary individuals ignore. He or she responds to the insights generated by the imagination, using what Emerson calls a "very high sort of seeing" that allows the poet to recognize these implications. The poet, according to Emerson, becomes one with the natural world, drawing upon a power of mind that is separate from the intellect or consciousness through which the energy of the universe makes itself knowable. Emerson considers the suggestive power of language, how words function as symbols, and how the poet can use language to reveal the order that pervades the natural world. He calls the poet "Namer, or Language-maker," crediting poets with having given us all words, and claims that words themselves contain "pictures" that affirm the order the poet reveals.

Emerson laments that he does not find poets who will sing of the present and of the meaning of daily life. He proclaims America a poem, influencing the later assertions of Walt Whitman, and calls for poets who will convey the meaning of America with originality and courage. He again charges poets to turn away from tradition and even the customs and views of their contemporaries in order to be receptive to the muse, which they will only discover in solitude. He admits that the work of the poet is demanding, but that the rewards will be great, for the poet will possess the whole world and see beauty in all that exists.

3

Edgar Allan Poe
"The Raven" and
Selected Stories

No other nineteenth-century American author has enjoyed the sustained popularity and mass appeal that Edgar Allan Poe garnered in the twentieth century. His gothic short stories, such as "The Fall of the House of Usher" and "The Masque of the Red Death," inspired horror films that revitalized the genre, while his poem "The Raven," which created a sensation when it appeared in 1845, introduced an iconic symbol that continues to resonate with readers today. No other nineteenth-century American author, however, has been the source and subject of more controversy than Poe, both in life and afterward. In addition to debates over the value and meaning of his work, commentary on Poe, both from his contemporaries and later biographers and critics, wrestles with the problematic elements of Poe's life and conduct.

A writer who craved recognition and status, Poe often undermined his chances for success, both through his volatile relations with others and through his abuse of alcohol. An insightful critic with high standards, Poe frequently attacked the work of his contemporaries, highlighting their failures and missteps. His pointed remarks and sometimes false accusations stirred resentments that alienated people who might have been helpful to him. Through his reviews, he also argued for the principles of unity and effect as key components of the short story, defining the genre that was to become a mainstay of American fiction. While he struggled with poverty, his wife's death, and his own failing health, Poe wrote many of the poems and tales that have secured his place in the literary canon. For more than one hundred years after his death, critics and scholars debated the significance of Poe's work, but the continuing presence of his work in school anthologies and on college reading lists indicates the significance of Poe's contributions, both to popular culture and to literary art.

BIOGRAPHICAL CONTEXT

The turmoil that defined Poe's personal life began in his earliest years. The son of actors David and Elizabeth (Arnold) Poe, Edgar was born on January 19, 1809, in Boston, Massachusetts, where his parents were members of a theatrical company. Poe's father abandoned the family in 1810, shortly after the birth of Poe's sister. His mother attempted to continue in the theater, relocating to Richmond, Virginia, but illness and her premature death in 1811 left Edgar and his siblings orphaned. Each was taken in by a different family, Edgar becoming the ward of John and Frances Allan, a childless couple. John Allan, a tobacco merchant, had a prosperous business and opened an office in England, where he moved the family in 1815. Edgar, who at this time used the surname Allan even though not legally adopted, attended schools in greater London. The Allans returned to Richmond in 1820, where Edgar continued his education, focusing on classical literature, and began to write poetry. He also resumed the surname Poe, distancing himself from John Allan.

In 1826, Poe enrolled at the University of Virginia, where he studied classical and modern languages. Poe did well in his studies but lost substantial sums playing cards, debts that John Allan refused to pay. Allan also refused to supply further funds for Poe's education. Despite Poe's affection for Frances Allan, he left the household in Richmond and went to Boston. Little is known of his activity there, except that he arranged to publish anonymously his first volume, *Tamerlane and Other Poems*, in 1827. That same year, he enlisted in the army under the name Edgar A. Perry. Poe considered a military career and sought John Allan's help in getting an appointment to the West Point military academy to train as an officer. While waiting to secure his appointment, Poe published a second volume, *Al Aaraaf, Tamerlane and Minor Poems*, in 1829. He also mourned the death of Frances Allan and attempted to reconcile with his foster father.

Poe enrolled at West Point in 1830, where he again studied languages. His relationship with John Allan collapsed when Allan remarried, endangering Poe's hopes of a substantial inheritance. Poe decided to abandon a military career, engaging in conduct that provoked a court-martial and expulsion from the army. He moved to New York City in 1831, where he published *Poems*, a volume subsidized by contributions from his former classmates. Desperately poor, Poe moved to Baltimore, where he joined the household of his grandmother, his aunt Maria Clemm (Muddy), and her young daughter Virginia. He began submitting work to literary contests in hopes of winning prize money. Some of these stories, including "Metzengerstein," a gothic tale, were published in Philadelphia's *Saturday Courier*. He submitted more work to an 1833 contest sponsored by the Baltimore *Saturday Visiter*, in which his tale "MS. Found in a Bottle" earned first place. Even with these successes, Poe was nearly destitute.

Publication of a story in the nationally circulating *Godey's Lady's Book* in 1834 gained Poe a wider readership. That year, however, John Allan died, having written Poe out of his will and dashing any hopes of financial relief. Fortunately, Poe was recommended for the assistant editorship of a new magazine, the *Southern Literary Messenger*, which ironically took him back to Richmond. His departure from Baltimore aggravated the financial distress of his aunt Maria Clemm and his cousin Virginia. Maria's pleas for assistance prompted Poe to bring her and Virginia to Richmond in the fall of 1835, and in the spring of 1836 he married his cousin, who was barely 14. Battling depression and bouts of drunkenness, Poe assumed responsibility for support-ing his family. Writing reviews and notices for the *Messenger* at a feverish pace, Poe hoped to have a volume of his tales published, but his efforts came to naught. In what became a pattern for Poe, he argued with Thomas White, publisher of the *Messenger,* and resigned his post. Moving to New York, Poe did not find steady work, although he continued to publish tales and poems. He completed *The Narrative of Arthur Gordon Pym* (1838), his one novel, but returned to the medium of the short story, where, over the next several years, he demonstrated both range in and mastery of the genre.

In hopes of finding steady work, Poe moved his family to Philadelphia, where he contributed reviews and some tales, including "The Fall of the House of Usher" and "William Wilson" to *Gentleman's Magazine*. In 1839, these two tales, along with other pieces he had written, appeared in his collection *Tales of the Grotesque and Arabesque*. Poe was dismissed from the *Gentleman's Magazine* after arguing with the publisher, but when that publi-cation came under new ownership and was retitled *Graham's Magazine*, Poe was hired as editor, which for a brief period in 1841–1842 provided him with financial stability. He contributed more tales to this periodical, including "The Murders in the Rue Morgue," "A Descent into the Maelstrom," and "The Masque of the Red Death."

While Poe appeared to be establishing himself more securely in a literary career, Virginia Poe suffered a respiratory hemorrhage. Her failing health added to Poe's anxieties, but he continued to write, publishing "The Tell-Tale Heart" and "The Black Cat" in 1843. He also traveled to Washington, D.C., in hopes of securing a government clerkship, but he got drunk and ruined his chances. His success with "The Gold-Bug," which won a $100 prize from a Philadelphia paper, increased his popularity but did not solve his financial problems. Poe returned to New York in 1844 and found work at the *Evening Mirror*, to which he contributed articles and reviews and in which he published "The Raven," his best-known poem, in 1845. In 1845, he also published *Tales*, a collection of 12 stories, and late in the year *The Raven and Other Poems*. During this period, he also cultivated relationships and engaged in flirtations with a number of literary women. As Virginia's health declined precipitously, he was torn between his devotion to her and his need for attention from others. When she died early in 1847, Poe went into a tailspin, suffering from grief and illness. He produced little work that year, except for the somber and mournful poem "Ulalume."

By 1848, he had recovered his energies and focus, going on the lecture circuit and visiting with various women in the hopes of remarrying and having an element of domestic stability in his life. In his final year, Poe was actively writing and lecturing, but again engaged in alcohol abuse that brought on hallucinations. Hoping to wed Elmira Shelton, one of his earliest loves, he joined a temperance society and pledged sobriety. On a journey from Richmond to New York, he stopped in Baltimore, where he was found in a feverish delirium, possibly brought on by alcohol poisoning. The circumstances that led to this final illness remain a mystery, although much speculation has occurred over the years. Poe died on October 7, 1849, and was buried in the Westminster Burying Ground in Baltimore, where ceremonies to honor him occur each year on the anniversaries of his birth and death.

POE'S LYRICS

Poe was devoted to the theory and practice of poetry. From an early age, he had definite opinions about the nature of the poet and the purpose of poetry, ideas he continued to refine throughout his career. He gave voice to these ideas in his reviews of other poets' work, in prefaces to his own volumes, and in lectures such as "The Poetic Principle." Poe's ideas about poetry were influenced by the English Romantic poet Samuel Taylor Coleridge, and his early verse reflects his reading of another English Romantic, Lord Byron. For Poe, the central purpose of poetry was to give pleasure, to awaken the recognition of the beautiful through the musicality and effect of verse. He rejected the commonly held belief that poetry should also instruct and reveal some truth, and he frequently reprimanded his fellow poets for making explicit the moral or "lesson" embedded in their poems. He argued that the best poems adhered to a principle of brevity in order to preserve unity, a "totality of effect or impression" (*Essays and Reviews* 71) that could only be achieved when a poem could be read in a single sitting. He also paid particular attention to the rhythm of poems and to patterns of rhyme, alliteration, and assonance that contribute to the sensuousness of verse. Poe frequently revised his own poems, always seeking to express what he called "supernal beauty," the apprehension of which would elevate the soul.

Poe's study of classical literature influenced the imagery and allusions that give shape to his poems. His poetry expresses Poe's sense of the chasm that exists between the mythic and the mundane realities of life. Unlike Emerson, who believed that beauty could be found in the everyday, Poe sought a more elevated sphere. In an early poem, "Sonnet—To Science," Poe's speaker rejects the empirical method, which he associates with "peering eyes" and "dull realities" (*Poetry and Tales* 38), in favor of the imagination. He accuses science of undermining beauty by offering rational explanations of phenomena that had once been the province of myth, dragging "Diana from her car" and tearing "the Naiad from her flood" (*Poetry and Tales* 38). To accept knowledge gained through science would cost the speaker his imaginative access to the ideal, his "summer dream beneath the tamarind tree" (*Poetry and Tales* 38).

For Poe, archetypal feminine beauty can transport the poet toward the realm of the ideal, "his own native shore," according to the 1831 version of "To Helen." This poem alludes to the figure of Helen of Troy, a woman of legendary beauty, who inspires the speaker to journey "home / To the glory that was Greece, / And the grandeur that was Rome" (*Poetry and Tales* 62). In many poems, such as "Lenore," "To One in Paradise," and "Ulalume," Poe explores the effect of the loss of a beloved woman and, through the speaker's reactions, suggests that love and loss, pleasure and pain, are inseparable. Although he often dismissed the role of narrative in poems, Poe uses it as a source of structure and coherence in a number of these poems, as his speakers recount their experiences of loss. The women who are the objects of their love and the cause of their grief are idealized by the speakers, who reveal few specific details about them. Instead, their deaths underscore the powerlessness of the speakers. In "Annabel Lee," one of his best known poems, Poe presents a speaker who mourns the loss of one who loved him "with a love that was more than love" (*Poetry and Tales* 102), so that the angels in heaven envy their happiness. Poe suggests that such happiness is unearthly and as such, it cannot last. The speaker believes that their love was the cause of Annabel's death, that it provoked the chill wind that led to her demise. The speaker cannot thwart the wind, nor can he stop her "high-born kinsmen" who "bore her away" in order "To shut her up in a sepulchre" (*Poetry and Tales* 102), reinforcing their separation. However, the speaker claims that their love is stronger than death, that death cannot "dissever" his soul from hers. In the last stanza, he admits that he regularly dreams of her, unable to relinquish her. Instead he lies down by her side, figuratively, if not literally, embracing her again.

"The Raven"

When "The Raven" was published in 1845, it became a widespread success, appealing to readers in England as well as the United States and bringing Poe, at least briefly, the degree of fame he desired. In "The Philosophy of Composition," which Poe wrote as a commentary on the poem, he claimed that melancholy was the most appropriate tone for poetry and that the "death, then, of a beautiful woman is, unquestionably the most poetical topic in the world" (*Essays and Reviews* 19) because it provokes the deepest melancholy. In "The Raven," his grieving speaker mourns the loss of Lenore, another idealized woman about whom little is revealed other than that she was "rare and radiant" (*Poems and Tales* 82). In his depressive solitude, the speaker is visited by "a stately Raven" whose only utterance shapes the poem's famous refrain, "Nevermore" (*Poetry and Tales* 83). Poe may have taken the idea of a talking raven from Charles Dickens's novel *Barnaby Rudge* (1841), a volume about which Poe had written a lengthy review. He also draws upon the traditional association of the bird with ill-omen and death, investing the bird with power and authority so that its response intensifies the speaker's anguish.

The setting Poe establishes for this narrative poem complements the mood he wishes to convey, incorporating gothic elements to create uneasiness. The speaker sits alone at midnight, a time associated with life's end, reading volumes of "forgotten lore" in an attempt to lull himself into forgetfulness. The time is "bleak December," the start of winter, a season associated with the end of life. The room is warmed and lighted by "dying embers" whose "ghosts" call up associations with the supernatural, an example of Poe's effective use of diction to create multiple layers of meaning. The purple curtains, whose color is also associated with funereal custom, inspire "fantastic terrors" in the speaker, revealing his susceptibility to suggestions of the supernatural. Likewise, his choice of a chair upholstered in "velvet-violet" later in the poem reasserts the connection to death and mourning. The darkness of the night, emphasized in stanzas four and five, unsettles the speaker, its silence heightening his apprehension.

Poe's speaker, like many of the personae who give voice to his poems, grieves the loss of a woman he loved, and, although he claims to seek "surcease of sorrow" in the volumes he peruses, he wallows in his melancholy. When the raven enters his chamber and responds to the speaker's first question with "Nevermore," the speaker acknowledges that "what it utters is its only stock and store / Caught from some unhappy master" (*Poetry and Tales* 84). His reaction is rational, and yet, as the poem continues, the speaker turns away from his own rational abilities. Instead "linking / Fancy unto fancy," he poses questions to the raven whose "Nevermore" increases the speaker's feelings of pain and loss. This pattern of self-inflicted torture builds in intensity until the speaker breaks down emotionally and demands that the raven "Take thy beak from out my heart, and take thy form from off my door!" (*Poetry and Tales* 86). The last stanza, however, reveals that the speaker cannot free himself from the presence of the bird and what he has come to represent, the futility of his hope for reunion with his lost love.

The raven assumes symbolic import within the poem as a bird associated with both good fortune and bad. In addition to its associations with death and foreboding, the raven also symbolizes knowledge and divine providence, at times treated as a messenger who bears the truth. The speaker in Poe's poem attributes knowledge to the raven through the pattern of questions that he asks. The raven's choice of perch, the bust of Pallas Athena, also connects him to wisdom, although some readers see this juxtaposition as ironic, since the speaker seems to abandon rational knowledge in favor of superstition in the presence of the raven. The raven's repeated utterance of the word "Nevermore" adds to the sense of authority and conclusiveness in his responses, drawing upon the raven's role in some myths as a bearer of messages from the dead. In this respect, the raven's response to the speaker's question of whether he will ever again "clasp a sainted maiden whom the angels name Lenore" (*Poetry and Tales* 85) conveys both the finality of death and the possibility of rejection by the speaker's beloved. Throughout the poem, the raven does nothing more than state a single word, but Poe allows readers to see how words and symbols acquire meaning through imagination.

Although "The Raven" has its weaknesses, it continues to inspire imitations and parodies, its blend of gothic overtones and mesmerizing rhythm and rhyme making it unforgettable. Some readers see the poem as a parody of meditative Romantic poems, such as Keats's "Ode to a Nightingale." In "The Philosophy of Composition" Poe offers explanations and analysis of his choice of meter, his use of alliteration and repetition, and his refrain. He makes the composition of the poem seem more a mechanical exercise than a creative act. But one can also read the essay as a lesson on the art of close reading; Poe demonstrates how a reader should approach any poem, considering which elements within the poem create its effect and why the poet might have made those choices.

GENRE

The gothic tradition in fiction emerged in the eighteenth century, the term "gothic" denoting narratives set during the medieval period. The authors of gothic tales, such as Horace Walpole and Ann Radcliffe, were not interested in writing historical romances; instead, they were intent on creating plots and atmospheres that would inspire terror in their readers. The plots of gothic novels often hinged on mystery and suspense, impelling readers to continue reading despite the horrors to come. These novels, such as Walpole's *Castle of Otranto,* were set in dark castles that featured hidden passageways and dungeons. They often included encounters with the supernatural, innocent maidens in distress, and devilish villains. The authors of early gothic novels were attracted to such fiction as a means of rebelling against the emphasis on rationality and order that dominated much of the eighteenth century. Their novels often exploited the irrational and inexplicable, suggesting that there was more to human experience than could be determined by empirical evidence.

By the nineteenth century, the term "gothic" was applied to any fiction that inspires terror or horror, even those not set during the middle ages. Such narratives continued to incorporate the supernatural, the irrational, suspense, a sense of foreboding, and an atmosphere of gloom. Influenced by German romanticism that encouraged greater exaggeration of the horrible and more reliance on the supernatural or uncanny, Poe makes use of gothic elements in most of his short fiction. For Poe, the effects produced by these elements were a means of raising questions about both the psychological states of his characters and the power of the unconscious to influence perceptions and behaviors. He also used the gothic tales at times to raise questions about the cultural anxieties of his era, especially those experienced by an increasingly urban population who feared the anonymity and dangers of the city. He sometimes used his gothic tales to challenge assumptions made by the Transcendentalists about the inherent goodness and improvability of humans. The unsettling presence of the supernatural in Poe's tales also challenged those who embraced technology and progress as sure remedies for human ills.

POE AND THE SHORT STORY

During the first half of the nineteenth century, the short story emerged as a distinct genre. Through his criticism as well as in practice, Poe defined the nature and scope of the short story. As in his comments on poetry, he underscored the value of brevity and focus in order to achieve a single, unifying effect. He also claimed that during the "hour of perusal" of a short story, the "soul of the reader is at the writer's control" (*Essays and Reviews* 572). To maintain this control, the writer must quickly identify characters and their attributes, initiate action that will lead to the climax, and pare away any detail that does not contribute to the overall unity of the story. Free to choose the point of view and whether to emphasize character or plot, the author, according to Poe, must always have in mind the ending of the tale. Poe often creates a five-part structure for his tales, including an exposition, rising action, a crisis, further action leading to the climax, and a denouement. The exposition and denouement in each of these tales is brief, Poe concentrating instead on the relationship between action, suspense, and crisis.

"The Fall of the House of Usher"

One of Poe's earliest and most successful gothic tales, "The Fall of the House of Usher," (1839) culminates in the literal collapse of a physical house and the psychological undoing of the central character. Poe employs a popular gothic convention in making two of his characters, Roderick and Madeline Usher, the end of their family line. Both they and the house they inhabit are repositories of their family legacy, which includes a tendency toward madness. The singular pattern of descent among the Ushers has intensified all of the eccentricities and extremes of the family, and Poe hints that incestuous desire shapes the relationship between brother and sister. Poe also suggests that as twins, Roderick and Madeline are two halves of a whole, neither can exist without the other.

Point of View

As in many of Poe's tales, "Usher" employs a first-person participant narrator. The narrator's sensibility contributes to the suspense of the tale, for throughout the story, he attempts to distinguish between what is real and what is imagined, between what is rational and what is mad. The narrator arrives at the House of Usher as an outsider but quickly finds himself under its influence. He speaks of the melancholy and gloom that affects him before he even enters the house. Prior to his entrance, he examines the inverted image of the house reflected in the black tarn (pond) that lies before it. This inverted image suggests that the narrator is entering into an environment in which things may not be what they seem, that the abnormal or irrational will predominate. Poe also makes use of water as a symbol for the unconscious, leading some readers to speculate that the tale that unfolds is the narrator's nightmare. Initially the unnamed narrator positions himself as a voice of reason in the mad world of the Ushers, but as the tale progresses, he admits that the terrors of the house have worked upon him as well.

Setting and Plot Development

In gothic tales, setting plays a crucial role in generating feelings of suspense and anxiety and is closely intertwined with the plot. From the opening sentence of "Usher," the setting is marked by darkness and decay. The house, with its "Gothic archway," maze-like passages, "phantasmagoric armorial trophies," and heavy tapestries (*Poetry and Tales* 320), has all the trappings of a medieval castle, including a dungeon that had served "the worst purposes" in its long history (*Poetry and Tales* 328). Marked by a fissure that runs down through its crumbling masonry, the house suggests a divided self, this sign of instability foreshadowing the collapse that occurs at the end of the tale. As the climax of the tale approaches, a storm lashes the house, suggesting that nature mirrors the mental turmoil that plagues Roderick and the narrator. Just as he had attempted to explain away other unsettling feelings, the narrator attempts to offer rational explanations for the storm's effects, that "electrical phenomena" (331) are causing the strange sensations he perceives. By closing the window, the narrator attempts to shut out the terror, but the true terror comes from within the house.

The exposition includes the narrator's approach to the house, his comments upon the history of the Ushers, and his description of the current condition of the house. This material provides necessary background and establishes the atmosphere. When the narrator passes through the gothic archway into the house, he initiates the rising action, which focuses on the condition of Roderick Usher and the mysterious ailment that affects his sister, Madeline. During the rising action, the narrator reveals more of Roderick's condition: his nervous anxieties and the signs that belie a disordered mind. The creative pursuits in which Roderick engages—his wild performances upon the guitar and his abstract paintings that resemble vaults or sepulchers—reflect a sensibility stimulated to extremes. Roderick's poem "The Haunted Palace" reinforces this impression as it recounts the transition of a great house and its monarch from fair and radiant to "desolate" and "discordant" (*Poetry and Tales* 327). The books read by the narrator and Roderick all focus on the occult, torture, and death, reinforcing the troubled state of Roderick's mind. The rising action ends with the death of Madeline Usher, her entombment marking a turn or crisis in the narrative that governs the fate of Roderick.

The portion of the narrative that follows the crisis builds to the climax of the tale, which occurs with Madeline's reappearance. Between the time of her entombment and her return, both Roderick and the narrator hear strange sounds, and the narrator remarks upon Roderick's further decline. The narrator and Roderick read a fabricated gothic tale, "Mad Trist," that aggravates rather than soothes their troubled psyches; the narrator is now as enveloped in the madness as Roderick. They hear the high-pitched grating of metal, which sets the narrator's nerves on edge, while Roderick slips into a catatonic state, rocking back and forth. His "gibbering murmur" (334) reveals his horrified realization that Madeline was buried alive. The appearance of the enshrouded and bloodied Madeline initiates the apocalyptic collapse of the house, as she falls upon her brother, bringing them both to the floor as corpses.

The denouement records the narrator's terrified flight as he witnesses the widening of the fissure and the rushing collapse of the house into the tarn, whose black waters "close sullenly and silently" over its remains.

Characters

In a number of his tales, Poe uses a pattern of doubling, or what is known as the doppelganger motif. The term *doppelganger* originally referred to a ghostly double of a living person, but it can also be applied to other types of doubles, including twins. Authors frequently introduce a doppelganger in order to reveal internal conflicts within a character, using the double to represent qualities or traits that are personally or culturally problematic. In "Usher," Roderick and Madeline are twins who have an uncanny relationship. Roderick occupies center stage in the tale, while Madeline appears only once while living; her mysterious condition puzzles the narrator and frightens Roderick. Some readers also see the narrator and Roderick as doubles, the narrator's initial connections to rationality standing in contrast to Roderick's madness. Through this doubling, Poe suggests that the narrator may attempt to repress his own fear of the irrational.

Roderick's maladies and anxieties define the circumstances of the narrator's visit. His "cadaverous complexion" (321), overly acute senses, and mood swings reflect a troubled being. Roderick claims these are manifestations of a "family evil" (322), hinting that his madness may be inherited. He has retreated from the outside world, never leaving the family home, and Poe implies that this isolation has caused his malady to fester, that the house itself has toxic effects on its inhabitants. The narrator remarks on the precarious state of Roderick's stability, his reason giving way completely in the aftermath of his sister's death. His abject fear of Madeline's return drives his actions and responses, and he seems to anticipate retribution for wrongs he has committed.

Madeline, who appears ghostly even while alive, has no substance, but her presence in the house pervades the consciousness of Roderick both before and after her death. She exerts a power over Roderick, representing a side of himself that he attempts to repress or deny, possibly his sexuality and sexual desire. She may also represent the feminine aspect of Roderick's character, which he must stifle in light of cultural definitions of manhood in the nineteenth century. Yet his own condition worsens when he believes that Madeline is dead, suggesting that Roderick cannot survive without her, that he cannot achieve wholeness while rejecting a part of himself. When Madeline reappears in the full horror of her premature burial, she falls upon Roderick, asserting her claim upon him before they both collapse in death.

Themes

"Usher" explores a number of themes and issues, including the sources and stability of identity and the relationship between the normal and abnormal mind. Poe insinuates that sanity or rationality is a thin veneer beneath which chaos reigns. He also indirectly critiques the nature of aristocracy and its exclusivity, the custom of inbreeding that accentuates eccentricities and accelerates decay. He draws upon archetypal images to explore the realm of the unconscious and the power of dreams or nightmares. By the end, the narrator feels trapped in a nightmare that may or may not be of his own making.

"The Masque of the Red Death"

Although Poe regarded allegory as a less successful art form because of its ties to the didactic, his tale "The Masque of the Red Death" (1842) relies heavily on symbolic elements that carry allegorical import. Masques originated in the medieval period, but reached the height of their popularity during the Renaissance. They were elaborate spectacles that featured elegant costuming, detailed scenery, and complex music. These were entertainments offered at court, designed to please the elites in European societies.

Setting and Plot Development

Poe creates a fantastical setting for "Masque," a palace decorated in the eccentric tastes of Prince Prospero. The palace has attributes of a fortress to keep out the Red Death and anyone not among the select thousand that Prospero has invited to join him. It also contains "all the appliances of pleasure" (*Poetry and Tales* 485), so that those who reside within its walls do not have to think and can simply revel in sensual delights. The seven rooms of the palace are laid out like a maze, with sharp turns that lead from one chamber to the next. The number seven is associated with the days of the week, but also with the deadly sins. Each room is decorated in a different color, lit only by braziers that shine through stained glass, intensifying the color's effect. Decorated in black, the final room glows with red light, the two colors associated with passion and death. In this last room stands the ebony clock, whose chiming of the hour marks the passage of time. This has a profound effect upon Prospero's guests, who all freeze when they hear the sound. It is the one pause that permits reflection and reminds the guests of their mortal natures.

The plot structure of the story reinforces the symbolic elements of the set-ting. A brief exposition describes a pestilence, the Red Death, which is rav-aging an unnamed country. The rising action begins when Prince Prospero, the country's ruler, takes 1,000 of his knights and ladies to a secluded retreat to escape the plague and defy death. Poe highlights that these guests are of the elite, that they have left the common people, "the external world" to "take care of itself" (*Poetry and Tales* 485). While the plague is at its worst, the prince entertains his guests with a fantastical masked ball, everyone's costume marked by Prospero's "delirious fancies" (*Poetry and Tales* 487). The crisis occurs when an uninvited guest whose costume resembles the physical signs of the Red Death appears at the ball. This presents a turn for Prospero and his guests as their mood changes from festive to fearful.

The uninvited guest provokes a rage in Prospero, who orders him seized for execution. The climax approaches as Prospero chases the mysterious guest through the maze of rooms while the revelers are paralyzed with terror. Prospero confronts the figure with dagger drawn, intent on destroying his foe. The other guests, suddenly emboldened, seize the figure, only to discover that no one inhabits the costume. In the denouement, the Prince and his guests recognize the presence of death in their midst, and they succumb to the Red Death in an apocalyptic closure like that which ends "The Fall of the House of Usher."

Characters

Only two figures emerge as distinct characters in this tale, Prince Prospero and the uninvited guest. Prospero, whose name alludes to the magician in

Shakespeare's *The Tempest*, manifests sensual and decadent eccentricities. He seems uninterested in the welfare of his kingdom, seeking only to preserve his own life and that of his favorites. While the plague is raging, he is "happy" and plans to escape the plague in the company of "hale and lighthearted friends" (*Poetry and Tales* 485). He responds to the crisis with overweening pride and self-confidence, believing that he is powerful enough to escape contagion and death. When the uninvited guest appears, Prospero asserts his earthly authority, but his powers are ineffective in the face of death, which stands as the great equalizer.

The uninvited guest who wears the costume of the Red Death is the personification of Death. Like the Grim Reaper, this uninvited guest strikes fear into the hearts of Prospero and his company. He turns their masked ball into a *danse macabre*, or procession to the grave, reminding them all that no privilege bestows immortality.

Themes

In addition to addressing the inescapability of death, Poe also considers the relationship between time and change—often referred to as mutability, a favorite topic of Romantic writers. Prince Prospero attempts to construct an ideal world in which he and his chosen subjects will escape the plague, but time, represented by the ebony clock, as well as death cannot be avoided. Again Poe critiques an aristocratic mindset that values privilege and exclusivity over the well-being of the masses. When Prospero cuts himself off from the people he rules, he in effect seals his own fate, for he no longer serves a purpose.

"The Tell-Tale Heart"

Perhaps the most famous of Poe's tales, "The Tell-Tale Heart" (1843) traces the performance of a perfect crime, discovered only through the mental breakdown of the perpetrator. In this tale, Poe exploits fears of urban crime and the city's anonymity that were beginning to affect American sensibility.

Point of View

Crucial to its success, Poe's use of a first-person participant narrator in "The Tell-Tale Heart" controls the mood and the progress of this tale. From the outset, the narrator raises the question of madness by denying that he is afflicted and claiming that his control over the narrative proves it. Like

Roderick Usher, this narrator suffers from over-acuteness of the senses, suggesting that he is more susceptible to stimuli. His ability to manipulate the flow of information and his analysis of his actions reveal his egocentricity and his delusions of superiority. His deliberate impeding of the forward pace of the narrative reflects his need for control and adds suspense. His chilling emphasis on the methodical nature with which he disposes of the body in his view reaffirms his rationality, but only further convinces readers that they are listening to the voice of a madman.

Setting and Plot Development

The narrator recounts events that take place over the course of seven nights, culminating on the eighth in murder and discovery. He chooses the hour of midnight, often associated with death and the darkest part of the night, to conduct his surveillance and ultimately to commit the crime. To conceal his actions, he relies upon the darkness of the hour and of the old man's room, whose shutters have been fastened "through fear of robbers" (*Poetry and Tales* 556). The events take place in what appears to be an ordinary old house in a city, thus transferring the terrors of the medieval castle to the familiar world of domestic space. This adds to readers' suspense and discomfort, for it makes deadly crime possible in what is supposed to be a sanctuary from the hostile world. Poe uses sound as his primary gothic effect within the tale. The noise of the lantern, the old man's groans, the pounding of his heart (or that of the narrator), and the old man's shriek when the narrator assaults him all play upon readers' anxieties. The beating of the heart becomes a recurrent motif, the sound that drives the narrator to murder and then compels him to confess.

The brief exposition in this tale focuses upon the narrator's assertions of sanity and his justification for what he has done. The rising action begins as he details the procedure he followed for spying on the old man. Here the narrative builds tension by heightening the reader's awareness of time, for the narrator describes how slowly and stealthily he proceeded, how he seemed to gain control over time. His constant interjection and repetition of adverbs such as "slowly" and "cautiously" slows the forward movement of the plot. The narrator then compares his nightly behavior to his actions during the day, his feigned interest in the old man's well-being, contrasting what he does in daylight to what he pursues in darkness.

The eighth night begins as usual, but the narrator's actions precipitate the crisis, when he makes a sound that wakes the old man. Here again the narrator impedes the forward motion of the plot, this time by focusing on the old man's terror. This has the effect of creating a sympathetic bond between readers and the victim, as the narrator dismisses the typical rationalizations used to dispel fears in the night. When he shines the lantern beam on the old man's eye, the narrator grows irate. Having transformed the eye into a symbol of evil, the narrator feels impelled to strike out against it, further motivated by what he believes is the drumbeat of the old man's heart. This marks the moment of crisis, from which the narrator will not turn back. After killing the old man, the narrator continues to hear the heartbeat, at which point readers realize that it may be the narrator's own heart.

Having committed a heinous crime, the narrator proceeds toward the climax of the tale. He disposes of the body beneath the floorboards, confident that he has left no trace of his actions. When the police arrive at the behest of a neighbor, the narrator believes they will find nothing out of order. As agents of social control and practitioners of reasoned analysis, the police function as new antagonists to the narrator. He believes that he can control them as he imagines he has controlled time. His hubris asserts itself as he seats the officers directly over the spot where he has concealed his victim. But his acute senses initiate his undoing, for he believes he hears the beating of the old man's heart. As the sound grows in intensity, he believes the police know all and are simply tormenting him as he tormented the old man. The climax of the story occurs as he blurts out his confession, unable to conceal what he thought was the perfect crime.

Characters

Only the narrator develops as a character; throughout the story, he reveals his nature, his obsession, and his undoing. Little else is known about him: he remains nameless and his relation to the old man remains obscure. His fixation on madness and his need to proclaim his sanity immediately arouse the reader's suspicions. His preoccupation with time and the minute detail in which he conveys his actions demonstrate his mania. The pleasure he takes in watching the old man's psychological suffering reveals a streak of sadism. The old man, who may have some wealth and status, serves only as the object of the narrator's obsession.

Themes

"The Tell-Tale Heart" examines the power of obsession to drive the behavior of a character and to overwhelm his reason. The narrator feels impelled to conduct his surveillance and to commit his crime, unable to control his impulses, even though he believes he is in control at all times. Throughout, the narrator expresses an antagonism toward what he perceives as controlling external authorities, but he cannot master his own impulse through self-control. Poe plays upon this irony, and, as the tension of the story escalates, he reveals the fracturing of the narrator's calm and the full eruption of his insanity.

"A Cask of Amontillado"

Frequently cited as Poe's most perfectly constructed tale, "A Cask of Amontillado" (1846) presents a case of single-mindedness and revenge. From the opening paragraph in which Montresor describes his desire to avenge the wrongs (or perceived wrongs) done to him by Fortunato, the tale moves forward with an intensity of focus and a unity of design that makes a lasting impression.

Point of View

Montresor, the perpetrator of the crime, narrates the tale, which some readers have taken to be a death-bed confession. However, unlike many of Poe's narrators who breakdown as madness overtakes them, Montresor keeps his wits about him, feels no remorse for what he has done, and still takes pride in his deception years later. He intersperses his narrative with ironic puns and double entendres, reflecting his pleasure as he ensnares his victim. This tale, more so than many by Poe, relies heavily upon dialogue to advance the plot and to heighten the irony, as Fortunato walks unknowingly toward his doom.

Setting and Plot Development

This story does not have a particular, named setting, but details place it somewhere in Europe. The meeting of Montresor and Fortunato takes place during carnival, a time of revelry and celebration when chaos and misrule predominate. It is a brief period during which normally regulated and repressed impulses and desires are acted upon, when excess is the norm. During the carnival, Montresor leads Fortunato through a maze of streets to the Montresor catacombs, which hold family remains and where supposedly Montresor keeps his collection of wines. The pair descend into the catacombs until they reach the chamber that lies beneath the river. Poe uses this process of descent to accentuate their increasing distance from the crowd and to suggest that they have entered an underworld over which

Montresor rules. Fortunato follows him into a literal land of the dead. Montresor calls attention to the nitre (potassium nitrate) covering the walls, creating an eerie glow when illuminated by his torch, again emphasizing the unnaturalness of the space. When they reach the final chamber, the degree of Montresor's premeditation becomes clear, for beneath a pile of bones he has concealed the masonry supplies that he will use to seal Fortunato into his tomb.

Poe again relies on a brief exposition, as Montresor explains his desire for and obsession with revenge. He remarks on Fortunato's weakness, his pride in connoisseurship, which Montresor will exploit to gain the upper hand. The rising action begins when Montresor encounters Fortunato, whom he calls "my friend" with one of his ironic touches, and mentions the Amontillado. Fortunato, whose pride in his expertise keeps him from saying no, falls for Montresor's trap. When Montresor offers to consult Luchesi instead, Fortunato protests and insists on accompanying Montresor to test the wine. The third portion of the tale encompasses the journey through the catacombs, each step and turn taking Fortunato closer to his demise. Montresor stops their progress periodically, calling attention to the dangers of the catacombs, but each time mentions Luchesi, ensuring that Fortunato will proceed. He continues to supply Fortunato with wine, abetting his intoxication to keep him unaware of the true danger he faces. Montresor continues to make ironic comments and gestures, toasting to Fortunato's long life and flourishing a trowel when Fortunato mentions the Masons. The crisis occurs as Montresor chains Fortunato to the wall, much like a spider catching its prey on a web. Once Montresor has his victim ensnared, there is no going back for either man.

Having succeeded in luring his victim into the trap, Montresor begins building the wall that will enclose Fortunato in the catacombs. While his victim screams and struggles, Montresor works methodically to complete his task, much like the narrator of "The Tell-Tale Heart." A final conversation ensues between the two men, during which Fortunato tries to pass off the incident as a joke, then pleads for his life. Occurring at midnight, an hour viewed as unfavorable or unlucky in Masonic symbolism and traditionally associated with endings, the conversation ends in silence. In the brief denouement, Montresor claims that 50 years have passed while his deed remains undiscovered. The last words of the tale, "*In pace requiescat*" (854), have been interpreted in a variety of ways. Some think they are the blessing of a confessor who has listened to Montresor's tale; others claim they are Montresor's final ironic comment upon Fortunato and his fate.

Characters

In this tale, Poe develops the characters of both the perpetrator and the victim. Montresor, who sees himself as the victim of Fortunato's insults, fixates upon revenge to redress those wrongs. He has overweening pride in his family and in his ability to commit the perfect crime. During the carnival, he dresses in a black mask and cape, a costume that evokes death and the executioner. While he criticizes Fortunato's pride, Montresor's own governs his responses. Although he gives Fortunato warnings that things are not what they seem, many of them are conveyed in terms that sound innocuous. Once he has Fortunato trapped, Montresor drops his pretense of friendship and allows his animosity to show as he torments his victim. He quickly explains away his remark that his "heart grew sick" (*Poetry and Tales* 854) and hardens himself against any sympathy for his victim.

Fortunato, whose name (meaning "fortunate one") proves to be a misnomer, is a proud man, but obtuse. His fool's costume for the carnival is apt, for he is easily drawn into Montresor's trap. Fortunato's hubris clouds his judgment, aggravated by his competition with Luchesi and by his intoxication. The jingling bells of his costume, a sound associated with merriment, become his death knell as his mood shifts from enthusiasm and trust to suspicion and dread. Although he is a victim, little in his character inspires readers' sympathy.

Themes

In "Cask" Poe explores the nature of monomania, the fixation on or preoccupation with a single thought, in this case revenge. Telling this tale in retrospect, Montresor still revels in his success, empowered by the act he has committed. Unlike the narrator of "The Tell-Tale Heart," Montresor never loses his composure. He demonstrates a mastery of himself and his circumstances to meet his deepest need. His attitude and his obsession anticipate in nature, if not in degree, that of Captain Ahab in *Moby-Dick*.

4

Henry Wadsworth Longfellow
Evangeline
1847

In 1824, at the age of 17, aspiring poet Henry Wadsworth Longfellow wrote an essay, "The Literary Spirit of Our Country," in which he joined many of his contemporaries in calling for the emergence of a distinctive American literature, one that would "make America in some degree a classic land" (794). In this essay, published in *The United States Literary Gazette*, Longfellow noted that the consciousness of the poets who would initiate this transformation would be shaped by nature, particularly as it unfolded in the American landscape. While he expressed the conviction that it was the uniqueness of the American setting and the political and social culture emerging from the legacy of the American Revolution that would give rise to a recognizable national literature, Longfellow was, perhaps more than any of his contemporaries, influenced by European traditions and sensibilities. His extended sojourns on the Continent and his study of classical and modern languages exposed him to materials he incorporated into his work, at times by adapting European legends and folklore to American settings and circumstances.

During his lifetime and at the beginning of the twentieth century, Longfellow enjoyed a reputation as a significant voice in American literature. In both England and the United States, his popularity equaled Tennyson's, and he was the first American poet to be honored in the Poets' Corner of Westminster Abbey in London. His work as a literary translator broadened the tastes and awareness of American readers, especially his translation of Dante's *Divine Comedy* that sparked broad interest in the medieval Italian poet. Many of his narrative poems, like those of the other "fireside poets" (William Cullen Bryant, John Greenleaf Whittier, Oliver Wendell

Holmes, and James Russell Lowell) were memorized by students, who found Longfellow's metrical cadences and regularity of rhyme easy to recall. These very qualities, however, in addition to Longfellow's genteel decorum and sentimentality, contributed to his loss of stature with the emergence of modernism, a twentieth-century literary movement that prized experimentation in form and a more subjective and critical approach to content. But many of Longfellow's shorter lyrics reflect issues that were important to his nineteenth-century readers, including definitions of masculinity, the tension between the home and the world, the importance of work in defining the self, and the role of poetry in daily life. His long narrative poems, including *Evangeline*, also engaged in significant cultural work as he looked at America's past to consider how it shaped American identity.

BIOGRAPHICAL CONTEXT

Growing up in an active household, Henry Wadsworth Longfellow, in the company of his seven brothers and sisters, enjoyed a happy childhood. The second son of Stephen and Zilpah (Wadsworth) Longfellow, he was born on February 27, 1807, in Portland, Maine, where his father practiced law. With his older brother Stephen, he attended Portland Academy, but much of his early interest in literature and music was cultivated by his mother, herself an avid reader of poetry. While a boy, Longfellow learned to play the piano and the flute, pastimes that trained his ear toward the melodic and harmonious, qualities that later marked much of his verse. At the age of 13, he published his first poem in a local newspaper, the verse imitative of the eighteenth-century poets he had been reading. The following year, he passed the entrance exam for Bowdoin College but delayed attending for a year, because his family was concerned that he might be too young to leave home. In 1822, he arrived at Bowdoin, a classmate of future author Nathaniel Hawthorne.

In college, Longfellow was a conscientious student who enjoyed his studies and excelled, particularly in languages. He was a commencement speaker in 1825, delivering an oration, "Our Native Writers," in which he asserted that a national literature would not flourish as long as poetry and the arts in general were perceived as secondary in an American culture focused on the practical and commercial. When Longfellow wrote to his father expressing his desire to achieve success as a poet, his father suggested he plan to study the law as a means of supporting himself. With little interest in law, Longfellow was relieved when he was offered a place as professor of modern languages at Bowdoin. To qualify himself for the position, he traveled in Europe for three years, becoming immersed in the languages and literatures of France, Spain, Italy, and Germany. Longfellow loved the opportunity to study languages and literature at length, but he lamented that his efforts and his travels consumed all his time so that he produced little poetry during this period. He discovered, once he began his teaching career, that the demands of instruction and administration likewise limited the time and energy he could devote to his own composition.

Longfellow remained at Bowdoin for six years, where he taught French and Spanish and lectured on the literature of the Middle Ages. While there, he married Mary Potter of Portland and they set up house in Brunswick, but Longfellow was tiring of the limited life Brunswick offered compared to the European cities in which he had lived. Fortunately, George Ticknor at Harvard recommended Longfellow as his replacement. This new appointment as professor of modern languages at Harvard entailed another trip to Europe, this time to focus on German and Scandinavian languages. Pleased to be returning to his studies and further travel, Longfellow also saw his first literary volume published, *Outre-Mer: A Pilgrimage beyond the Sea* (1835), a collection of sketches based on his first trip to Europe. His happiness soon turned to grief when his young wife, who suffered a miscarriage shortly after their arrival in Amsterdam, became ill and died in Rotterdam. Seeking consolation in his studies, Longfellow moved on to Heidelberg, where he continued his work in German. By June of 1836, Longfellow took a break from his studies and traveled to Switzerland. There he met the family of wealthy American industrialist Nathan Appleton, whose daughter Frances, better known as Fanny, attracted his interest.

In the fall of 1836, Longfellow returned to the United States and, by the spring of 1837, began some of his teaching duties at Harvard, where he was to remain as a professor until 1854. He also returned to writing, including an 1837 review of Hawthorne's *Twice-Told Tales*. In 1839, Longfellow published *Hyperion*, a prose romance, and *Voices of the Night*, his first volume of poems. During this period he also courted Fanny Appleton, but she remained cool to his advances; Longfellow persisted, and they were married in 1843. Meanwhile, he published *Ballads and Other Poems* (1841), and, on his way back from another European sojourn, he wrote the pieces that comprised *Poems on Slavery* (1842). Finding his work well received, Longfellow channeled more of his energy into writing, producing a drama, *The Spanish Student* (1843), and editing a major anthology of translations, *The Poets and Poetry of Europe* (1845). He followed this with another collection, *The Belfry at Bruges and Other Poems* (1845) and began work on *Evangeline*, which he published in 1847.

Happy in his married life, Longfellow continued his streak of productivity, publishing another poetry volume, *The Seaside and the Fireside* (1849), and his last attempt at prose fiction, the novel *Kavanagh* (1849). In 1853, Longfellow resumed work on the translation of Dante's *Purgatorio*, a project that would eventually expand to encompass all of the *Divine Comedy*. The following year, influenced by his reading of the Finnish epic *Kalevala*, he began *The Song of Hiawatha* (1855), a poetic record of Native American myth and folklore. Well received at the time of publication, *Hiawatha*, with its distinctive trochaic tetrameter verse, became one of the most parodied of American poems. In 1858, he published *The Courtship of Miles Standish and Other Poems*, which, with its sales of 25,000 copies in two months, testified to the established popularity of Longfellow's work.

The 1860s proved to be a difficult decade for Longfellow. Although he welcomed the election of Lincoln as president, he, like many of his contemporaries, closely followed the South's move toward secession and the outbreak of the Civil War. While this tragic episode emerged on the national scene, Longfellow suffered a personal tragedy as well. In July of 1861, his wife accidentally dropped a match or burning wax and set her dress on fire. Although Longfellow attempted to save Fanny, she was too severely burned and died the next day. He, too, was severely injured and could not attend her funeral. Deeply stricken by his loss, Longfellow again turned to work as a means of coping, continuing with his translation of Dante and writing the pieces that made up *Tales of a Wayside Inn* (1863). In 1865, he founded the Dante Club with his friends James Russell Lowell and Charles Eliot Norton, who assisted with revisions of Longfellow's translations. Out of the Dante Club eventually grew the Dante Society of America, a group still active today.

In 1868, Longfellow made his last trip to Europe, where he received honorary degrees from Cambridge and Oxford Universities. He continued writing sustained works, such as *The New England Tragedies* (1868), and shorter pieces gathered in collections, including *Flower-de-Luce* (1866), *Aftermath* (1873), *The Masque of Pandora and Other Poems* (1875), *Kéramos and Other Poems* (1878), *Ultima Thule* (1880), and *In the Harbor* (1882). His 70th birthday in 1877 was an occasion for literary celebration. His health, which had troubled him through much of his adult life, grew progressively worse in 1881, and in 1882, he contracted peritonitis and died on March 24. Following a funeral service in Craigie House, his home for more than 40 years, he was buried in Mount Auburn Cemetery in Cambridge, Massachusetts.

LONGFELLOW'S SHORT POEMS

Longfellow was less concerned with the techniques and theories of poetry than he was with the melody and the purpose of the poem. He wrote in traditional verse forms, demonstrating his ability with quatrains, couplets, and ballad stanzas, as well as sonnets and blank verse. He often modified these forms to suit his needs, but his changes were minor, reflecting his belief that art evolves slowly. Unlike some of his contemporaries, including Walt Whitman, who were seeking new forms to express what they felt were new American ideas and values, Longfellow was content to work within accepted structures, forms that were familiar to both his audience and himself. Much of his work reflects an interest in the didactic—the attempt to instruct readers and guide them in contemplation of moral and ethical issues.

He was aware that the United States in the 1830s, 1840s, and 1850s was undergoing profound changes, not only through continuing westward expansion, but also through the rise of the industrial-commercial culture that was redefining the country. Many of Longfellow's poems offered reassurance to readers that, despite the transformations occurring in the world around them, certain values and beliefs would continue to provide meaning and stability. The melodic quality of many of the poems offered a soothing balm to readers who felt the pressures of competition and the drive for success in their lives. He often positioned the home as a place of security and shelter from a difficult world, the speakers in his poems giving voice to the desire for rest and escape from the cares of the day. Unlike Harriet Beecher Stowe, who used the values associated with domesticity to challenge the values of the marketplace, Longfellow simply posited them as an alternative.

Longfellow had absorbed from his family and his education a belief in duty and purpose in life. From an early age he set high goals for himself to achieve eminence in his chosen field. In his poem "The Psalm of Life," the popularity of which established him as a major public voice, Longfellow articulates a prevailing sentiment of his day—the belief that "Life is Earnest!", that one must act with serious intent and the desire to accomplish one's purpose. The opening stanza of "Psalm" has a muted quality, with words like "mournful," "empty," "dead," and "slumbers" conveying a somberness and resignation that the speaker must resist. The second stanza emphasizes life and sets up a contrasting attitude that shapes the remainder of the poem. The poem closes with the shared admonition, "Let us then be up and doing," suggesting action, and yet its last line, "Learn to labor and to wait," implies acceptance of what life brings. The mixed messages of the poem suggest the mixed feelings of the poet, the desire to achieve something of significance coupled with a realization that it may be beyond his power to determine if and when this will happen. Longfellow's later poem "Mezzo Cammin" (see below) conveys his continuing thought on this issue.

In another well-known poem, "The Village Blacksmith," Longfellow captures the simplicity of village life that moves at a slower pace than the urban and industrial world that many of his readers inhabited. Its alternating lines of iambic tetrameter and trimeter arranged in six-line stanzas create a regularity of cadence and rhyme that supports the feeling of stability and assurance that the poem evokes. The smithy is part of a world in which manhood is measured by physical strength, evident in the "muscles of his brawny arms," and steadiness of temper, rather than the aggressive competitiveness expected of men who function in the world of commerce. Again Longfellow returns to the themes of work and patience, "Toiling,—rejoicing,—sorrowing,/Onward through life he goes," his diction underscoring the idea of continuity of action. He closes the poem by calling attention to the value of the smithy's life and honest labor, but Longfellow spells out the lesson, rather than trusting his readers to discern it, a tendency that weakens the effect of many of his poems.

Throughout his career, Longfellow wrote nearly 80 sonnets, some about other writers or artists, others about nature and travel. All of his sonnets follow the Italian or Petrarchan form, consisting of an octave that presents a narrative or develops a question and a sestet that offers a response to it. One of Longfellow's sonnets that addresses a more personal subject is "Mezzo Cammin." Influenced by his study of Dante, Longfellow takes the title from the opening line of the Divine Comedy. The phrase means "midway through the journey," appropriate for a poem that reflects upon the midpoint of one's life. Here the octave provides a narrative in which the speaker expresses his feeling that he has not achieved his potential, that he "has not fulfilled / The aspirations of . . . youth" to achieve eminence as a poet. His image of "the tower of song with lofty parapet" symbolizes that eminence and alludes to the courtly traditions of poetry. He explains the reason for this failure, "a care that almost killed," referring to the death of his first wife, but ends the octave with a renewed belief in his potential, "what I may accomplish yet." The word "yet" signals the turn that is the center of the Petrarchan form, as it marks the point at which the speaker introduces his response to the situation in the octave. The sestet that follows creates a metaphor that likens the speaker's life to climbing a hill, from which perspective he views the past and anticipates the future. The future, associated with the "autumnal blast" of aging, is unknown, and, although the speaker hopes to achieve greatness, he also feels the pressure of time's passage, underscored by the "cataract of Death" that sounds from the distance, connoting his finite existence.

Although many of Longfellow's poems incorporate nature to serve a fixed purpose, in some lyrics he allows aspects of the natural world to convey meaning without the didactic impulse overriding the power of his images. "Aftermath," written later in Longfellow's career and after the Civil War, presents a speaker responding to an autumnal moment, a time of last gatherings before the onset of winter. Although the speaker uses plural pronouns "we" and "ours," suggesting shared experience, there are implications in the poem for an individual who has entered into later life as well. The speaker begins by describing fields in the late days of autumn, when birds have flown, leaves and early snows have fallen, and only the "cawing of the crow," a bird associated with death, is heard. A last labor of the season is performed: "Once again the fields we mow / And gather in the aftermath" emphasizes a harvest of remnants. The second stanza underscores the difference between this mowing and earlier ones in the season that brought in "sweet, new grass with flowers" and "upland clover bloom," suggesting freshness, innocence, and fertility. Instead, this last harvest brings in "rowen" (a second crop) that includes "weeds" and "tangled tufts." This image suggests a loss of innocence, which the title "Aftermath" plays upon, since this word means a consequence of disaster or misfortune or the period of time following a disastrous event. This may refer to the period following the Civil War, when families dealt with misfortune and loss, so that even the victorious North felt weary and spent. The perspective of the speaker may also be that of a poet who looks upon the work of his later years, his personal second harvest, with less buoyancy and optimism than he felt in youth.

GENRE

Although he abandoned writing prose fiction after the publication of *Kavanagh*, Longfellow was a talented storyteller. Many of his poems incorporate narratives, from the traditional ballad "The Wreck of the Hesperus" to the historical tale of "Paul Revere's Ride." In writing these poems, Longfellow at times draws on details from actual events but shapes them to his own purposes. He often takes advantage of the compression that poetry demands—the use of image, metaphor, and allusion—to enlarge the scope of the narrative he conveys, while incorporating elements usually associated with fiction—such as setting, plot, and character—to give substance to his subject. Longfellow's interest in the narrative poem reflects his own appreciation of the cultural work performed by classical poets, such as Homer and Virgil, whose epic poems both captured and influenced the world view and sensibility of their times and places. Longfellow also looked for inspiration to the work of earlier English poets, including Chaucer, whose *Canterbury Tales* provides the model for Longfellow's own *Tales from a Wayside Inn*.

A narrative poem relates an event as it unfolds in time, but often the poem attempts to capture not only how that event affects its immediate moment, but how in some way it continues to reverberate in time. Like his contemporaries who were writing historical fiction, Longfellow was interested in how events in America's past might have shaped not only the experiences of individuals living in the past, but might continue to speak to the experiences of his own day. In *Evangeline,* Longfellow confronts the problem of irrevocable change manifested in both physical and cultural dislocation. He attempts to show how certain ideals—such as loyalty, constancy, and perseverance—serve as antidotes to the futility and emptiness that such dislocation engenders. As his contemporaries grappled with their own reactions to the cultural transformations they saw happening around them, they responded to Longfellow's *Evangeline* with great enthusiasm, buying enough copies to warrant six printings of the poem within the first few months of its publication.

EVANGELINE: A TALE OF ACADIE

Longfellow heard the story that inspired *Evangeline* from Nathaniel Hawthorne's friend Horace Connolly, whose housekeeper, an Acadian, had told him the tale. Longfellow was moved by the disruption and hardship suffered by the Acadians and by the belief in an undying love that motivates the tireless search at the heart of the story. The young woman in the original tale searched for her beloved throughout New England, but Longfellow expands the scope of the setting by shifting much of the action in Part II to the region that eventually makes up the lower portion of the Louisiana Purchase. Although not true to the original tale, this shift was true to the experience of many Acadians, who made their way to Louisiana after having been driven from Nova Scotia.

Evangeline is divided into two parts, each consisting of five cantos, and the entire narrative is framed by a prologue and epilogue. Longfellow chose to write in hexameter verse, a particularly difficult meter to sustain in English, although it had been used successfully by German poets that he read, particularly Goethe. It was also a meter associated with the work of Greek and Latin poets, including Homer and Virgil, whose influence can be seen in the poem. The line length and rhythm create a melancholy tone suitable to the elegiac mood and somber unfolding of the action. The diction in the prologue and epilogue reinforces this mood, as Longfellow describes the "murmuring pines" with voices "sad and prophetic" whose "wail" is answered "in accents disconsolate" by the ocean (57). In the prologue, he also calls up the bardic tradition of poets who in their verse recounted the history of their tribes through his similes that compare the pines and hemlocks to "Druids of eld" and "harpers hoar" (57). But the history this poem recounts is not one of victory and celebration, but of dispersal and loss; only its recitation preserves a memory of what was.

Part I

The historical moment that defines Part I of *Evangeline* takes place in 1755, as the French and Indian War is erupting, although the incidents that take place are not directly tied to the war. Earlier in the century, France had ceded control of the region known as Acadia (present day New Brunswick and Nova Scotia) to its rival for dominance in North America, Britain. British colonists in New England felt hostility toward the Acadians, primarily because of religious and cultural differences. When the Acadians refused to sign an oath of allegiance that would have forced them to fight against France, the British, who also wanted the rich farmlands owned by the Acadians, expelled them from the province of Nova Scotia in the summer of 1755. To keep the Acadians from traveling to New France and supporting Britain's enemy, the British army and the colonial militia forced them onto transport ships, which carried them to distant regions, including Louisiana. Many families were separated during the transportation, and many Acadians died at sea. For years after the expulsion, families searched for lost loved ones; some returned to Acadia hoping for reunion but found their farms taken by British settlers. Acadia and what it represented existed only in memory.

Part I of Evangeline depicts Acadia up to the day of expulsion, focusing on the village of Grand-Pré that "Lay in the fruitful valley" (58). Longfellow draws upon elements of the pastoral in describing Grand-Pré, describing the nature of its rural inhabitants and the simplicity of their lives. He echoes ideas that emerge in Virgil's *Georgics*, a long poem that praised farming and the ability to live in harmony with nature. The Acadians live in "homes of peace and contentment" (59), the community united by language, tradition, and faith. Longfellow alters the season in which events take place to that of autumn, after a successful harvest, when the Acadians enjoy a period of "rest and affection and stillness" (64). The rhythm of their lives is governed by the daily rituals of maintaining their livestock, creating a sense of regularity and stability. This regularity and stability appears in the domestic ritual of the home of Benedict Bellefontaine and his daughter Evangeline, where she spins "flax for the loom" while he sings songs passed down from his ancestors.

The passage of time and the connection to the past are highlighted by the "measured motion" in which the "clock clicked" (66).

The opening canto introduces the five main characters whose experiences shape the tale. Like many characters in prose romances, those in *Evangeline* tend to represent certain values and ideals, rather than develop as well-rounded individuals. Benedict Bellefontaine, 70 years old, is the wealthiest farmer in the village, a man defined by bonhomie who prizes his heritage and who looks upon life with optimism. He is a figure tied to the past, who will not be able to withstand the trauma of removal. Evangeline, 17, with her dark eyes and dark hair, was "Fair . . . to behold" (60), her manner marked by a serene grace, so that "When she had passed, it seemed like the ceasing of exquisite music" (60). Like her father, Evangeline has an innocence or naiveté about her, trusting in the stability of the life she has known. She has many suitors, but Gabriel Lajeunesse has been her companion from childhood and has won her love and her loyalty. His surname defines his role in Part I, for the French word *jeunesse* means youth or youthfulness, and Gabriel has just reached the age when he is entering into adulthood and must begin to define his life. Gabriel's father, Basil the blacksmith, although friends with Benedict, is less passive; he is a strong and physical man who distrusts the British intentions. Although his occupation ties him to the past, Basil, who is younger than Benedict, proves to be more resilient in the face of change. Father Felician, who has been both priest and teacher in the village, represents one source of continuity and consolation—the Catholic faith and traditions that have defined Grand Pré.

Initially, the only change that appears on the horizon is the forthcoming marriage of Gabriel and Evangeline, but a sense of foreboding closes canto II, when Basil mentions the British ships at anchor in the harbor "with their cannon pointed against us" (67). Uneasiness intensifies in canto III, when the notary, who has arrived to complete the paperwork for the marriage, admits that the British purpose remains a mystery. He, like Benedict, refuses to contemplate the possibility of violence, despite Basil's protests. Legal matters completed, the rituals of hospitality ensue, as the fathers enjoy a game of checkers while Gabriel and Evangeline gaze at the evening sky. Their anticipated union reinforces the ideals of stability and the preservation of tradition, as Evangeline has prepared "the precious dower" of her handiwork that prove "her skill as a housewife" (72).

Canto IV begins with a day of celebration for the betrothal of Gabriel and Evangeline. Longfellow repeats the word "pleasantly" in the opening two lines, an example of anaphora (the repetition of a word or phrase at the beginning of two or more lines of verse) to underscore the congenial mood of the village.

In the third line, however, the British ships are mentioned, their presence a menacing note in an otherwise a cheerful occasion. The villagers ignore the ships, engaged in festivities that reinforce their ties to each other and to their traditions. The mood changes suddenly when, "with a summons sonorous / Sounded the bell from its tower, and over the meadows a drumbeat" (75), ominous sounds that portend trouble. This disruption announces the arrival of the British troops, whose commander delivers the edict from the king that all the Acadians' lands and livestock are to be surrendered and the Acadians themselves "transported to other lands" (76). Longfellow uses an extended simile comparing a powerful storm and the destruction it wreaks to the effect of the commander's words on the people. Sensing their lives are about to be shattered, the men panic. Above the tumult, Basil, who is compared to a spar "tossed by the billows" (76), rises up to challenge the edict but is quickly struck down by a soldier. Father Felician calms the crowd by reminding them of their faith, while the men remain captive in the church. Longfellow closes canto IV by contrasting images of harmony and plenty with those of distress and emptiness, as Evangeline awaits her father's return.

The last canto of Part I records the destruction of the town of Grand Pré. Evangeline finds Gabriel in the throng and tries to reassure him, but her own confidence is shaken when she sees the toll four days of captivity have taken on her father. As the villagers move toward the harbor, Longfellow's diction conveys the violence of the moment: "disorder prevailed . . . and in the confusion / Wives were torn from their husbands, and mothers, too late, saw their children / Left on land, extending their arms, with wildest entreaties". Gabriel and Basil are put on separate ships, while Evangeline remains on shore with her father. The separation of Gabriel and Evangeline on the day of departure not only affects their relationship, but symbolizes the dissolution of the family ties and traditions that have defined the village. Longfellow transforms the departure into an apocalyptic scene that figures the end of the world the Acadians have known. The burning of the village turns the night red and the stampeding livestock "madly rushed o'er the meadows" (84). Benedict, a man defined by the past and his prized heritage, cannot withstand the trauma. He dies, leaving Evangeline alone.

Part II

While Part I of *Evangeline* focuses on the community of Grand Pré, Part II of the poem focuses on a people in exile, "Scattered . . . like flakes of snow" (86) who have become wanderers in search of home and the ties of family and friendship. The hardship of this trek has its costs, for "Written their history stands on tablets of stone in the churchyards" (86), suggesting the number who die as a result of the transportation. Evangeline becomes the epitome of the wanderers and Longfellow draws upon the quest motif as Evangeline, initially in the company of Father Felician, sets out to find Gabriel and reclaim part of her life. This motif calls up associations with Homer's *Odyssey* and the Arthurian legends of the Holy Grail, but Longfellow inverts their pattern by having a woman make the journey. Until she turns eastward in the last stage of her journey, however, Evangeline always has a trusted male companion, a father-figure to keep harm at bay. Longfellow links this half of his poem to the epic tradition, invoking the muse to assist him in telling the tale. For Evangeline, "home" will be wherever she finds Gabriel, and, like Odysseus, she travels for years across a diverse geography, before achieving that reunion. During her quest, Evangeline's search for Gabriel also becomes a symbol of an inner journey toward spiritual fulfillment.

Evangeline's travels take her west to the Mississippi River, then south, as she follows the river toward Louisiana, where people claim that Gabriel has settled. Longfellow idealizes the movement on the river and bases his descriptions of the landscape on travel narratives written by others. He blends gothic and romantic images of nature when the travelers reach the Bayou of Plaquemine, creating another extended metaphor that compares the setting to an ancient cathedral. The landscape inspires feelings of "wonder and sadness,— / Strange forebodings of ill, unseen and that cannot be compassed" (90). The object of Evangeline's journey has also taken on a supernatural quality as "the thought of her brain ... assumed the shape of a phantom" (91). These references to the supernatural further link Evangeline's journey to an archetypal quest. Longfellow's blending of realistic details—such as the names of specific birds, animals, and flowers—with elements of the supernatural and extrasensory creates what Hawthorne termed the "neutral territory" of romance, where the ideal and the actual can merge. Through the creation of this neutral territory, Longfellow suggests that Evangeline's search has implications not only for her, but for an entire people that she comes to represent.

Heading further south, Evangeline's traveling party moves on to the Atchafalaya, a Louisiana river and its surrounding swamplands. Weary with their travels, the group stops on an island to sleep. Meanwhile, Gabriel, who has grown restless and "weary with waiting" (92), leaves his father's farm to go on a hunting and trapping expedition. In a painfully ironic moment, the boat in which he travels passes by the island where Evangeline rests, the two lovers thus unknowingly crossing paths. Evangeline senses his presence but wonders if it is a dream, "an idle and vague superstition" (93). This missed connection defines the pattern of Evangeline's quest, for each time she comes near to Gabriel's most recent location, he has moved on, and each stop becomes a testing ground for Evangeline's resolve. The implications of this missed connection are intensified when Evangeline arrives at Basil's farm, for it is set in the midst of fertile and productive ground, suggesting that here a new version of Acadia might have been established. Echoing what becomes one of the American myths, Basil has emerged as a new man, a prosperous farmer who now provides the bountiful hospitality once offered by Benedict Bellefontaine. He celebrates freedom from the rule of "King George of England" and claims that the only drawback to Louisiana is "the fever" (99). Friends and neighbors come to celebrate the arrival of the travelers, reaffirming their identity in the songs and dances of their tradition. Only Evangeline feels left out and incomplete, her thoughts on Gabriel and the next stage of her journey.

As her quest continues, Evangeline ventures into the territory of the unknown and undefined, the West, still controlled by tribes of Native Americans. Longfellow terms this the "wonderful land" (103) through which Evangeline travels, accompanied by Basil, who has replaced Father Felician as her guide. As they pursue Gabriel's path, Longfellow again recalls the Arthurian quest, comparing the mirages on the horizon to Fata Morgana, the shape-changing enchantress of legend. Evangeline encounters a Shawnee woman who tells her own sad tale and two tales of phantom lovers from Native American mythology. Through this encounter, Longfellow underscores archetypal elements of his narrative that transcend a single tradition. The band of travelers arrives at a Jesuit mission, where Evangeline decides to stay and await Gabriel's return. Basil, leaving her in the company of the mission's priest, returns home. To emphasize the passage of time and the agony of waiting, Longfellow uses repetition: "Slowly, slowly, slowly, the days succeeded each other" (108). Eventually, word comes that Gabriel is in Michigan, so Evangeline departs, for the first time without a male guide and protector. Her chastity becomes a source of her safety and, combined with her deep faith, makes her, like Galahad of Arthurian legend, deserving of a completed quest. Longfellow suggests that through the trials of her journey, Evangeline has become ethereal, more spirit than flesh, "Like a phantom she came, and passed away unremembered" (109).

The last canto describes Evangeline's arrival in the Quaker environs of Philadelphia. Although she has given up hope of achieving a reunion with Gabriel on earth, she has found a semblance of home, something that "made her no longer a stranger" (110). When an epidemic breaks out in the city,

Evangeline serves as a nurse in the almshouse, the "home of the homeless" (111), with whom she feels sympathy. While ministering to the sick one day, she recognizes Gabriel, weakened by age, illness, and a hard life. She whispers his name, and the sound of her voice briefly kindles for them both a vision of their lost Acadia and their lost youth, a past never to be regained. Their reunion, marked by the sharing of a single kiss before Gabriel dies, brings Evangeline peace and a sense that her quest has been accomplished. At the same time, it reminds readers of the loss that she and all Acadians have suffered.

The epilogue records the passing into anonymity of both Gabriel and Evangeline, buried in nameless graves "unknown and unnoticed" (114). Their story, repeated by the few Acadians who have returned to their original homeland, becomes part of an oral tradition but finds greater permanence through Longfellow's poem, much like the epic tales of the classical world that were preserved through the written word. In *Evangeline*, Longfellow addressed a particular example of diaspora and its implications, but his poem speaks to questions of cultural identity and the preservation of cultural memory faced by all peoples who endure forced separation from their homeland and the loss of traditions and folkways that provided meaning and defined community. Although the poem became a source of inspiration for many Acadians who wished to reestablish connections and celebrate the heritage that gave shape to their sense of self, it also suggests the impossibility of recapturing the past and the innocence associated with it. Evangeline's single-mindedness defines a purpose for her life, but it cannot erase the effect of change and the loss—both personal and communal—that accompanies it.

5

Nathaniel Hawthorne
The Scarlet Letter
1850

Unlike James Fenimore Cooper, whose early work brought him acclaim and financial rewards, Nathaniel Hawthorne published short stories and sketches for 20 years before he achieved significant recognition with the publication of *The Scarlet Letter* in 1850. Drawing upon New England's history, as he had in many of his short stories, Hawthorne offered in this romance an interpretation of life in seventeenth-century Puritan society, focusing on the relationship between the individual and his or her culture. Like Cooper, Hawthorne was interested in exploring through fiction the roots of American identity, how the people, events, and values of the past generated a legacy that shaped the American mind and culture of his own nineteenth-century world. Hawthorne had mixed feelings about this legacy and examined it more critically than did some of his contemporaries, seeing not only its successes but its limitations.

In *The Scarlet Letter*, Hawthorne explores the impact of censure and isolation on his central character, Hester Prynne, as she comes to terms with the punishment meted out to her by the magistrates and ministers. Found guilty of adultery, Hester is viewed as a criminal whose actions threaten disorder, working against the cohesiveness of the community. Her punishment, to wear a scarlet letter A upon her breast, singles her out and reminds her and everyone else of her sin and failing. Through Hester's experience, Hawthorne interrogates the romantic impulse toward self-definition and self-realization, but he balances this emphasis on the individual by considering Hester's need for connection to others. He also considers how the community, even in an oppositional role, has an impact on identity and understanding. Hawthorne's sympathetic exploration of the pain and turmoil that affects all four central characters allows this novel to transcend its historical setting and continue to speak to readers today.

BIOGRAPHICAL CONTEXT

Born in Salem, Massachusetts, on July 4, 1804, Nathaniel Hawthorne was the second child and only son of Nathaniel and Elizabeth (Manning) Hathorne. He was just four when his father died of yellow fever while serving as captain of a ship that had sailed to Surinam. Left with few financial resources, Elizabeth Hathorne moved into her parents' home and became dependent upon the Mannings for financial as well as emotional support, something that was true of young Nathaniel as well. Never fond of attending school, Hawthorne took advantage of an injury received while playing ball to remain at home and be tutored. During this time he became a constant reader and often reread personal favorites, including John Bunyan's *Pilgrim's Progress* as well as works by Shakespeare and Spenser, all of which influenced his later work. While he prepared for college, he continued to read fiction, enjoying new novels by Sir Walter Scott and the gothic novels of Ann Radcliffe and William Godwin.

Hawthorne enrolled at Bowdoin College in Brunswick, Maine, in 1821. During his years at Bowdoin, Hawthorne wrote fiction, working on drafts of a novel as well as short stories. His social life was as important as his studies, and he developed what became life-long friendships with the future poet Henry Wadsworth Longfellow and the future President Franklin Pierce. When he graduated from Bowdoin in 1825, Hawthorne returned to his boyhood attic room in the Manning home in Salem. At this time, he resumed the *w* in the spelling of his family name, as had been common in the sixteenth century. In Salem, he began what he often thought of as his long apprenticeship as an author. He recorded his observations of the life around him and spent time reading to learn more about New England's past and his family's role in it. He had no success with his early writings, however, and, discouraged by editors' responses, burned some of his manuscripts.

In 1828 Hawthorne published a novel, *Fanshawe,* anonymously and at his own expense. It received favorable mention in Boston periodicals, but Hawthorne, embarrassed by what he saw as the novel's failings, destroyed his own copy and refused to acknowledge the book in later years. During these early years of his career, Hawthorne cultivated the persona of a loner and an observer, but he did enjoy socializing with a small circle in Salem, including Susan Ingersoll, a cousin who lived in the House of the Seven Gables—the eventual setting for one of his romances. In the early 1830s some of Hawthorne's stories, including "The Gentle Boy," "My Kinsman, Major Molineux," and "Roger Malvin's Burial," were published in *The Token*, an annual gift book. Even though the stories appeared anonymously, Hawthorne thought this was the start of his authorial career, but he continued to need other employment to supplement his meager income from publication.

In 1837 Hawthorne published his first collection of stories, *Twice-Told Tales*, with his name on the title page. Longfellow, already established as a man of letters, wrote a positive review of the collection for the *North American Review*. That same year, Hawthorne met Sophia Peabody, the woman he would eventually marry. They became secretly engaged in 1838, but did not wed until 1842. Hawthorne's ties to the Peabody family benefited his career, mostly through the activities of Sophia's sister Elizabeth, a member of the Transcendentalist circle, who used her literary and social connections to promote his writings and to arrange a job for Hawthorne at the Boston Custom House, which he held from 1839 to 1841.

In the 1840s, many Americans considered the possibility of finding a better life through the establishment of utopian communities. Although he did not agree with many tenets of Transcendentalism, Hawthorne joined their community at Brook Farm in 1841. He left after eight months, having realized that the demands of farm work inhibited his writing. His time there was not wasted, however, for he later used the experience as the basis for his novel *The Blithedale Romance* (1852). In 1842, Hawthorne moved with his bride Sophia to Concord, Massachusetts, where they rented the Old Manse and became neighbors of various members of the Transcendentalist circle, including Ralph Waldo Emerson, Henry David Thoreau, and Bronson Alcott (father of Louisa May Alcott). He also became better acquainted with Margaret Fuller, another Transcendentalist who frequently visited Concord. Hawthorne often disagreed with his neighbors' ideas, expressing greater skepticism about human nature and human goodness.

The years in Concord were productive for Hawthorne as a writer, as he published 20 new stories and saw the publication of a second, expanded edition of *Twice-Told Tales*. To Hawthorne's dismay, however, his writing still didn't produce sufficient income, and he could not pay his rent. Hawthorne moved his family back to Salem in 1845 to join his mother and sisters. In Salem, Hawthorne benefited from his political connections with the Democratic party to secure a position in the Salem Custom House. While he worked at the Custom House, Hawthorne published *Mosses from an Old Manse*, a short story collection, but found again that his job hindered his writing. Hawthorne's dismissal from the Custom House in 1849 generated controversy, and a group of friends, including Longfellow, raised funds for his support. The turmoil in Hawthorne's life was compounded in July of 1849 when his mother died. These unsettling changes drove Hawthorne back to his writing, and in 1850 he published *The Scarlet Letter*, the book that secured his literary reputation.

Enjoying his success, Hawthorne moved west to Lenox, Massachusetts, in the Berkshire region not far from where Herman Melville lived with his family. An admirer of Hawthorne's work, Melville had written favorably of it, and for a time the two became good friends and encouraged each other's literary endeavors. By the time he was leaving Lenox, however, Hawthorne's feelings toward Melville had become more reserved and the two men drifted apart. During his stay in Lenox, Hawthorne wrote *The House of the Seven Gables* (1851) and *The Wonder-Book for Girls and Boys* (1851) as well as gathered a third collection of stories titled *The Snow Image* (1851). He was finally earning enough from his writings to support his family.

In 1852 Hawthorne purchased The Wayside in Concord. He also agreed to write the campaign biography for his college friend Franklin Pierce, the Democratic nominee for president. When Pierce won the election, Hawthorne was appointed to be American Consul in Liverpool, England. He served as consul from 1853 until October 1857. Pierce did not win renomination to his party's ticket, so Hawthorne resigned his consular appointment and with his family toured France and Italy from 1858 to 1860. In Italy, Hawthorne met many artists and writers and visited many galleries and museums, all of which influenced his last completed romance, *The Marble Faun* (1860).

In late 1860, after another stop in England, Hawthorne returned to the United States as the Civil War loomed. On his return voyage he met Harriet Beecher Stowe, author of the abolitionist novel *Uncle Tom's Cabin*, but did not pursue an acquaintance. The family settled in Concord, where Hawthorne resumed writing, but found he could bring little to completion. As the Civil War raged, Hawthorne's health declined, and he often sought relief through travel with old friends. In 1864 on a journey in New Hampshire with Franklin Pierce, Hawthorne weakened suddenly and died in his sleep on May 19, 1864. He was buried in Sleepy Hollow Cemetery in Concord, along what has become known as Author's Ridge.

GENRE

In the early nineteenth century, writers transformed the historical novel from a narrative that used a historical period merely as a source of costume and event to one that attempted to convey the mindset and understanding of the characters as shaped by historical circumstances. Following the lead of Sir Walter Scott, authors incorporated into their fiction the manners and mores of a given historical era and used them to develop more fully the individuality of characters and to explore the conflicts their characters faced. Hawthorne was drawn to the historical novel's potential, but he wished for greater latitude in defining the scope of his narrative so he preferred the term "romance." He felt the romance allowed an author the freedom to go beyond the everyday, to consider possibilities as well as probabilities. In Hawthorne's view, the romance permits a writer to enter into what he calls in *The Scarlet Letter* a "neutral territory." In that realm, the writer can "mingle" or merge the actual and the ideal. Calling his work a romance gave Hawthorne license to acknowledge that narrative is a product of the imagination while asserting the validity of the connections it makes between the tangible and the abstract.

Aware that earlier writers drew a line between fiction and fact, Hawthorne sought ways to suggest that truth stands behind fiction, even though fiction is a product of the imagination. He also wanted his readers to be aware that fiction may draw upon the record of history, but is not bound simply to repeat it. To Hawthorne, the romance invited an author to let the power of his or her imagination bring to light those aspects of experience that are usually hidden from public view. Drawing upon the New England past as he had come to understand it, Hawthorne used the narrative of *The Scarlet Letter* to explore issues such as the nature of passion, revenge, and guilt, as well as the power and meaning of symbols. By treating such issues through the dynamics of his characters' lives, Hawthorne recovered more of the human drama of a particular era than what the factual record of history alone can reveal.

Unlike many of his contemporaries, whose historical romances entailed high adventure, expansive settings, and complicated plot lines, Hawthorne focused his attention on the private conflicts and struggles experienced by his characters. The action is restricted to the small geographic area of the Boston settlement and its immediate surroundings. Many important scenes are placed in domestic interiors to underscore the dramatic tension in his characters' private lives. Even the public space, especially the scaffold, conveys an atmosphere of enclosure and restriction, contributing to the narrative's intensity. The only time Hawthorne's characters feel that they have any privacy and are free from the oversight of the Puritan community occurs in the forest, a space that Hawthorne associates with ideas of personal freedom, but which the Puritan community associates with moral danger and the devil's influence.

THE SCARLET LETTER

As a preface to *The Scarlet Letter*, Hawthorne wrote "The Custom-House," a lengthy sketch set in the Salem Custom House, where he worked for approximately three years. This sketch, with its satirical treatment of his former coworkers, critiques the system of political appointments. Beyond his personal complaints, Hawthorne also explores the dangers of being dependent on the government or political patronage for support. Commenting on the abrupt dismissal that anyone dependent upon political favor might face, he claims that "many people are seeking . . . to shelter themselves under the wing of the federal eagle," assuming they will find security there, not realizing that she "is apt to fling off her nestlings with a scratch of her claw" (123). He also critiques the position of many authors in American culture, forced to supplement their literary income with steadier though mundane employment to the detriment of their creative faculties. He admits that since beginning work in the Custom House he finds "literature, its exertions and objects, were now of little moment in my regard. . . . A gift, a faculty, if it had not departed, was suspended and inanimate within me" (140–141).

In this preface, Hawthorne explores the nature of authorship and authority. He explains how he discovered the record of events that shapes his narrative and the remnant of the letter A. He states that the real purpose of "The Custom-House" is to establish his role as the editor of the narrative that follows. This claim of veracity for the events incorporated in the novel reflects a common practice by eighteenth- and early nineteenth-century writers of fiction. Even in the nineteenth century, many people distrusted narrative that was the product of the imagination or fancy. By reporting that some physical evidence stands behind the story, Hawthorne attempts to circumvent questions about the truthfulness of his narrative. Hawthorne also calls attention to the power of symbols to stimulate the imagination, focusing on the remnant of the letter. Placing the letter on his breast, he "experienced a sensation not altogether physical, yet almost so, as of burning heat" (146), a foreshadowing of the passion and pain associated with the letter in the narrative proper. He also considers how symbols can represent abstract ideas, how they are invested with one meaning by a culture and another meaning by an individual. His sympathetic response to the power of the letter and its value as a symbol also links Hawthorne to the character of Hester Prynne, her artistry, and her role as an outsider in her community.

Setting and Plot Development

Set in seventeenth-century New England, *The Scarlet Letter* depicts the era during which the Puritans were founding their colonies. They had come to New England in hopes of establishing communities that would be models of the religious and moral rigor that they deemed necessary for salvation. Puritans lived by strict codes of conduct that encouraged confession of sin and public repentance. They meted out severe punishment to those who violated the law, believing that harsh discipline discouraged the actions of those who might threaten the unity of the settlement. The early settlers believed that if their experiment were successful, if they accomplished what they believed God had willed for them to do, others back in Old England would emulate them. They viewed their actions as part of a reform effort that would eliminate corruption in the Church of England and redefine broader English culture.

Hawthorne drew heavily on the histories of New England that he had read earlier in his life to capture the atmosphere and values of the early settlements. The Puritans believed it necessary to safeguard their experiment from anything or anyone who deviated from their plan. In the first decade of settlement, Puritan leaders felt threatened by what became known as the Antinomian crisis, centered around the ideas and activities of Anne Hutchinson. Hutchinson, who arrived with her family in 1634, was an active church member and well versed in religious issues. She disagreed with what she heard in sermons and began to hold religious meetings in her house. Some claimed that Hutchinson was questioning the teaching of the clergy and asserting the possibility of direct revelation from God. Her views, labeled "antinomian" because they were in conflict with the law, provoked the authorities, and she was charged with sedition and heresy. Banished from Massachusetts Bay, she and her family went first to Rhode Island, then to New York, where they were killed in an Indian attack in 1643. Hawthorne makes indirect comparisons between Hester Prynne and Anne Hutchinson in the opening of the narrative and alludes to Hutchinson at later points as well when he highlights Hester's opposition to commonly held ideas. His references to Hutchinson suggest that the fear of upheaval from within stayed with the Puritan community long after Hutchinson had departed the settlement.

The Puritans also feared interference and assaults upon their endeavor from supernatural powers, principally Satan and those in league with him. This anxiety manifested itself in their preoccupation with witchcraft. The persecution of witches was prevalent in Europe in the decades that preceded settlement, and the Puritans brought with them suspicion of anyone who seemed to possess unexplained powers and dangerous knowledge. The presence of witchcraft is introduced into *The Scarlet Letter* through Mistress Hibbins and her allusions to secret knowledge and to meetings in the forest. The historical Ann Hibbins, upon whom the character is based, was executed for witchcraft in Boston in 1656. The witchcraft hysteria that swept Salem and surrounding towns occurred in 1692 to 1693, nearly a half-century after the period of *The Scarlet Letter*. That such a panic erupted suggests that anxieties about supernatural threats to New England had increased rather than dissipated over time.

In the midst of such social and cultural turmoil, Hawthorne initiates the story of Hester Prynne, a young woman convicted of adultery, who is viewed by her neighbors as shameful and unrepentant. Hester's story begins in chapter 2, "The Market-Place," when she endures public humiliation and condemnation by the community. Mounting the scaffold while holding Pearl, the evidence of her sinful act, Hester stands as an isolated figure singled out for punishment. Sentenced to wear a scarlet letter A upon her dress, Hester is marked with a reminder of her crime, a punishment some of the women in the crowd find too lenient. The scarlet A also is a badge that signifies Hester's resistance to the public authority that tries to define her, her elaborate embroidery of the letter articulating her attempt to redefine its meaning. In their public questioning, the ministers urge Hester to name the father of her child so that he might also be punished for his sin. Resisting the pressure, Hester keeps silent. Her silence is viewed as another indication of her lack of repentance and her refusal to accept the authority of church and community. In light of this resistance, Hester is forced to live at the edge of the settlement, another physical reminder of her status as an outcast.

Hawthorne uses this opening scene on the scaffold to establish a point of reference in the narrative, for the scaffold represents both a place of isolation and punishment and later of redemption and reintegration into the community. The main characters are brought back to the scaffold in the middle of the novel and again at the end. When Hester, Dimmesdale, Chillingworth, and Pearl meet in this space, the emotional and psychological impact on each is intense. Between these scaffold scenes, Hawthorne explores the nature of his central characters individually and in pairs, in some chapters focusing on Hester and Pearl and in others on Dimmesdale and Chillingworth. The dynamics of these relationships allow Hawthorne to address issues of rebellion, denial, and revenge that underpin the narrative.

Hester's relationships with two men, her husband and her lover, have placed her in the position she occupies within the community, and yet she cannot publicly acknowledge her relationship to either. Hawthorne uses this element of secrecy and Hester's interactions with Chillingworth and Dimmesdale to illuminate the differences in the two relationships and to create symmetry in the plot line. Hester's encounters with Chillingworth in chapter 4 and with Dimmesdale in chapters 16 to 18 are mirror images of each other.

During "The Interview," Hester faces the husband she has wronged through her act of adultery. Having recognized him amid the crowd while she stood on the scaffold, Hester dreads this meeting, for she does not know what to expect from her husband. He visits her in her prison cell as night approaches, the gloom and oppressive atmosphere of the prison echoing Hester's feelings about her marriage. Repeating the pattern on the scaffold, Chillingworth, as he has chosen to call himself, engages in his own interrogation of Hester, encouraging her to name her partner in adultery. He also commands her to keep the secret of his identity, calling upon her sense of obligation to him. Although Hester initially faces Chillingworth with a degree of confidence and self-assertion, she fears the threat he poses to the man she loves. Her fears awaken in Hester a feeling of powerlessness that she struggles to overcome and invests Chillingworth with power over her.

Between Hester's private encounter with Chillingworth and her intimate conversation with Dimmesdale is another scene that takes place on the scaffold. This scene in chapter 12 recalls Hester's appearance before the authorities but focuses on Arthur Dimmesdale. Hawthorne develops the contrasts between these two scaffold scenes to highlight the differences between Hester and Dimmesdale's public roles and their personal characters. Unlike Hester's appearance on the scaffold that occurred in broad daylight, "The Minister's Vigil" takes place at night with no crowd present to witness Dimmesdale's imagined revelation. Although he envisions the terror of a public confession, Dimmesdale's "vain show of expiation" (248) brings him no more freedom from his guilt than do his secret scourgings or his rationalizations about concealing the past. Only Pearl, who with Hester joins Dimmesdale on the scaffold, makes demands of him, asking whether he will stand with her and Hester on the scaffold at noon the next day. Dimmesdale demurs, his fear of public exposure again haunting him. Dimmesdale's weakness is further exposed by his cowering submissiveness in the presence of Chillingworth, who discovers the little party on the scaffold and demands that the minister accompany him back to their lodgings.

In contrast to the prison meeting between Hester and Chillingworth, the encounter between Hester and Dimmesdale in the forest seven years later presents an inverse pattern of interaction. Initially, Hawthorne describes the forest as "dismal," providing an "intense seclusion" (280), not unlike the atmosphere of the prison. During their encounter, however, the atmosphere changes, as a "golden light" pervades the forest and creates an open and dream-like ambiance. This change indicates that the forest is not controlled by the Puritan culture and that this lack of regulation makes possible the hope for escape and freedom that Hester and Dimmesdale entertain there. When they first meet, Hester and Dimmesdale appear diffident, unable to trust each other, suffering from their respective isolations. Once they break through that isolation by clasping each other's hands, they engage in moments of confession. Dimmesdale admits his misery to Hester, and she reveals Roger Chillingworth's true identity. Shocked by this revelation, Dimmesdale turns his anger on Hester and attempts to withdraw from her. She calls upon her enduring love for him to plead her case, claiming that their love provided a "consecration of its own" for what they had done.

Finding her own strength renewed by this profession, Hester describes avenues of escape available to them. In a gesture that suggests what that freedom might offer, Hester removes the scarlet letter and the burden it represents, revealing the vibrancy that still defines her inner being. To complete her ideal picture of the future, Hester must draw her family together, beckoning Pearl to join them. Up to this point, Hawthorne has allowed optimism and the illusion of freedom to define the scene, in contrast to the dread and confinement Hester experienced in her meeting with Chillingworth. Pearl's entrance deflates that optimism, however, for she will not approach until Hester resumes her cap and the scarlet letter. For Pearl the reality of their situation is not so easily undone. Pearl continues to disconcert Dimmesdale, asking if he will walk back into town with them (an echo of her question on the scaffold), and washes away the kiss he bestows on her. While Hester is willing to excuse Dimmesdale's weakness and his inability to acknowledge their relationship and their child in public, Pearl refuses to do so.

Hawthorne brings his four characters back to the scaffold in chapter 23, "The Revelation of The Scarlet Letter." Again Dimmesdale is the central figure in this scene, but unlike his midnight climb up the scaffold steps, this trip takes place within the context of a public celebration with the entire community present. Having wrestled with the choice of escape or confession, Dimmesdale decides to bare his breast, figuratively, and then literally, before the crowd. Although weak and unsteady, he controls the scene, summoning Hester and Pearl to join him on the scaffold as he makes his public announcement. He compares his sin to Hester's and claims that her letter "is but the shadow of what he bears on his own breast" (338). Despite what his gestures signify, Dimmesdale never plainly states that he is Pearl's father. This leaves room for the ambiguity conveyed by the responses of the crowd, who cannot agree on what they have seen or what has happened. Hawthorne infuses this scaffold scene with symbolic actions, especially Pearl's kiss that seems to break "a spell" and visually affirms the unspoken bond that exists between her and Dimmesdale.

In the aftermath of the last scaffold scene, Hester has lost one of the two people who have provided meaning in her life. With Pearl she returns to England, where she remained "while the story of the scarlet letter grew into a legend" (343)—much like the story of Evangeline and Gabriel becomes part of an oral tradition in *Evangeline*. Although Hester finds temporary escape, she feels that there was "more real life" for her in Boston, and so returns. Reclaiming a part of her past and her self, she voluntarily resumes wearing the scarlet letter on her dress. Over the course of the narrative, the meaning represented by the letter has evolved so that instead of representing adultery, its associations have expanded to include "artist," "able," "angel," and "atonement," suggesting the ways that people's views of Hester have changed. By the end of the novel, the letter has also changed for Hester and instead of being a badge of resistance has become a sign of her belonging. Drawing upon the insights into human suffering and loss that she has gained through her own sad experience, Hester counsels women who seek her advice. Hawthorne brings the novel to a close with Hester's death but suggests that the power of her story revivifies the past and continues to shape the present. Many readers are troubled by the last chapter, disturbed by Hester's renunciation of claims to equality with men and the right to use her voice for change. They think that in undercutting what has appeared to be sympathy for Hester's views earlier in the narrative, Hawthorne asserts a conservative position that restricts the possibilities of self-realization for women.

Major Characters

The Scarlet Letter is sometimes referred to as a novel of character, since the plot entails minimal action. Hawthorne focuses on the development of characters through their interactions with each other and with the larger Puritan community. Some chapters enhance a single character and her or his motives, while in others Hawthorne presents a pair of characters whose dialogue reveals more about each. Each of the major characters struggles with issues of identity, and all but Pearl engage in patterns of concealment, safeguarding some element of the truth from public exposure. Hester, Dimmesdale, Chillingworth, and Pearl are joined to each other, but not necessarily in bonds of sympathy.

An attractive young woman at the novel's opening, Hester Prynne has a "regularity of feature and richness of complexion" (163) enhanced by natural grace and poise under duress. On the scaffold, she is compared to an "image of Divine Maternity" (166), signifying the importance her role as a mother will have in the novel. Her actions on the scaffold also reflect a core of personal strength that Hester will call upon as she faces numerous trials. As Hester enters a long period of isolation, she undergoes an outward transformation, becoming more subdued and less assertive. She dresses in drab colors that more fully set off the scarlet letter she wears as though she wants to call attention to the letter and not to herself. She has embroidered the letter extravagantly, revealing her artistic ability, which further incenses some who think she is mocking her punishment. Through this elaboration of the letter, Hester owns the symbol of her fall and claims the right to redefine it. In contrast to her own clothing, she dresses Pearl in shades of red, calling attention to Pearl's role as a living embodiment of the letter.

From the time she appears on the scaffold, Hester no longer feels that she is part of the community. The treatment she receives—the verbal abuse and scorn cast upon her by the clergy, her former neighbors, and their children—intensifies her feelings of isolation. Gradually, her quiet life and her acts of mercy cause the community to alter its view, to see Hester as a changed woman and to reinterpret the scarlet letter as standing for "Able" (257). While her outward transformation reassures the town about Hester's character, she conceals her inner self. As she spends time by herself, Hester develops independent ways of thinking, assuming a freedom of thought that allows her to reject the community's laws. Associated by the narrator with the rebellious Anne Hutchinson, Hester questions woman's place and the social system that consigns her to a subordinate role. This pattern of thought fuels Hester's resistance to the authorities that have punished her and bolsters the strength that allows her to endure her trials and to contemplate escape with Dimmesdale. But Hawthorne suggests that this process has hardened Hester and that she has lost some of the feminine qualities that can balance her nature. This hardness even affects her role as a mother, for in some scenes she lavishes affection on Pearl, while in others she silences Pearl in an attempt to exert the same restraint over Pearl that the community exerts over Hester.

The novel's final view of Hester suggests that her sufferings have brought about yet another transformation, one that restores the balance in her nature. When Dimmesdale dies in her arms, Hester is left to mourn the loss of the man whom she continued to love throughout her period of trial. In chapter 13, the narrator claims that the "scarlet letter had not done its office" (261), that Hester was still sustained by pride that inhibited her willingness to submit to the authority of the church and state or to seek God's mercy and forgiveness by admitting her sinfulness. By the end of the novel, her pride has been broken, and when she returns to Boston, she finds that there is there is "more real life" for her there than in England. She repudiates the role of prophetess of a new age that she had once envisioned for herself, instead accepting that change will come slowly and offering consolation to others who have suffered heartache not unlike her own.

While Hester performs as a figure of strength in the novel, her partner in adultery, the Reverend Arthur Dimmesdale embodies weakness, unable to own what he has done or to share in Hester's public disgrace. A young and talented minister called to a pulpit in New England, Dimmesdale seeks the approval of his congregation and of the senior clergy to affirm his sense of self and his calling. To protect his image, he conceals his relationship with Hester and distances himself from Pearl. Privately he tortures and accuses himself, but these actions bring him no relief because he resists doing what he encourages others to do, admit publicly one's sinfulness and failings. He fears what his own admission would cost him, both in terms of the punishment he would endure and the loss of status. His fears force him to live as a hypocrite, professing one thing, yet doing another. His inner pangs of conscience take a toll upon him, as he physically declines throughout the novel. With an irony that Dimmesdale himself perceives, his stature as a preacher continues to rise and he is perceived as "saintly" by his congregation.

Dimmesdale's meeting with Hester in the forest initiates the final stages of conflict for him. At first he is attracted to her plan for escape, especially when she promises that they will go together, but as he returns to town he experiences wild impulses to shock and hurt the people he meets, hardly able to restrain himself. Unsettled by these feelings and by his meeting with Mistress Hibbins, Dimmesdale begins to perceive escape as something akin to striking a bargain with the devil that ultimately will cost him his soul. In rejecting this bargain, Dimmesdale comes to a new understanding of himself and what he must do: accept responsibility in public for his actions and for his child. This new understanding shapes his plans for both his Election Day sermon and his final appearance on the scaffold.

Like Dimmesdale, Roger Chillingworth is confronted with choices, and, like Dimmesdale, he chooses to shield himself from public exposure. He appears in Boston just as his wife is being displayed upon the scaffold for the crime of adultery, a crime that shames him as well as her. Chillingworth decides to conceal his true identity as Hester's husband, thus avoiding any responsibility for Pearl as well. His skills as a physician make him welcome in Boston, and his learning provides him with a degree of status and respect, so that few question his motives or actions. Most people hope he will be able to cure Dimmesdale's mysterious illness and encourage their interaction, forwarding Chillingworth's obsession to discover Dimmesdale's secret. Chillingworth's very presence in their shared household, his constant surveillance and probing, adds to Dimmesdale's torment. Using the term commonly applied to early physicians, Hawthorne refers to Chillingworth as a "leech" but implies that this term also signifies the parasitic relationship that develops between doctor and patient.

Easily labeled a villain, Chillingworth is also a victim—of his wife's actions but, more significantly, of his own drive for revenge. Chillingworth attempts to commit what Hawthorne sees as the basest of crimes, the violation of another's heart. As he begins to probe Dimmesdale's nature, Chillingworth becomes more self-assured and willing to cross the boundaries of privacy that should protect another's inner being. When he finds Dimmesdale asleep one afternoon, he goes so far as to pull back the vestment covering Dimmesdale's breast, a physical manifestation of Chillingworth's desire to find what lies in Dimmesdale's heart. His reaction to what he sees, the "ghastly rapture" and behavior compared to "how Satan comports himself" (237), links Chillingworth to the devil. The more fixated he becomes on pursuing his plan for revenge, the more twisted Chillingworth's body appears. Hawthorne suggests that his anger and his inability to forgive have deformed Chillingworth's inner being. When he fears that Dimmesdale will escape his control during the Election Day scaffold scene, Chillingworth attempts to "snatch back his victim" (336), then cries out, "Thou hast escaped me!" (338). Without his victim's anguish to feed upon, Chillingworth shrivels and dies within a year, but before doing so makes a gesture of restitution by leaving all his properties to Pearl.

Only a child, Pearl occupies the most difficult position in the novel, for she is attempting to discover her own identity within the context of the many identities placed upon her by others. Her mother names her "Pearl," a reminder that she has come to Hester at great price, but Pearl seems conscious at a very early stage that she lacks a father and therefore lacks the identity that a father's surname bestows. Those around her wonder if she is Satan's child rather than God's gift, speculation prompted by Pearl's elfish and sprite-like behavior. Hawthorne draws connections between the scarlet letter and Pearl, suggesting that Pearl functions as a living symbol of her parents' sin. Drawn to the letter as an object of curiosity and speculation, Pearl frequently asks her mother about its meaning and import. She perceives that her own identity is tied to this symbol and believes that discovering its meaning will provide clues to her own nature. She attempts to fashion versions of the letter out of seaweed for herself, assuming that she will discern its meaning if it appears on her own garments. For Pearl the letter signifies her bond with her mother, so that when Hester removes it in the forest while in Dimmesdale's company, Pearl demands it be replaced, reasserting her claim over her mother's affections and loyalty.

Hester's situation defines Pearl's world, and she, too, lives as an outcast, denied the companionship of other children. Growing up on the fringes of Boston's Puritan culture and under her mother's at times unorthodox care, Pearl does not absorb the Puritan view of the world and retains a natural innocence and freedom. This innocence and the honesty that emanates from it allow Pearl to perceive the secrecy of others. She frequently asks her mother about the letter and questions the minister about his relation to her. Pearl confronts Dimmesdale, claiming that he is "not true," implying his lack of both honesty and loyalty. Pearl's innocence also allows her to enjoy a different relation to the natural world, and she often looks to it for companionship, finding it in the woods, sunshine, and babbling brook. In these moments, Pearl reflects a romantic connection to nature: she does not see herself as living an existence separate from it, nor does she see it as something she must fear and conquer. But this connection to the natural world does not entirely ease Pearl's loneliness. Only at the end of the novel, after Pearl has experienced a public moment with her father, does her own conflict resolve in the kiss she bestows upon Dimmesdale. The narrator claims that Pearl's adult life in England affords her a happier existence than she had experienced as a child in Boston.

Minor Characters

By using actual figures from New England's past, Hawthorne creates a more realistic setting for the major characters and ties the narrative to the region's history. In shaping these characters, Hawthorne uses some historical facts but also highlights aspects of character that suit his purposes. As the governor of the colony, Bellingham gives voice to the legal authority of the state. He exercises his power in conjunction with that of the clergy, reflecting the strong bonds between church and state in New England. Bellingham has personal traits that mark him as an unusual Puritan, however, including a preference for elaborate dress and ornate decoration. The historical Bellingham had been accused of improper conduct, so setting Hester's story during his governorship raises questions about the hypocrisy of those who pass judgment in this Puritan colony.

The Reverend John Wilson reveals the powerful influence of the clergy within the community. Unlike Bellingham, Wilson is a devout and righteous man, often described as fatherly in appearance and manner. He takes a stern view of human failings and focuses on God's judgment rather than mercy in dealing with sinners like Hester Prynne. As a senior member of the clergy, Wilson influences community attitudes, particularly how the townspeople view Hester and her crime.

Like Bellingham and Wilson, Mistress Hibbins exists in the historical record. Sister to the governor, she appears in the novel as a disruptive force, an eccentric who hints at the practice of witchcraft and associations with the devil. She frequently unsettles Hester with her questions and prompts discomfort in Dimmesdale, who fears the secret knowledge she claims is hers.

The unnamed townspeople also play an important role in the novel, although they exist primarily in the background. During the first scaffold scene, they provide commentary on what has occurred, and they reflect the community's standards and expectations. For the most part, they are not sympathetic to Hester at the outset and believe she deserves her punishment. In the middle of the story, their attitude changes, as they see Hester as a helpful presence within the community. They begin to modify their desire to see her pay for her sin. At the end of the novel, the townsfolk make up the crowd present for the Election Day ceremonies and the scaffold scene. They are less unified in their responses to what happens when Dimmesdale addresses them, contributing to the ambiguity of the scene. Their presence at both scaffold scenes builds a cultural framework for the novel, revealing the contexts in which the central characters must function.

Themes

The Scarlet Letter contains a number of themes that address issues important during the Romantic period, especially those that focus on the nature of the individual and the individual's relationship to the community. In dealing with the individual, Hawthorne raises questions about the implications of self-reliance, the difference between the private and the public persona, and the consequences of passion and repression. He also explores tensions between nature and culture.

The community in *The Scarlet Letter* places extensive restrictions on individuals. The focus on the prison in the opening chapter immediately establishes the power of the community to punish those who violate its laws and to demand obedience as a means of maintaining social order. This strict regulation of behavior may be necessary to ensure the survival of a new settlement, but it also leaves little room for the expression of individual will, especially in a culture as legalistic as the Puritan settlement. Those who question basic principles or the exercise of authority, as did Anne Hutchinson, face ostracism and retribution. As the narrative unfolds and Hester begins to explore the possibilities of self-realization, she embraces the possibility of acting on her own insights and of being self-reliant rather than following the dictates of the community. While Hawthorne is sympathetic to Hester, he expresses reservations about what happens to an individual, especially a woman, who turns away completely from the moderating influences of the community. When Hester returns to New England, she accepts the community's influence on the individual will.

To protect herself from the retribution she might face as an independent thinker, Hester conceals her rebellious impulses beneath a calm and even drab exterior. This introduces a second theme that Hawthorne explores, the contrasts between the private self and the public self. To protect himself from public exposure and punishment, Dimmesdale constructs a public persona. He appears to his congregation a righteous and devout man, one who follows the rules and is a model for others. His public image, however, increases Dimmesdale's inner torment, for he is aware of his own hypocrisy. Torn by this conflict, Dimmesdale tries to evade any situation that brings it to the fore, especially encounters with Pearl, who sees through his mask. Likewise, Roger Chillingworth allows his public persona to conceal his true aims and identity. The townspeople believe that he genuinely wishes to help Dimmesdale, not knowing that, as Hester's husband, he seeks revenge on the man he believes has wronged him. Instead of healing, Chillingworth uses his considerable knowledge and skill to probe into the minister's psyche to inflict both mental and physical distress. Gradually, Chillingworth's inner self gains mastery over his outward appearance, as his body deforms, suggesting how powerful his drive for revenge has become.

In addition to developing themes that focus upon the nature of individuals and their experiences, Hawthorne considers issues of a wider scope, especially the tensions that exist between nature and culture. For Hawthorne, nature presents ambiguities. It can appear sympathetic to the human condition, such as the rose at the prison door, "a token that the deep heart of nature could pity and be kind" (158). Nature brings solace to Pearl in her moments of loneliness, reflecting the romantic belief that nature offers a healing balm to the human spirit. But Hawthorne also describes "that wild, heathen Nature, of the forest, never subjugated by human law, nor illumined by higher truth" (293). Thus, nature is never all positive or all negative, but reflects the very ambiguity that Hawthorne manipulates in his fiction.

The word "subjugated" reflects the Puritan attitude (and that of the later American culture that endorsed westward expansion) toward nature. This attitude toward nature is challenged by the thinking of many Romantic writers, especially the Transcendentalists, who see nature as a source of truth. The tensions between these two views, between a wild and a cultivated nature, reflect the tensions between what Hawthorne sees as two sides of the self. One retains the impulses and instincts characteristic of natural beings, the other reflects the socializing power of culture and its institutions.

6

Herman Melville
Moby-Dick
1851

Given the presence of his work on so many required and suggested reading lists, students find it hard to believe that in the late nineteenth century, Herman Melville had all but disappeared from the literary scene in America. In the 1840s, he had attained a literary reputation and audience through the publication of novels based in part on his experiences as a sailor. Readers were drawn to his descriptions of exotic locations and peoples and to his accounts of adventure at sea. In the 1850s, Melville increasingly incorporated philosophical musings and spiritual questioning into his narratives, elements that readers rejected. Neither *Mardi* nor *Moby-Dick* sold well, and *Pierre*, a novel that treated incest, madness, and murder, brought condemnation and the end of Melville's ability to earn his living by writing. Although he continued to write, Melville's work went unreviewed and largely unread. He eventually supported himself and his family through work as a customs inspector in New York. When he died in 1891, a number of his books had gone out of print, and he was all but forgotten. Not until the 1920s did the rediscovery of Melville begin, along with the debate over his place in American letters. By the 1950s, his role as a major American author was confirmed.

Now an American cultural icon, *Moby-Dick* introduced the white whale as a mythic symbol that resonates with meaning much like Poe's raven or Hawthorne's scarlet letter. Even those who have not read the novel recognize the name Captain Ahab and know the tale of his obsessive pursuit of and final destruction by Moby Dick. The novel sold about 4,000 copies during Melville's lifetime, only 500 of which were purchased outside the United

States. Today the novel has been translated into over 30 languages, and abridged versions are sold as children's books. It has also been the basis of a number of films, the best of which is John Huston's 1956 version for which Ray Bradbury wrote the screenplay. Unlike Stowe's *Uncle Tom's Cabin*, *Moby-Dick* did not generate a nineteenth-century market for material goods associated with the novel. During the twentieth century, however, the name Moby Dick was used to label fighter planes and race cars. Today images of the white whale appear on paperweights, jewelry, pocketknives, and bookmarks, an indication of this symbol's hold on the popular imagination.

BIOGRAPHICAL CONTEXT

Like a number of his literary contemporaries, Herman Melville lost his father at a young age, and this loss had a profound impact that resonated throughout his life. Born in 1819, the third child of Allan and Maria (Gansevoort) Melville, Herman spent his early years in New York City, attending school amid the cultivated and genteel world of his parents. His mother, descended of old Dutch stock, was socially ambitious, but her desires were frustrated when Melville's father, a merchant, saw his business fail. The family moved to Albany in 1830. After a struggle to regain his financial security, Allan Melville collapsed physically and mentally and died in January 1832, deeply in debt. His death left the family in financial straits, forcing Herman to leave school and work as a bank clerk. Although family fortunes revived briefly, allowing Herman to return to school, the Panic of 1837 undermined what little financial stability the family had. Herman took a job as a schoolmaster. From this point on, his relationship with his mother was a stressful one. Often forced to support her and some of his sisters financially, he felt an acute lack of emotional support from his mother while at the same time chaffing under her domineering ways. Eager to escape his mother's house, Melville went to sea in 1839.

Melville's first voyage was on the *St. Lawrence*, a merchant vessel that took him to Liverpool and back. He had the lowest position in the hierarchy of a ship's crew and was forced to do the most menial jobs and suffer abuse and bullying from the more experienced crew members. As a counterbalance to the romantic sense of adventure that many associated with going to sea, Melville also saw the dark underside of life, both aboard ship and in the port of Liverpool. Difficult as some aspects of this trip may have been, it later provided Melville with much of the material for his novel *Redburn* (1849), one of his successful sea romances. After another period of teaching and travel, he again set sail in 1841, signing on to the whaling ship *Acushnet* out of New Bedford. Melville spent 18 months on board before he and his friend Richard (Toby) Greene jumped ship in the Marquesas, a group of islands in the South Pacific. Melville spent a month there, observing and experiencing the natives' life-style. Initially drawn to their simple and seemingly carefree life, Melville became unsettled when he discovered evidence of their cannibalism. Determined to escape, he was picked up by the whale ship *Lucy Ann* and put ashore as a mutineer in Tahiti. There he and another friend, John Troy, explored the island before setting sail on another whaling ship, the *Charles and Henry*, in November 1842. Melville's experiences in the South Sea became the basis for his first two books, *Typee* (1846) and *Omoo* (1847).

Melville remained on the *Charles and Henry* for six months. After working at odd jobs in Honolulu, he enlisted in the U.S. Navy and sailed aboard the *United States* to Boston. This 14-month journey included stops in South America. During his time on a man-of-war, Melville witnessed the cruelty of naval discipline, particularly the use of flogging. He drew on his warship experiences when he wrote his fourth book, *White Jacket* (1850). Upon his arrival in the States, Melville returned to his mother's house, where he began reading extensively and working on his first manuscript. His brother Gansevoort, who had been named to a diplomatic post in London, took the completed manuscript with him, where it was accepted for publication by John Murray. Appearing in England under the title *Narrative of Four Months' Residence among the Natives of a Valley of the Marquesas Islands* in February 1846, the novel received positive reviews and was released a month later in the United States under the title *Typee*. This success launched Melville on his writing career, and he engaged in a period of intense productivity between 1847 and 1852, producing six more novels, including the monumental *Moby-Dick*.

While he was establishing himself as an author, Melville also married Elizabeth Shaw, daughter of Lemuel Shaw, the Chief Justice of the Massachusetts Supreme Court. After their 1847 wedding, the Melvilles settled in New York in a household that included two of Melville's sisters. In 1849, Melville's first child was born, increasing the financial pressures on him. He decided to move his family out of the city and, with a loan from his father-in-law, in 1850 purchased Arrowhead, a farmhouse in Pittsfield, Massachusetts, where he and his family lived for 13 years. While living in the Berkshires, he met Nathaniel Hawthorne, whose work Melville praised in reviews, and with whom for a period of time he formed an intense and influential friendship. Melville was working on the manuscript of *Moby-Dick* as his friendship with Hawthorne developed. In appreciation for the long discussions the two writers shared on philosophical and metaphysical questions, Melville dedicated the novel to him.

Although Hawthorne recognized the greatness of *Moby-Dick*, many readers did not, and a number of reviewers criticized Melville for what they saw as a rambling and disjointed narrative. Writing the novel took its toll emotionally and psychologically upon Melville, but he no sooner saw *Moby-Dick* into print than he began work on his next novel, *Pièrre* (1852), which was rejected in more strident terms by reviewers. Plunged into depression by his failure to find an understanding audience, Melville struggled to obtain employment that would enable him to support his family. He wrote tales and sketches that were published in periodicals, including his now famous "Bartleby, the Scrivener," and produced a novel, *Israel Potter* (1855); a collection, *The Piazza Tales* (1856); and another novel, *The Confidence Man* (1857). These went unnoticed and unsold. Melville was only 36 when his literary career had, in effect, come to an end.

For Melville, marriage and family life did not provide consolation. His financial difficulties, his restlessness and preference for the company of men, and his struggle with depression created tensions in his domestic life. His wife's family had provided financial support over the years, but by the 1860s they viewed Melville as unstable and encouraged Elizabeth to consider a separation from him. Melville gave up Arrowhead in 1863, moving his family back to New York. In 1866 he published *Battle-Pieces and Aspects of the War*, poems that recorded his responses to the Civil War. That year, he also secured an appointment as a customs inspector at the port of New York, where he worked until 1885. In addition to his long poem *Clarel* (1876), he had two volumes privately printed before his death, *John Marr and Other Sailors* (1888) and *Timoleon* (1891). When he died in September 1891, he left among his papers the manuscript for one of his most highly regarded works, *Billy Budd* (1924). Having retreated into private life in the 1860s, his passing was barely noticed by the press. Unacknowledged by a large memorial service like those accorded a number of his literary contemporaries, Melville was buried quietly in Woodlawn Cemetery in the Bronx, New York.

GENRE

Although traditions of the sea narrative can be traced back to the classical world of Homer and later to the sagas that recorded the journeys of the Vikings, the modern sea narrative emerged as a complement to the political, geographic, and economic activity occurring in Europe in the fifteenth century. Monarchs and merchants desired new trade routes, markets, and natural resources to enrich themselves and to secure greater power for their nations. By the late fifteenth century, what is sometimes called the Age of

Expansion was underway, as many countries sent explorers out upon the high seas to discover trade routes and new lands. For the next two centuries, explorers claimed territory for their home countries, fueling the competition to establish colonial empires for England, Spain, France, Portugal, and the Netherlands. Frequently, the explorers or those who traveled with them wrote about their journeys, describing exotic lands, the perils they faced at sea, and the peoples they encountered. They often wrote to promote interest in further exploration as well as economic development and conquest of new lands. Books such as Richard Halkuyt's collection *The Principal Navigations, Voyages, Traffiques and Discoveries of the English Nation* (1598–1600) emphasized the connections between exploration, empire, and nationhood.

As exploration and sea travel continued, personal narratives of sea-going experiences became popular. Often these narratives revealed the concepts of manhood important to a particular cultural era and treated the sea journey as a type of quest in which the individual faced various tests and trials in pursuit of self-knowledge as well as commercial success. Many of these narratives included stories of survival, whether of shipwrecks, mutinies, or encounters with pirates. Fictional versions of such survival experiences also emerged, one of the most famous being *Robinson Crusoe* (1719) by Daniel Defoe. Readers looked to both personal and fictional accounts for tales of adventure and for explanations and interpretations of the differences in customs, values, manners, and religion that voyagers encountered in foreign lands. Through comparisons of foreign cultures to European values and expectations, many of these narratives asserted the supremacy of European culture and Christianity, supporting the ideology of conquest and empire. In the United States, sea narratives continued as a popular genre from the post–Revolutionary War era through the nineteenth century as the United States began to emerge as a trading and commercial power. As whaling expanded as an American industry, tales of whaling voyages became an important part of American sea lore. Whether written as factual or fictive accounts, whaling narratives recounted the dangers encountered in hunting whales and the unpredictability of life at sea.

Melville was familiar with many sea narratives and aware of the form's conventions when he began his writing career. Much of his own fiction from *Typee* on drew on these conventions as well as on his experiences as a sailor. For Melville, the quest embedded within the sea narrative assumed greater significance as he continued to write, for it presented him with a motif within which he could grapple with questions of human nature and consciousness, the nature of God, and the search for truth. As one of his biographers notes, "the voyage or quest was not simply a subject or an occasion for him; it was an archetypal pattern of experience to which his whole nature instinctively turned" (Arvin, *Melville* 79). In *Moby-Dick*, Melville created a multilayered quest within the sea narrative, enriched by symbolism and realistic detail, that some have labeled an American epic.

MOBY-DICK

One of the most encyclopedic novels written by an American author, *Moby-Dick* reflects the range of Melville's reading, his love of the arcane and the obscure, and his fascination with the power of symbols and myth. In developing the novel, Melville made use of material from contemporary periodicals, such as the stories of Mocha Dick that had appeared in the *Knickerbocker Magazine* in 1839. He also drew on personal accounts of other men's experiences at sea, including that of Owen Chase, one of the survivors of the shipwrecked whaler *Essex*. Melville also consulted scientific works such as Thomas Beale's *The Natural History of the Sperm Whale* (1839) to ensure accuracy in his details of whale biology and behavior. An avid reader of philosophy and literature, he was influenced by the work of those authors he believed had a deep insight into the human condition. Among this group he placed Shakespeare; the philosophers Plato, Thomas Browne, and Michel de Montaigne; the English Romantics Coleridge and Carlyle; and his contemporaries, Hawthorne and Emerson. In writing *Moby-Dick*, Melville joined the company of these thinkers, generating a work of fiction that reflects the complexity of his vision.

Unlike most adventure narratives in which plot predominates, the plot of *Moby-Dick* shifts to the background for much of the novel. Melville deliberately impedes its forward movement through the use of multiple digressions into the biology of whales, the history of whaling, the depiction of whales in art, accounts of meetings with other whaling vessels, and factual details about whaling. In some of these digressions, Ishmael pursues his philosophical explorations or offers interpretations of the deeper implications or symbolic import of the processes and objects being described. Periodically Melville draws plot to the foreground, through episodes of hunting whales, the movement of the ship on its journey, and finally the sighting and pursuit of Moby Dick. By constructing the narrative in this way, Melville conveys the rhythm of a whaling voyage, long stretches of waiting and routine interrupted by brief periods of intense activity. He also develops some chapters through the use of dramatic conventions, including dialogue and stage direction, suggesting that the *Pequod* is a stage upon which Ahab's tragedy will be acted.

Melville also enriches the story through allusions to the Bible, classical mythology, and earlier works of literature. Instead of providing a conventional preface that might instruct readers on how to approach the novel, Melville begins with two sections labeled "Etymology" and "Extracts." In "Etymology" he presents the origin of the word "whale," and in "Extracts" he quotes numerous texts—literary, popular, and scientific—to demonstrate the continuing presence and significance of the whale or leviathan in Western thought. In doing so, he lays the groundwork for the symbolic value that will accrue to Moby Dick. By starting with this material, Melville suggests that readers must engage in a process of interpretation and analysis to decipher the symbolic import present in the narrative. Like Ishmael, readers cannot remain content with the surface details if they hope to grasp the novel's underlying meanings.

Setting and Plot Development

Many people think of *Moby-Dick* as a sea narrative, but the first 21 chapters take place on land, from the famous opening, "Call me Ishmael" (795) uttered in New York, to Ishmael's meeting Queequeg in New Bedford, to their signing on to the *Pequod* together in Nantucket. This time on land allows Melville to introduce and develop the point of view, attitude, and mood of his narrator, Ishmael. Ishmael claims that he must leave his land-bound life and conventional occupation to go to sea whenever the "hypos"—or depression and a restlessness of mind and spirit—gain the upper hand with him. As Ishmael's character unfolds in these opening chapters, Melville suggests that Ishmael's quest and the tests he will face have as much to do with his need to discover what meanings stand behind the symbols he encounters as they do with the need to escape his life on shore.

The restlessness generated by Ishmael's frame of mind is evident in the amount of movement that goes on in these land-based chapters. In addition to his travel from New York, Ishmael spends time walking in search of lodging in New Bedford and, once in Nantucket, a ship on which to sail. But he also has a need to explore, to consider the relationship between people and place, to observe customs and mannerisms that define particular communities, especially those connected to a sailor's life. In New Bedford he enters the Whaleman's Chapel, where he hears a sermon based on the book of Jonah delivered by Father Mapple. Mapple preaches on the human impulse to disobey God and the need to submit to God's will to have hope of salvation. Melville juxtaposes Mapple's service and its orthodox Christian vision with Queequeg's religious practice that entails ritual offerings to a small idol. Ishmael finds that he cannot judge Queequeg's practice as wrong and asks himself, "But what is worship?" (849), as he joins in Queequeg's ceremony. Melville uses this comparison as one means of calling into question the assumptions that have shaped Ishmael's sensibility. Ishmael's friendship with Queequeg reveals that part of Ishmael's quest is shaped by his need for comradeship, for connections anchored in the common bond of humanity. Such connections offer a balance to his sense of individuals being what he later terms "isolatoes" (921), who must face the existential crises of life alone. Ishmael's openness to difference also allows him to accept the variety of individuals who will make up the crew of the *Pequod*.

Through Ishmael's search for a ship on which to sail and his inquiries on the *Pequod*, Melville also introduces the mystery of Ahab. Ishmael refers to him as "dark Ahab" (879), an impression reinforced by the encounter with eccentric Elijah. Elijah, who bears the name of an Old Testament prophet, unsettles Ishmael with his hints about what destructive fate may await those who sail with Ahab. Ahab's lack of visibility adds to the question about his character and how he will shape the journey. Ahab does not appear in the novel until chapter 28, once the *Pequod* is out to sea and there is no going back for those who have signed on to the voyage. He does not mix with those aboard ship, keeping his own counsel and concealing much of what he thinks from those on the voyage. Unlike Ishmael, who seeks connections, Ahab consciously shuns them.

Chapter 22 marks the transition from the land-based portion of the narrative to that of life at sea, as the setting shifts to the *Pequod* and the open ocean. Chapters 23 to 47 describe the activities aboard ship and introduce the members of the ship's company. Through the diverse group of men on the ship, Melville suggests that the *Pequod* exists as a microcosm of the world itself. To reinforce the dignity and importance that he ascribes to whaling and to emphasize the connection between whaling and other quest traditions, Melville uses the terms "knights" and "squires" to describe certain individuals and their roles on board. The knights or boat-headers, each of whom commands a whaling boat, include the chief mate, Starbuck; the second mate, Stubb; and the third mate, Flask. Ishmael describes each of them and draws contrasts between them, suggesting that their personalities will influence how they direct their boats and how they respond to Ahab as their captain. Their squires, who serve as seconds in command on the boats, are the harpooners, Queequeg, Tashtego, and Daggoo. By using feudalism as a metaphor for the ship's hierarchy, Melville implies that Ahab serves as king of a rigidly structured chain of command and that he demands the loyalty and submission of those who serve him. Melville also uses this metaphor to indicate that those who have signed on to the *Pequod* have in a sense surrendered their individual rights and independence, a reality brought home to Stubb when Ahab commands him, "Down, dog, and kennel!" (928).

In this early portion of the voyage, Melville also reveals more of Ahab's character, his force of will and his obsession with avenging himself against the white whale. Addressing his crew from the quarter-deck, Ahab quickly molds their purpose to his own when he nails the doubloon to the main-mast, promising it as the reward to whomever raises the white whale. His action is followed by disclosure of the whale's name, Moby Dick, by the har-pooners, investing the name as well as the whale itself with totemic signifi-cance, making it a symbol of the bond of unity among the men as well as the object of their hunt. Ahab gives the order to pass a great draft of grog among the crew as a type of communion rite, another means of underscoring their shared purpose and the crew's commitment to him. Only Starbuck attempts to resist this assertion of Ahab's will over his own, challenging the sense in imputing motive to a "dumb brute" like a whale (967). Ahab, however, senses that even Starbuck, who believes in rules and order, will come under his sway rather than openly rebel.

Once Moby Dick has been identified by name, Ishmael relates his own mixed feelings about what lies ahead, his dread yet his desire to embrace the crew's unity. He also provides more detail about Moby Dick, the legends that have grown around him, his strength and cunning, the supernatural powers associated with him, the way his name alone inspires terror in those at sea. He begins to explore how the stories of Moby Dick have been woven together to form a myth, making the whale "ubiquitous" and "immortal" (987). These tales credit the whale with an "intelligent malignity" (988) that suggests a consciousness driving his actions. This ensures that, while Moby Dick is not seen, as the object of the quest he remains constantly before the crew and Ahab.

Ishmael also reveals that Ahab's fixation on the whale derives not only from the bodily injury he has suffered but from his transformation of the whale into the embodiment of evil upon which he can exercise his rage and hatred. Ishmael calls Ahab's attitude a monomania, and each "gam" or encounter with another ship underscores this singular vision when Ahab repeatedly asks others whether they have seen the white whale. Some of the stories related in these encounters add to the fearful impression of the white whale, while others, such as the "Town-Ho Story," foreshadow the fate of those who challenge Moby Dick. Ishmael also asks himself what the white whale means to him, and what whiteness signifies. He begins with white's associations with innocence and goodness, then considers how, as the absence of any positive color, it can also be a sign of a ghostly presence, a source of terror, a figure of evil.

At the close of chapter 47, Melville introduces the challenge and physicality of the whale hunt, for the cry of "There she blows!" (1022) stirs the mates and crew to action. Chapters 48 to 116 record the hunt for other whales while the search for Moby Dick continues. Melville traces the path of the journey across the Atlantic, around the Cape of Good Hope, through the Indian Ocean, and, after a fortunate escape from pirates in the Strait of Malacca, entry into the Pacific. In this portion of the book, Melville also considers the nature of whaling as an industry—an enterprise that straddles two worlds, one tied to the primitive ritual of the hunt, the other to the demands and values of the modern marketplace. He considers how the whale or products derived from whales have become commodities whose monetary worth is determined by landsmen. In various chapters, Melville continues to develop Ahab's character and singular drive as well as the conflict between Ahab's vision and that of Starbuck. He uses the many gams that occur as opportunities to develop contrasts between Ahab and other ships' captains, revealing Ahab's dismissal of any that he perceives as frivolous, cowardly, or soft-hearted.

The chapters that depict the pursuit of whales are action packed, as Melville reveals the determination of the men and their need to work as a single unit to achieve a kill. They face danger not only from the whale and from the implements they use, but from the unpredictability of the sea and from their own ship. After his first experience of a lowering, Ishmael considers the real possibility of death as an outcome of the voyage, a realization that remains an undercurrent through the rest of the story. Despite the possibility of death, the crew readies to lower boats and embark on the chase whenever whales are sighted, driven by both the desire for profit and the exhilaration of the experience. These chapters also prepare readers for the climax of the novel—the attempt to take Moby Dick. The various lowerings can be read as rehearsals for the ultimate battle that Ahab and his crew will face.

Once a whale has been killed and fastened to the ship, the process of harvesting its oil begins. Ishmael, over several chapters, describes the dismemberment and beheading of the whale and the operation of the try-works to rend the oil so it can be stowed away in the ship's hold. He also spends a great deal of time describing whale physiology, attempting to discern what part of the whale defines its essence. Among the most valuable parts of a whale, the spermaceti—a whitish, waxy liquid found in the head—requires preparation before going into the try-works. Ishmael's description of the manual squeezing of the spermaceti in chapter 94, during which he experiences a rapture as he grasps and squeezes the hands of his fellow whalers, echoes the idea of a communion that binds the crew. Some readers also see in the language Melville uses in this episode an expression of homoerotic desire on the part of Ishmael (and Melville).

Interspersed between the descriptions of the pursuit and processing of whales are chapters that raise more questions about Ahab's intent and the means that he will use to find and slaughter Moby Dick. Although Ahab has revealed his purpose for the voyage, he has concealed his own preparations for it until the first whales are sighted. As the boats are being lowered to begin pursuit, the men discover that Ahab has staffed his own boat with a crew that has been secreted below decks. Headed by the mysterious Fedallah, whom Ishmael links to dark spirits and sorcery, this crew arouses the superstitions of the rest, and the irregularity of Ahab's conduct disturbs both Starbuck and Stubb. Fedallah, described at times as standing in Ahab's shadow, seems the manifestation of the dark side of Ahab, an alter ego who exerts influence on the choices Ahab makes.

Chapter 99, titled "The Doubloon," highlights the different sensibilities and understandings of a number of characters. In this chapter, Melville also considers how symbols can contain multiple meanings, none of which is ultimately the "right" one. As each man studies the doubloon, his responses to it reveal aspects of his inner nature, for, as Ahab remarks about the doubloon, "to each and every man [it] in turn but mirrors back his own mysterious self" (1254). For Ahab, the images that appear on the doubloon are reflections of his own power and supremacy. To Starbuck, the images recall ideas of the Trinity and the steadfast love of God, but he worries that the "sun of Righteousness" (1255) is not visible in the dark of night, a reference to what he perceives as the condition of the *Pequod* under Ahab. Other characters respond to the doubloon in keeping with their nature, until Pip refers to it as the navel of the ship, suggesting that as a corollary to Moby Dick, it serves as a constant center for the voyage.

The simmering conflict between Ahab and Starbuck erupts into open disagreement as the voyage continues. When challenged by Starbuck, Ahab draws a loaded musket on him. Starbuck cautions Ahab to "beware of Ahab" (1300), suggesting that Ahab's obsession with the white whale has overtaken his better judgment and will prove costly to him. Ahab relents, but the drawing of the musket signals a defining moment in the conflict between the two men. Starbuck later considers using the musket to kill Ahab. He debates the merits and risks of taking such action, engaging in a soliloquy that recalls the musings of some of Shakespeare's tragic figures. Melville uses this device to reveal Starbuck's wavering; his doubts prevent him from taking action, much like Shakespeare's Hamlet.

To add to the mythic implications of Ahab's pursuit of the white whale, Melville includes Fedallah's prophecy of Ahab's death. Ahab believes that the conditions of the prophecy cannot be met, making him "immortal on land and sea" (1325), making him God's equal. This prophecy, recited in chapter 117, marks the end of the long preparation for the confrontation with Moby Dick and the beginning of the fateful chase. The *Pequod*'s encounter with a typhoon in chapters 119 to 124 adds to the ominous mood. The storm wreaks havoc with the ship and alters the reading of the compasses. Ahab creates a new compass, reinforcing his control of the ship's direction. During the storm, the three masts catch fire from the lightning, as does Ahab's harpoon. Stubb takes these fires as signs of good luck, but Starbuck views them as additional omens of disaster, that God has declared himself against Ahab and his obsession. Ahab determines that the appropriate response to what is happening is defiance, which fuels his determination and hubris.

The single-mindedness of Ahab's pursuit costs him his ability to sympathize with others. When the captain of the *Rachel* asks for help in searching for his lost son, Ahab refuses, claiming that he is pressed for time in his hunt for Moby Dick. Ahab begins to question his need to prosecute revenge, but admits that he cannot let go of his obsession. Melville reveals Ahab's struggle in the contrast between chapters 130 and 132, "The Hat" and "The Symphony." In "The Hat" Ahab convinces himself that he must have the doubloon, that he must be the first to call out the presence of Moby Dick. In "The Symphony," in a rare moment of calm before the crisis, Ahab senses his connection to the world around him and sheds a tear, a sign that his own humanity and sympathy have not completely deserted him. In a conversation with Starbuck, he asks "Why this strife of the chase?" (1374) and admits the toll his life has taken on him and on his family. Starbuck sees this as the opportunity to press the case for turning homeward, but Ahab refuses. Instead Ahab asks what drives him on, what impels him to go against his longings for home, family, and rest: "Is Ahab, Ahab? Is it I, God or who that lifts this arm? . . . By heaven, man, we are turned round and round in this world, like yonder windlass, and Fate is the handspike" (1375).

Although his presence has been felt in the novel since chapter 36, Moby Dick finally appears in chapter 133, his reputation as a killer of men and his role as a multifaceted symbol having developed over the course of the narrative. Ahab believes that since he spots the white whale first, fate has sealed his charge as the man to avenge the wrongs of Moby Dick. At first Moby Dick seems uninterested in the *Pequod*'s presence. But "with that malicious intelligence ascribed to him" (1381), he outmaneuvers Ahab's boat and snaps it in two with his powerful jaw. More determined than ever, Ahab continues to chase his foe, his drive and the excitement of pursuit forging his crew into a single unit that responds to his command. Ahab's frenzy also seems to fuel the frenzy of Moby Dick, for the whale attacks the boats, again wreaking destruction upon them, and drags Fedallah, who gets tangled in the web of lines, to his death. In the aftermath of two days of failed assaults upon Moby Dick, Starbuck urges that they give up, that to continue is to invite destruction. Ahab again refuses, claiming that he, like other mythic figures, must act out what the Fates decree.

On the third and last day of the chase, Ahab again sets out with the boats, finding reassurance in the impossibility of Fedallah's prophecy. But Ahab's confidence begins to erode when he sees Fedallah lashed to the side of Moby Dick, fulfilling part of that prophecy. Ahab then watches in horror as Moby Dick rams the *Pequod* and the ship begins to sink. Hurling one last harpoon at Moby Dick, a final gesture of resistance and vindication, Ahab gets caught by the line as it wraps around his neck, pulling him into the sea. In an apocalyptic moment similar to the close of Poe's "The Fall of the House of Usher," the *Pequod* is swallowed by the vortex and disappears. As he reveals in the epilogue, only Ishmael survives the ordeal, floating on Queequeg's coffin until he is picked up by the *Rachel*, still combing the seas for Captain Gardiner's missing son.

Major Characters

Although Melville often pushes plot to the background, he does not develop a typical novel of character. His characters do not change or evolve through the course of action, but instead remain consistent types. Melville reveals more about them as the narrative unfolds, exposing their dominant traits, weaknesses, and inconsistencies. Many of these traits are revealed through interactions with other characters, speeches and soliloquies, and responses to symbols such as the doubloon and the white whale. Characters often serve as foils for each other, allowing Melville to highlight distinctive qualities, especially in Ahab.

As the sole survivor of the *Pequod*, Ishmael narrates most of the novel, although some chapters are constructed so that his voice does not intrude. The name Ishmael foreshadows his experience, for it refers to the Biblical son of Abraham who is cast into the desert wilderness by his father. Like the Biblical Ishmael, the narrator endures, but he labels himself an orphan in the end, emphasizing his isolation and feelings of abandonment. Like Melville, the narrator Ishmael enjoys plays on words, the history embedded in names and terminology, and the ways that people mangle names and words to humorous effect. His frequent allusions, analogies, and digressions suggest that he is well-read and has an associative mind, even though he reveals little of his personal background. Being assigned the 300th lay—the smallest portion of the proceeds from the voyage—suggests that Ishmael is perceived as insignificant, making him the perfect observer. Rather than placing himself center stage once the voyage begins, he relates incidents that he observes, offering interpretations about the meaning of what transpires.

Ishmael reveals his need to speculate on the nature of experience and the meaning of life. Much of his questioning focuses on the differences between what he has been taught and what he encounters in the world, whether in relation to religion, to civilization's progress, or to the tension between free will and predestination. Shaped by both Calvinist and Romantic influences, Ishmael struggles to understand the underlying implications of surface realities and to read the world to discern the meaning of human experience. He wrestles with the problem of which ideology offers the truest way of reading nature, humanity, and the relationship to God. Conscious of the power of symbols, Ishmael speculates on the meaning of the whiteness of the whale, but ultimately he offers no definitive answer, suggesting that some truths are unknowable or indeterminate.

In contrast to Ishmael's role on the sidelines, Ahab takes center stage in the drama that unfolds, his will and obsession shaping the meaning of the voyage and its ultimate outcome. His manner of speaking, a forceful, assertive style that incorporates elevated or poetic diction, reinforces his central position, for he commands the attention of his crew and of readers. Ahab's striking appearance—with the "slender rod-like mark" that evokes the image of a tree struck by lightning (924) and the "barbaric white leg" (925) carved of ivory to replace his missing limb—reinforces his singularity and distinctiveness. A complex man who sees himself as embattled against the challenges of human experience, Ahab struggles against feelings of vulnerability, his injury having called into question his control over his life as well as his manhood. Having faced his insignificance before the white whale, Ahab rebels, raging at times against God, against fate, and against the power of the natural world. His desire to avenge himself against Moby Dick reflects his desire to reassert power and control. He knows that such single-mindedness has costs, but he is willing to bear those as part of his personal quest. For Ahab, this quest entails proving himself against God and nature. By killing Moby Dick, he will be able to do what no man has done, taking revenge not only for what he sees as the wrongs done against him, but against humankind in general.

Named after a Biblical king of Israel who worshipped pagan gods and provoked the wrath of God, Ahab, too, seems to have made his own bargain with the devil. He is at times associated with Lucifer, the angel who in his pride rebelled against God and was cast out of heaven. His reliance on Fedallah, a Zoroastrian fire-worshipper who has mysterious powers of foresight, reinforces Ahab's association with dark powers. Ahab also speculates on the meanings of events and objects, but, unlike Ishmael, he reads them to reinforce his already established views. At times, Ahab questions his own motivations and his need to forsake all for his chance to vanquish Moby Dick, but his obsession has taken such hold of him that he cannot listen to voices such as Starbuck's that argue for an alternate course.

As chief mate, Starbuck is second in command on the *Pequod* and stands in contrast to Ahab. A product of his culture, he believes that the purpose of the *Pequod's* voyage is to engage in the commercial activity of whaling, and he questions Ahab's right to redefine the nature of the journey. A professed Quaker, Starbuck relies on his piety to guide his responses to what occurs and to what he sees. He views many of Ahab's choices, words, and actions as blasphemy or sacrilege when they call into question God's power and sovereignty or when they appear to mock conventional Christian practice, such as Ahab's ritual blessing of the harpoons. Starbuck also feels strong ties to the family he has left behind on Nantucket, which influence his reaction to what he believes is Ahab's suicidal quest. Although he believes Ahab is wrong, he is not strong enough to stand against him. At times, his faith seems to waver, as he struggles to determine the right course of action.

In contrast to the at times ascetic Starbuck, the second mate Stubb lives through his senses, taking what he calls a "jolly" approach to life. He does not wish to be troubled by the deeper implications of experience, taking a more fatalistic view of what comes. When Stubb succeeds in killing a whale, he celebrates by eating a whale steak for dinner, a confirmation of his prowess and success as a whaleman. In his encounter with the French captain of the *Rosebud*, Stubb plays the trickster, stealing the smelly carcass of a whale from which he then harvests the valuable ambergris. During this encounter, the word play between Stubb and the Guernsey-man who acts as his translator adds an element of humor. Stubb tends to look for positive signs and affirmations and gives voice to a sense of equality that he feels with his fellow whalemen.

In his first appearance in the novel, Queequeg is definitely viewed as Other. His distinctive tattooed appearance, his probable practice of cannibalism, and his peddling of shrunken heads initially cause Ishmael to fear him. However, Ishmael soon begins to consider Queequeg's differences insignificant, for "You cannot hide the soul. Through all his unearthly tattooings, I thought I saw the traces of a simple honest heart" (846), especially once

Queequeg reveals his own background. A South Seas islander, Queequeg shipped aboard his first whaling vessel because he wished to know the world beyond his island and the cultures of men different from his own. Their friendship, which Ishmael likens to a marriage in its intimacy, grows quickly. On the voyage, Queequeg proves to be an able harpooner and a loyal friend. He faces the tests of the voyage with courage and a calm that suggests his inner confidence. When he becomes ill and believes he might die, he has a "canoe" (coffin) built and makes the ritual preparations for his final voyage. Once he satisfies himself that he is ready to face death, he wills himself back to health, as though death is simply one more test he faces. That his coffin becomes the life-buoy that sustains Ishmael suggests that the bonds of their friendship transcend death.

Not a character in the conventional sense and only physically present in the novel for three chapters, Moby Dick affects the destinies of all aboard the *Pequod*. Although Starbuck argues that it is senseless to attribute consciousness and motive to a non-human creature, many on board the *Pequod* and many of the sailors encountered during the gams have done exactly that, seeing Moby Dick as vindictive and malicious. For many of the sailors, Moby Dick becomes the embodiment of all the dangers they face at sea and a reminder of their own vulnerability and insignificance in the natural world. When he does encounter the *Pequod*, Moby Dick seems to act with cunning and take pleasure in the destruction he wreaks, making him a fit opponent in a mythic battle.

Minor Characters

Many minor characters appear in the novel, some only once, others with frequency. They all give dimension to the narrative; some serve as additional foils to Ahab, and some provide information or add to suspense and foreboding. Many contribute to the diversity of the ship's crew and reveal the varied ways that individuals approach the whale hunt and experience the voyage.

Many ships' captains appear, all in contrast to Ahab. Peleg and Bildad, owners of the *Pequod*, reveal the commercial interest of whaling and their hope for profit from the voyage. Melville explores the irony of these old whalers' profession of Quakerism, a religious tradition that upholds pacifism, and the violent trade they pursue. Captain Boomer of the *Samuel Enderby* has also encountered Moby Dick and lost an arm in the process. Unlike Ahab, he is glad to steer clear of another encounter with the white whale, believing that such an opponent is best left alone. Captain Gardiner of the *Rachel*, who fears he has lost his young son through an encounter with the white whale, seeks help from Ahab, only to be disappointed. His search underscores the bonds of paternal love and humanity that Ahab has forsaken to pursue his quest.

A number of characters prophesy or foretell future events. Elijah and the Manxman hint at trouble that awaits the Pequod, playing upon the superstitions of the sailors and arousing readers' suspicions of Ahab. Fedallah offers a vision of what awaits Ahab, but his cryptic account may be interpreted in different ways. Ahab chooses to hear in it predictions of a positive outcome for his quest and a confirmation of his own power. The most significant of these characters is Pip, the young black sailor who out of fear jumps from Stubb's whaleboat and is left behind while Stubb and his crew pursue a whale. Rescued by the *Pequod*, Pip has gone mad from fear and the realization of his abandonment. He becomes a version of the holy fool, modeled on many of the fools in Shakespeare's plays who give voice to powerful insights in the midst of their twisted speech. Ahab takes him in as his cabin boy, believing that there is wisdom in Pip's utterances. Ishmael also compares himself to Pip in terms of his own abandonment at sea and rescue by the *Rachel*.

Themes

Just as characters see a multitude of meanings in the white whale and the doubloon, readers have identified a multitude of themes in *Moby-Dick*, issues with which its narrator Ishmael and readers must grapple. Ishmael, like Melville, questions the assumptions that most individuals of his day live by, seeing them as buffers between the individual and the unanswerable questions of life. He wrestles with philosophical inquiries, including the problem of knowledge, the human relationship to God or deity, and the place of humans in the natural world. He also considers questions about social conditioning, particularly the expectations and definitions of manhood in mid nineteenth-century America.

As narrator, Ishmael is conscious of the human desire for answers to life's questions, the human need to seek truth. His telling of the story of the *Pequod* is one way of attempting to satisfy that desire, for in telling of his experience he hopes to make sense of it. He attempts to fit all the pieces together to provide some coherent and definite answer about the truth of human experience. Melville calls upon varied resources in constructing Ishmael's account, from literature and history to biology and natural science to the Bible and religion, in an attempt to provide explanations for what occurs. No matter what branch of knowledge he considers, however, it does not provide definite answers or a singular path to truth. Ahab also struggles with the question of meaning and purpose for his own life. He speaks of coming up against a wall—symbolized by the white whale—and believes that if he can just break through it, truth will be revealed. Many characters in the novel also attempt to read omens and prophecies to discern the future. This, too, reveals the desire for answers or reassurance about life's questions.

Melville also raises questions about the human relationship to God. The sermon of Father Mapple establishes a conservative view of the relationship between man and God, one that Ishmael would have learned in the Presbyterian church of that era. In this tradition, the God of the Old Testament predominates, a figure of omnipotence and omniscience who demands submission and abnegation of self. Ahab rebels against this God, his pride and sense of self making the thought of submission and acceptance unpalatable, especially when he considers what he perceives as God's unfair treatment of humankind. Starbuck voices belief in a God of love who sustains those who believe in Him, but his own faith wavers in the presence of Ahab and during the final confrontation with Moby Dick. In contrast to this distant and demanding image of God, Queequeg worships a small idol that he carries with him and treats in a familiar way, a practice that surprises and intrigues Ishmael.

As do many Romantic writers, Melville considers the human relationship to nature and the natural world. In contrast to many Romantics, however, he sees in nature a power and unpredictability that underscores the insignificance of the individual and of humans in general. In response to this insignificance, humans attempt to conquer nature and subdue it. In hunting and killing whales, the largest creatures on earth, humans assert their supremacy in the natural order. In *Moby-Dick,* the sea functions much like the wilderness in *The Last of the Mohicans,* a place where individuals are tested and where they discover the skills necessary to survive in their environment. Melville also considers the human need to inscribe meaning upon nature: the whiteness of the whale, like a blank slate, invites each individual to invest Moby Dick with particular personal significance.

In addition to these questions, Melville explores gender expectations for men during his era. Although Melville makes allusions to the feminine and to the mythic maternal, these concepts remain abstract and few women are mentioned in the book. Instead, Melville creates a man's world in which definitions and expectations of manhood are examined and tested. All the male characters are aware of the importance of manliness, as references to it are used to drive the men when rowing whaleboats. Ahab's loss of a limb, a symbolic emasculation and sign of his lack of wholeness, calls into question his manhood and suitability for command at sea. In the end, Starbuck gives voice to his fear that he not "die in a woman's fainting fit" (1404). Melville also acknowledges the changing nature of manhood in the nineteenth century, as men engaged in business and professional enterprises—whose success depends on their mental rather than physical skill—are redefining the nature of masculinity while exerting control of the marketplace.

7

Harriet Beecher Stowe
Uncle Tom's Cabin
1852

Other American authors had more influence on the shape of high culture in the United States, but none had as much influence on the moral debates and political will of the country as did Harriet Beecher Stowe with her anti-slavery novel *Uncle Tom's Cabin* (1851). Anecdotes claim that during the Civil War Abraham Lincoln credited Stowe with being "the little lady who made this big war" (Rugoff 365). Although Lincoln argued that the war's purpose was to preserve the Union, many anti-slavery factions believed that the war was really about bringing an end to slavery in America. Anti-slavery parties viewed slavery as a great moral wrong in a country whose Declaration of Independence proclaimed that "all men are created equal" and that called itself the land of the free. Stowe's novel, which depicted the physical cruelties of slavery, the destruction of slave families, and the corruption of slaveholders by the very system they defended, intensified the debate over how and when to bring slavery to an end. Serialized in the *National Era* in 1851, *Uncle Tom's Cabin* appeared as a book in 1852 and sold an astounding 300,000 copies its first year in print. By the end of the decade, it had been translated into more than 20 languages and was second in sales only to the Bible.

The novel became part of America's popular culture almost immediately—it was adapted for stage performances, magic lantern shows, and as a children's book within a year of publication. The narrative also provided the basis for board games, jigsaw puzzles, commemorative plates, and other objects that testify to its mass appeal. What is remarkable is the narrative's sustained popularity after the Civil War, when the stage play of *Uncle Tom's Cabin* continued to be performed regularly, its plot pared down to emphasize its sentimental effect. In the twentieth century, it was parodied in vaudeville productions and was the basis for numerous silent films, cartoon parodies, and even popular feature films. Today many of these productions are considered offensive, with white actors in blackface playing up racist stereotypes of African Americans. Although these popular renditions of the novel perpetuated the racial divide in U.S. culture, they also elevated the characters of Little Eva, Uncle Tom, and Simon Legree to the status of mythic characters in American consciousness, their names recognized by individuals who have never read Stowe's novel.

BIOGRAPHICAL CONTEXT

The daughter of ardent evangelical preacher Lyman Beecher and his first wife Roxana (Foote), Harriet Beecher was born on June 14, 1911, in Litchfield, Connecticut. She was the seventh child and fourth daughter born into a lively household, but Harriet's world altered considerably in 1816, when her mother died from tuberculosis. Initially devastated by the loss, Lyman Beecher remarried fairly soon. Beecher believed in the value of education for girls as well as boys, so Harriet attended school in Litchfield. She was also encouraged to read widely, not only the Bible, John Bunyan's *Pilgrim's Progress*, and Cotton Mather's *Magnalia Christi*, but also the novels of Maria Edgeworth and Walter Scott and the poetry of Lord Byron.

From 1824 to 1827, Harriet attended the Hartford Female Seminary, which was run by her older sister Catharine who was a pioneer in innovative and practical education for women. While a student, Harriet had a conversion experience. As the child of an evangelical household, Harriet recognized the importance of this event in her spiritual life, but during her adult life she had various experiences that challenged her beliefs and led her to question the rigors of the theology her father preached. In 1827, Harriet made the transition from student to teacher in her sister's school, but she did not enjoy teaching. Her introspective ways inclined her toward writing and reflection rather than the activities of the classroom.

When Lyman Beecher was invited to head the Lane Theological Seminary in Cincinnati, Ohio, in 1832, numerous members of the Beecher family moved with him. There Catharine established a new school, and Harriet resumed her duties as a teacher. The years in Cincinnati were very influential on Harriet Beecher, both professionally and personally. She joined the Semi-Colon Club, a literary group that met to critique each other's work. Members of this circle encouraged Harriet in her literary aspirations. She won a literary competition and, in addition to the prize money, saw her story "A New England Sketch" in print. While living in Cincinnati, a city across the Ohio River from slave-state Kentucky, Harriet gained direct knowledge of the conditions of slavery and attempts at escape by fugitive slaves, information that would prove invaluable in the writing of *Uncle Tom's Cabin*.

The most significant personal change for Harriet occurred through her friendship with and then marriage to Calvin Stowe, a Biblical scholar at Lane Seminary. Marriage was not something Harriet Beecher had seriously anticipated, and the demands of marriage were physically and emotionally draining. She bore five children, including a set of twins, within the first seven years of marriage. Calvin's temperament, which included a tendency toward melancholy, and his limited income as a professor placed additional emotional and financial demands upon her. As Harriet Beecher Stowe, she continued to write, often to bring in additional income to keep her household stable, but the duties of running a household and caring for her children limited the amount of time and energy she could devote to literary production.

The Stowes remained in Cincinnati until 1850. During this period, Stowe began to publish stories in various national magazines, including the popular *Godey's Lady's Book*. The money she earned allowed her to hire additional domestic help to free up time for writing. In 1843, Stowe's sister Catharine arranged for the publication of Harriet's first collection of fiction, *The Mayflower*. The volume revealed both the strengths and weaknesses of Stowe's work: her ability to capture characters, especially those from New England, with great accuracy of manner and voice and her tendency allow sentimentalism to overwhelm some pieces. Stowe had hoped that this first volume would mark the beginning of steady literary output, but most of her energies still went into the care of her children and her husband. While the Stowes lived in Cincinnati, the debate over slavery became more heated. As other members of her family became more fervent in their opposition to slavery, Stowe gradually embraced the abolitionist cause. When her husband was offered a position on the faculty of Bowdoin College in Maine, Stowe was happy to return to New England, where she felt more at home.

The passage of the Fugitive Slave Act in 1850, which allowed runaways to be hunted in free states, added fuel to the slavery debate. Now fully committed to the abolitionist position, Stowe began to write anti-slavery pieces for the *National Era*, an abolitionist newspaper. In 1851, her novel *Uncle Tom's Cabin* appeared serially in this paper and was an immediate sensation. When it appeared in book form, the first printing of 5,000 copies sold in two days. The novel was not without controversy and provoked rebuttals by Southern readers who thought Stowe had misrepresented the slave system and Southern sensibilities. The success of the novel made Stowe a literary celebrity and a public figure. It also brought a degree of financial security to her still struggling family. She continued to write for magazines and in 1853 published *A Key to Uncle Tom's Cabin* to offer proof of the veracity of her narrative. That year she also traveled to Europe, where she was warmly welcomed by the public and by government officials. She wrote of her travels in *Sunny Memories of Foreign Lands*, which appeared in 1854. Her second antislavery novel, *Dred: A Tale of the Dismal Swamp*, appeared in 1856.

While Stowe had been caught up in the whirlwind following her literary acclaim, her husband accepted a position at Andover Theological Seminary in Andover, Massachusetts. Although she had faced other losses in her life, the sudden death of Stowe's eldest son Henry in a swimming accident shook her to the core. Out of this tragedy eventually came the first of Stowe's New England novels, *The Minister's Wooing* (1859). During the Civil War, she continued to write fiction and in 1862 published *The Pearl of Orr's Island* set in coastal Maine and *Agnes of Sorrento* set in Italy. During the war, the Stowes moved to Hartford, Connecticut, and there, following the death of her father in 1863, Stowe joined the Episcopal Church. The war took its toll on Stowe's family. Her son Fred was wounded at Gettysburg and never recovered, eventually succumbing to alcoholism. In the year the war ended, Stowe published *House and Home Papers*, a contribution to the ever-popular field of domestic advice.

Over the next two decades, Stowe published several novels, including *Oldtown Folks* (1869), based upon Calvin's boyhood reminiscences; *Pink and White Tyranny* (1871), a domestic novel that critiques the preoccupation with social status and material excess; *My Wife and I* (1871), a social novel that treats among other questions the issue of women's rights; and its sequel, *We and Our Neighbors* (1875). She was honored on her 70th birthday in 1882 with a celebration hosted by her publisher, Houghton Mifflin, and her last volume, *Our Famous Women*, appeared in 1884. Stowe spent her remaining years quietly in the company of her family in Hartford, her memory and awareness failing her. She died on July 1, 1896, and is buried in the Academy cemetery in Andover, Massachusetts.

GENRE

The sentimental novel emerged as a popular literary genre in the eighteenth century with the publication of works such as Laurence Sterne's *A Sentimental Journey* (1768), Henry Mackenzie's *The Man of Feeling* (1771), and Johann Goethe's *The Sorrows of Young Werther* (1774). Like the gothic novel that appeared during the same period, the novel of sentiment grew out of the desire to rebel against the emphasis on rationality that had dominated the earlier half of the century. The interest in sentiment also revealed a desire to acknowledge factors other than self-interest and the drive for power as motivating human action. Narratives of sentiment or sensibility featured protagonists who expressed their emotional responses to situations in their own lives or in the lives of others. In some novels, this sympathetic response was seen as a sign of innate human benevolence and good will, a rejection of the Calvinist concept of an inherently depraved or sinful human nature. Writers who incorporated elements of sentiment or sensibility in their fiction often linked the ability to empathize with the plight of others to the ability to act morally. Their narratives were also constructed to provoke readers to respond sympathetically to the plight of various characters. They saw emotion, rather than reason, as a valid avenue toward truth. Writers whose narratives had a didactic purpose believed that triggering emotional responses in readers provided a means of driving home the import of the lesson they wished to teach.

In the nineteenth century, many American women writers wrote what have been labeled sentimental or domestic novels. These narratives encompass a range of subjects and plots, some focusing on the growth and development of a central female character, others on the dynamics of family life or the value of female friendships. Many reflect the importance of what has been called the cult of domesticity, popularized by women's magazines of the day, in which women were defined by their role within the home and were charged with being moral and spiritual guides for their families. Women, it was believed, exercised their power through influence rather than direct argument, and, for many, domestic values stood in opposition to the values of capitalist individualism that defined the marketplace. Because of this oppositional role, domestic and sentimental fiction allowed writers to question and critique social and political issues of their day, including the role of women in a democracy, in what appeared to be conventional and even conservative narratives.

A product of the evangelical tradition of American Protestantism, Stowe claimed that God had used her to write the novel that moved many to embrace the anti-slavery cause. Like many women writers of her day, Stowe made remarks that were either self-effacing or that undercut the possibility of artistic merit in her work, accentuating instead the narrative's didactic purpose. She recognized, however, that the sentimental novel, with its emphasis on sympathy, conduct, and morality, was the perfect vehicle for addressing the issue of slavery and the damage it did to families, both black and white.

She wanted readers to recognize, through their emotional responses to the distress of Eliza and the suffering of Uncle Tom, the true evils that slavery entailed. Further, through their own feelings, readers were to recognize the anti-slavery position as the morally correct choice. Stowe wanted her female readers to acknowledge, much like Mrs. Bird does in the novel, a bond of sympathy with slave women, rooted in the role of motherhood. The language of Stowe's narrative, which combines the rhetoric of domesticity and the rhetoric of evangelical Christianity, draws on two powerful traditions that were familiar and meaningful to her readers.

UNCLE TOM'S CABIN

In keeping with the traditions of domestic fiction, Stowe used various households as focal points for organizing the narrative of *Uncle Tom's Cabin*. These households are set in different parts of the North and South, and each allows Stowe to highlight specific elements in her argument against slavery. The episodes set within these households are held together by narratives of journeys—for Eliza and her son, north to freedom and, for Uncle Tom, further south toward death. Through these two journeys and the households she depicts, Stowe explores the impact of slavery on families, both black and white.

Setting and Plot Development

The novel opens in the Shelby household on a plantation in Kentucky, a border state across the Ohio River from the free states of the North. Two men, Mr. Shelby and the slave trader Haley, are discussing Shelby's sale of some of his slaves to settle debts. Stowe draws sharp contrasts between Shelby and Haley, accentuating Shelby's gentlemanly nature as opposed to the coarse and cruel sensibility of Haley. But she makes clear that the slave system and economics create interdependency between these two men, forcing Shelby into dealings that he finds distasteful but necessary. Haley drives a hard bargain; he is willing to purchase the slave known as Uncle Tom if Shelby will also part with another slave, Eliza's young son Harry. Shelby hesitates, claiming he is a "humane man" (15), but Haley applies pressure, arguing that slaves "an't like whites folks" (15). Shelby stalls by saying that he must discuss the transaction with his wife, but the opening conversation and economic transaction between these two men sets in motion the action that will shape the entire novel. Stowe uses this opening to undermine the idea that slavery can function as a benevolent patriarchal institution, because finances—not human feeling—rule the day.

The early portion of the novel also explores familial and domestic relationships between husbands and wives, parents and children, and masters and slaves. Stowe points out how slave families feel the same emotional ties and bonds of commitment as do the masters, but that slave families have no protection under law, that they may be broken up at any time by the decision of owners or the force of necessity. She introduces George Harris, Eliza's husband and the father of young Harry, who lives on another plantation. Humiliated and forced into drudgery by his master, Harris resolves to flee to Canada, leaving his wife and child behind in what he believes is the protection of a kind master. He plans to buy them out of slavery once he can earn a living as a free man. Stowe also describes Uncle Tom's cabin, where his wife Aunt Chloe has created a domestic space that mirrors that of the plantation house; her domestic skills create and sustain the order and functioning of both households. Tom and Chloe's household, shaped by their Christian beliefs, embodies the ideals of the home that resonate with Stowe's readers.

The values of the home are pitted against the values of the marketplace in the actions that transpire following Haley's second visit. Tension erupts within the Shelby household when Mr. Shelby admits that he has sold Tom and Eliza's son. Mrs. Shelby had assured Eliza that this would not happen, and she reminds her husband of the many times he had promised Tom his freedom. To Mrs. Shelby, breaking these promises makes liars of them both. Mr. Shelby justifies his actions by arguing that he is sacrificing two slaves to preserve the existence of their entire plantation. Mrs. Shelby sees this choice as undermining the values that she has followed in guiding her own household and that she has shared with her slaves. When the household discovers that Eliza has run off with her son, Mrs. Shelby subtly conspires with a number of the slaves to delay Haley's pursuit, using the code of hospitality as a weapon against him. As a woman, Mrs. Shelby has no power in the economic transactions that have occurred, and her influence over her husband has had limited effect. She uses domestic arts and the loyalty of the household to engage in covert acts of resistance to the demands of the marketplace and the slave system.

Eliza's departure from the Shelby plantation separates the narrative into two parallel threads, one that will follow her progress north, the other tracing Uncle Tom's movement south. Stowe alternates chapters that detail Eliza's and Tom's experiences, thus delaying the progress of both narratives and increasing suspense. Eliza's escape and Haley's pursuit of her contains one of the most dramatic scenes in the novel, for standing between Eliza and the hope of freedom lies the Ohio River. In a scene that has become one of the story's mythic moments, Eliza, pursued by Haley, jumps down onto the ice of the partially frozen river, running barefoot across the ice floes, in a desperate attempt to reach the northern side.

Helped to safety by a man who sympathizes with her plight, Eliza makes her way to the home of Senator and Mrs. Bird. The Bird home presents the typical separation of spheres that characterized mid nineteenth-century households, with Senator Bird engaged in public business while his wife maintains their domestic order. A model of the domestic ideal who guides by influence, Mrs. Bird openly challenges her husband on the Fugitive Slave Law, condemning it for its cruelty and promising to break the law when she gets the chance. That chance arrives when Eliza appears. Eliza, perceiving that Mrs. Bird, who is dressed in mourning, has probably lost a child, draws on another mother's sympathy when describing her plight. Her words also touch the heart of Senator Bird, who, despite his claims of abiding by the law, chooses to aid Eliza by moving her to a farm where it will be easier to hide from the slave hunters. This episode emphasizes the notion that parental love transcends the color line and prompts readers to recognize similarities between themselves and those who are held in bondage. Stowe also demonstrates how feelings lead Senator Bird to take right actions, to make the moral choice, despite what he had reasoned earlier.

Eliza moves to another household, the home of the Hallidays, in an unnamed Quaker settlement. The Hallidays, whose lives are defined by spiritual commitment and domestic industry, provide a stable and supportive environment for Eliza and Harry. While there, Eliza is reunited with George Harris, who has made his escape from the South. The Hallidays treat George as an equal, an experience that allows George to claim his manhood and his role as protector of his family. The Harris family prepares to continue on the Underground Railroad, assisted by the pacifist Quakers, when they learn that slave hunters are planning to seize them. In the confrontation between Tom Loker's band of slave hunters and the fugitives, Stowe justifies George Harris's willingness to threaten violence to protect his family and secure his freedom. After another period of waiting, the Harris family, disguised to elude the slave hunters who await them at the shores of Lake Erie, cross the border to Canada and freedom.

In contrast to Eliza's journey and the households that have sustained her along the way, Uncle Tom faces a far different fate as he is carried down the Mississippi River by Haley. Stowe wants readers to compare the households in which Eliza has been sheltered to those in which Tom remains enslaved. Prior to the departure, Stowe depicts the household of Tom and Chloe, but shows that its apparent stability is only an illusion. Under the system of slavery, no slave family has security. In a moving scene, Tom bids good-bye to

Chloe and their children as he is shackled in the wagon by Haley, a reminder of his status as property. Despite the promises of rescue made by Mrs. Shelby and young George, Tom begins the journey south powerless to change his situation.

Stowe uses Tom's journey with Haley as a transition between the Shelby and St. Clare households. The journey exposes more of the horrors of the slave system, particularly the conditions of the slave auctions, where men, women, and children are debased and treated like livestock. Families are destroyed as mothers watch their children sold away and are driven to desperation and death. Haley casts all the transactions that take place in economic terms, rationalizing his trade in humans as servicing a market demand. To carry out some of his dealings, however, Haley and the slave owners engage in patterns of deception, as much to calm their own uneasy consciences as to fool their victims.

On the journey down the Mississippi, Tom encounters Augustine St. Clare and his daughter Evangeline, better known as Eva. When Eva falls from the riverboat, Tom rescues her, and she persuades her father to buy him. With this transaction, Stowe takes readers into a wealthy household of the Deep South, where Tom initially works as a coachman. Stowe compares Tom's situation in the St. Clare household to that of the biblical Joseph in Egypt. Sold by his brothers into slavery, Joseph became a trusted steward of the Pharaoh; likewise, Tom becomes St. Clare's trusted servant, given responsibilities for making purchases and handling money. The first two years of his servitude in the St. Clare household pass uneventfully, his friendship with Eva deepening over time. For a portion of the story, Tom recedes into the background as Stowe develops the characteristics and conflicts within the St. Clare household. The time that Tom spends within the St. Clare household creates another false image of stability and security in the life of a slave.

Unlike the Shelby household or those in Ohio that sheltered Eliza, the St. Clare household is marked by opulence, indolence, and disorder. Mrs. St. Clare, who has assumed the role of an invalid, takes no hand in running the household or in her daughter's upbringing, leaving these duties to others. To remedy the chaos that plagues his home, Mr. St. Clare invites his New England spinster cousin, Ophelia, to New Orleans to manage his domestic arrangements. Miss Ophelia plans to put the household in order and to educate the slaves on matters of housekeeping and management, but Ophelia also gains an education, for she begins to encounter firsthand the cruelties of slavery, including the death of old Prue from whipping. Ophelia questions her cousin on his unwillingness to try to change the system, while he challenges her Northern hypocrisy.

To put Miss Ophelia's arguments to the test, St. Clare brings home a slave child, Topsy, for Ophelia to educate. Initially Ophelia professes that she doesn't want her and doesn't know what to do with her. She questions Topsy about her origins, only to discover that the child has not known mother or father and has already suffered whippings and abuse, her body bearing the scars of her maltreatment. Ophelia's program for Topsy focuses on practical housekeeping skills, reading, and sewing. Topsy quickly develops proficiency at many of the tasks assigned to her, but only does them well when she feels like it, following her own whims and engaging in mischief as often as not. Ophelia also instructs her in the catechism, but it, like all the other lessons, seems to have little effect. Only Eva, who speaks to Topsy with words of kindness, has a calming effect upon her. When Topsy visits Eva on her deathbed, Eva's profession of love and compassion achieves what punishment does not, for Topsy resolves to be better. Eva's behavior gives Ophelia the key to her own relationship with Topsy, for she realizes that until she can embrace the child with genuine affection, she will have no lasting influence upon her.

Eva emerges as the spiritual center of the St. Clare household. Uncorrupted by the social world around her, Eva believes that love and compassion transcend race and status. Her death functions as the central moment of the St. Clare episode, and Stowe prolongs her passing over a period of days. During this time, Eva assumes a more Christ-like aspect, speaking to those around her in phrases that echo the New Testament. Eva's death plunges the entire household, black and white, into mourning, briefly illustrating the interconnection of all who reside there. The household is shaken by her death, but none as much as her father. Uncle Tom, concerned for St. Clare's state of mind and soul, spends a great deal of time with him, encouraging his spiritual reflection. In gratitude for Tom's devotion, St. Clare promises him his freedom, but, as with many of his resolutions, St. Clare fails to act, never putting his intention for Tom or any of his slaves in writing. When he is fatally stabbed during a café brawl, St. Clare's procrastination proves disastrous for all. Left unprotected by any directive from their owner, all the slaves of the household are sold at auction, and Stowe once again highlights the precarious situation that slaves endure. A kind and benevolent master is no real protection from the legalities or brutalities of the slave system.

At the slave warehouse, Tom is purchased by a new owner, Simon Legree, a character whose name has become synonymous with evil cruelty. In a symbolic gesture that marks the change of Tom's circumstances, Legree forces him to don his most worn work clothes and a pair of rough shoes. Legree takes the clothing Tom was accustomed to wearing in the St. Clare home and strips away the identity that Tom had preserved there. Legree also confiscates

Tom's hymnal, as though by doing so he can strip away Tom's faith as well. In the journey to Legree's plantation, Stowe creates another transition between households in a chapter titled, "The Middle Passage." The title invokes the name given to the journey of slave ships from West Africa to America, during which many slaves died from starvation, disease, and overcrowding. Despite the large loss of life, the slave trade was profitable to sea captains and slave traders. This pattern of taking profit despite the toll in human misery defines life on the Legree plantation, for Legree claims that his means of operation is to "Use up and buy more" (395) when it comes to his human property.

Despite its elements of disorder, the St. Clare household had a level of refinement and gentility that kept it from sinking into absolute disarray, but the Legree cotton plantation presents the complete absence of domestic organization. Filled with broken crockery, moldy wallpaper, and refuse, the house is not a home in any sense of the word, frequently the scene of drunken and violent revels on the part of Legree and his two henchmen. This tainted environment mirrors the corruption of its inhabitant, a man who loves no one and takes pleasure in the sadistic cruelty he practices. The Legree plantation is significantly removed from signs of civilization, and, in this isolated realm, the worst horrors of the slave system are manifest. Legree operates his plantation under a reign of terror, brutalizing all who live there through degraded living conditions, near starvation, and physical abuse. On the Legree plantation, Stowe details the sexual exploitation of female slaves alluded to in earlier episodes.

For the field slaves, life consists of unceasing toil and hardship. Even though Tom is a model worker, Legree has an inherent dislike for him, what Stowe calls "the native antipathy of bad to good" (408). Tom's sympathy for the suffering of his fellow slaves awakens in them a sense of their humanity, which Legree has attempted to repress. Although Tom commits no open acts of rebellion, his faith in God and his compassion for others are perceived by Legree as threats to Legree's control. In order to break Tom, Legree orders him to flog another slave, a woman already weakened by her labors. Tom refuses the order, which infuriates Legree. When Tom says that Legree can never possess his soul, Legree orders his two slave drivers, Sambo and Quimbo, to flog Tom to weaken his resolve. Enduring the abuse, Tom refuses to capitulate to Legree's demands. Tom experiences a religious vision that empowers him to withstand Legree's assaults and to retain his compassion for his fellow slaves. He will not lower himself to Legree's level, refusing to kill Legree when Cassy presents him with the opportunity.

Legree has one weakness—a fear of the supernatural—and Cassy, a female slave he has exploited, determines to use it against him to effect her and

Emmeline's escape. She stages a series of events to make Legree think that the attic of his house is haunted, then conceals Emmeline and herself there after feigning flight. Convinced that Tom knows where they have gone, Legree commands him to speak. When Tom refuses in another act of passive resistance, Legree determines to have him whipped until he speaks or dies. In this scene, Stowe completes the transformation of Tom into a Christ-figure, who will liberate others through his suffering and death. The beating of Uncle Tom initiates the novel's emotional climax. George Shelby, now a young man, arrives at the Legree plantation in search of Tom, only to find him near death. After Tom dies, George kneels at his grave and makes the moral choice to which his feelings have guided him. He prays, "oh, witness, that, from this hour, I will do *what one man can* to drive out this curse of slavery from my land!" (489). Stowe's persuasive rhetoric urges in readers the impulse to abolish slavery that she reiterates at the novel's end.

Modern readers think that Stowe relies on too many coincidences to create a believable and satisfying ending in the book's last chapters. On George Shelby's return to Kentucky, he is accompanied by Cassy and Emmeline, who have escaped from Legree's plantation. They encounter another traveler, Madame de Thoux, who questions Shelby about the slave George Harris, who turns out to be her brother. Overhearing this conversation, Cassy believes that Eliza Harris is her missing daughter. The families are reunited in Canada, through which Stowe underscores the argument that domestic life and family ties are sources of stability for blacks as well as whites. After a period of time in France, this extended family decides to emigrate to Africa to be part of the new nation of Liberia. Meanwhile, Topsy, who has grown up in Vermont under Miss Ophelia's care, becomes a missionary to Africa. When George Shelby frees all of his slaves, they pledge their loyalty to him, remaining as farm hands and house servants, rather than seeking independent lives. Critics today see Stowe's resolution of the story lines as problematic, for she offers no picture of an integrated or egalitarian American society.

Major Characters

Given the geographical and social territory that it covers, *Uncle Tom's Cabin* contains a substantial cast of characters. In addition to their individual traits, the main characters of the novel embody specific qualities that are tied to Stowe's political and moral arguments. Characters' lives are defined by specific gender roles and by race and the conditions of slavery.

Although Stowe argues that all whites are affected by the existence of slavery in America, she focuses on Southern whites who reflect different degrees of corruption brought on by their roles as slaveholders. In keeping with her emphasis on domestic life and the importance of social networks, Stowe develops these characters within family groupings, with the exception of Simon Legree, who displays the deepest level of corruption and immorality. Stowe wants readers to view these characters on a continuum from the Shelbys to the St. Clares to Legree.

Trapped by his financial dilemma, Mr. Shelby finds that he must break his word and go back on promises that he has made to both his wife and his slaves. He is ambivalent about and ashamed of what his role as slaveholder demands of him. Shelby attempts to shield himself from feelings of guilt and failure by removing himself from the scene of emotional turmoil and heartache when his devoted slave Tom is taken away. Shelby rationalizes his actions on the grounds of economic necessity, but he also wants to distance himself from Haley the slave trader, whom he perceives as corrupt. He recoils when Haley suggests that the two are in some ways partners in the business of slavery.

Mrs. Shelby, on the other hand, has firm convictions about her role as a Christian woman and her responsibilities toward the slaves who have put their trust in her. She believes she can exert influence on her husband to make moral decisions. When he rebuffs her questioning, she devises other strategies to thwart the sale of Tom and Harry. When it becomes obvious that she cannot dissuade her husband, Mrs. Shelby focuses her attention on comforting Chloe and on finding a way to buy Tom back. As a married woman, she lacks power over financial affairs on the plantation, despite her willingness to sacrifice consumer goods and creature comforts to secure Tom's safety. Although her husband tells her that she does not understand business, the narrator claims that she is far more practical and has a stronger character than her husband. When she gains control of the estate following her husband's death, Mrs. Shelby works to set things to rights and prepare the way for her son to emancipate their slaves. George Shelby, influenced by his mother's force of character and his loyalty to Uncle Tom, pledges to bring an end to slavery, beginning with his own plantation.

Augustine St. Clare has greater ambivalence toward the system of slavery than does Mr. Shelby, and Stowe suggests that if he had had a wife like Mrs. Shelby, he would have been persuaded to make the moral choice to free his slaves. Influenced by the saintly nature of his mother, St. Clare feels the wrong of slavery, but he lacks the strength of character to act upon his sensibility. St. Clare tries to appease his wife, a shallow and self-centered woman who thinks slavery is justified, by avoiding open challenges to the system. Instead, he attempts to find a middle way by accommodating the various foibles and infractions of his slaves, refusing to allow brutal punishment for what he perceives as minor offenses. His procrastination, a sign of his hesitancy to act against a system he believes he cannot change, ultimately leads to the very suffering on the part of his slaves that he had hoped to prevent.

Marie St. Clare, dissatisfied with life and dismissive of her husband's affection, provides no moral or practical guidance within their home. While her husband has qualms about the slave system and believes it is wrong, Mrs. St. Clare accepts it without question, because it preserves her privileged status and allows her to maintain her self-centeredness. She sees nothing wrong with inflicting brutal punishment on slaves to reinforce the rule and superiority of their masters. Stowe presents Mrs. St. Clare as one of the figures fully corrupted by the slave system, a woman whose lack of purpose and principle contributes to the dysfunction of her household and her moral failure.

In the St. Clare household, St. Clare's daughter Eva exerts the moral and spiritual influence that counterbalances her mother's selfish and petulant nature. As an innocent who has not been corrupted by the ways of the world, Eva gives voice to those truths that her parents attempt to deny. She especially understands the humanity of the slaves and her emotional bonds with them, something her mother finds disturbing. Eva's angelic appearance and demeanor underscore her role as a sentimental heroine, one who is too good for the fallen world that surrounds her. Her deathbed distribution of locks of her hair creates communion between Eva and those who love her, marking her as a salvific figure to those who accept the truth to which she bears witness. Although it is hard for present-day readers to appreciate the impact of sentimental deathbed scenes, Eva realizes a form of power as death approaches and attempts to use the emotional intensity of the situation to move her father toward the moral decision she wants him to make—to end slavery in his household and beyond.

In many ways a caricature of the industrious, dutiful, and thrifty Yankee, Miss Ophelia despises "shiftlessness" (189). Although she professes to disapprove of the system of slavery, she has internalized a deep-seated racism that causes her to recoil when Eva embraces the household's many black servants. Stowe uses Ophelia's opinions to confront the issue of Northern hypocrisy, as individuals decry the sins of their Southern counterparts while ignoring their own prejudices. Despite her mixed feelings, Ophelia is surprised by the callousness of Marie St. Clare, for Ophelia recognizes black slaves as fellow humans while Mrs. St. Clare considers them a "degraded race" (206) fit only for servitude. Ophelia has kept her emotional distance from the slaves, including Topsy, but when she witnesses Eva's compassion and response to

Topsy's need to be loved, Ophelia discovers her own nurturing instincts. Her desire to protect Topsy and provide for her moves Ophelia to action. Knowing her cousin's tendency to procrastinate, she insists that St. Clare give her papers of ownership for Topsy, thus ensuring that Ophelia can take Topsy out of the South and secure her freedom.

The only character presented without family attachments, Simon Legree has spurned those attachments, ignoring the pleas of his good mother and burning her last letter and a lock of her hair. The disarray of his household and the brutishness of his appearance reflect the lack of female influence upon him, and these outward signs of decay symbolize the corruption that exists within him. Legree has hardened himself against all others, bringing out the worst attributes in them to perpetuate his own power and accumulate wealth. Legree's fear of the supernatural, however, reveals his underlying anxieties and his fear that he will eventually be called to account for what he has done. The supernatural is the one thing that he believes lies outside his control and against which he feels powerless. When he sees what he believes is a ghost at his bedside, he takes to drinking heavily in an attempt to drown his fear of retribution. His dying moment finds him with no company but this ghostly figure, a final torment for the pain he has inflicted on others.

As a parallel to the white families and their interactions with slavery, Stowe presents black families and the trials they endure as victims of the slave system. For black families, however, the system of slavery thwarts their attempts to preserve family ties and to provide stability and security for children. Every black family that Stowe presents is, at least for a period of time, broken apart, and one of the driving forces for all black characters in the novel is the desire to draw their families back together. Although Stowe intended to arouse sympathy for her black characters, modern readers have criticized her reliance on racial stereotypes, finding black characters in the novel limited and predictable. They also object to her tendency in the novel to endow mixed-race characters with greater intellectual capability than their counterparts of African origin.

Even at the novel's outset, some slave families endure separation. Eliza lives on the Shelby plantation with her son Harry, where she labors as a house servant. Her husband, George Harris, is owned by another planter who controls his movement and his work. A bright and perceptive young woman, Eliza has grown up under Mrs. Shelby's tutelage. Although Eliza feels a strong loyalty to Mrs. Shelby, she realizes that Mrs. Shelby cannot protect her or Harry if Mr. Shelby goes through with the sale. She elects to flee with her son, taking a chance on her inner resources and drive, to make a bid for freedom. Likewise, Harris, who suffers under the abuse of a brutal and domineering master, makes his escape, running north to Ohio. He, too, is a resourceful and independent thinker, rejecting the oppressive limitations of slavery. George articulates abstract concepts about freedom and its implications in his willingness to fight for what he believes is the truth. Reunited once they have found safety in a Quaker settlement, George and Eliza move forward as a family, finding freedom and the opportunity to thrive in Canada, where they are safe from the slave hunters who pursue them.

The other slave family that Stowe develops on the Shelby plantation enjoys a greater degree of stability, for Tom and Chloe live together in a trim cabin with their children, working diligently for their owners. Chloe tends to be more assertive and questioning, while Tom accepts what comes, placing his faith in God. Their stability is shattered when Tom is sold to meet Shelby's debts, and this event highlights further the differences in their outlooks. In league with Mrs. Shelby, Chloe works to delay Haley's hunt for Eliza and then to delay his departure with Tom, drawing on domestic skills and ingenuity. Both women believe they must do what they can against a system designed to leave them powerless.

In contrast to Chloe's action, Tom accepts his situation, believing that his faithfulness to God provides him with a different source of resistance to the evils of slavery. For many readers today, Tom is the most problematic figure in the novel because he seems too willing to go along with what happens rather than attempting to escape or fighting against his oppressors. He, like George Harris, desires freedom, but he sees that freedom differently. Although he longs to be reunited with his family, Tom, as a Christian, believes that his real freedom comes from his spirituality and that his ultimate goal is heaven. He also feels a strong bond with other slaves and is willing to sacrifice himself for their spiritual redemption, to accept his own suffering to bring about their salvation. The problematic nature of Uncle Tom's character has been evident since the 1960s, when the term "Uncle Tom" became a derogatory label for African Americans perceived as too willing to accommodate the status quo of racial discrimination and limited opportunity.

Despised by the field slaves because she has enjoyed a certain amount of privilege by living with Legree, Cassy tells her story to Tom and, through her narrative, emerges as an emblem of all the women whose conditions of bondage entailed sexual abuse. She describes a pattern of being used emotionally and sexually by men and then sold to meet their debts. Coerced into compliance through threats against her children, she is unable to prevent their being sold away and broken by the system. To prevent this from happening to her last child, Cassy kills him in his infancy, portraying the desperation of slave mothers. When yet another master dies, she is "sold, and passed from hand to hand" until she ends up on Legree's plantation (427). After five years of living in hellacious conditions there, Cassy's reason wavers and she experiences bouts of madness. To avoid being vulnerable any longer, Cassy has hardened herself against others, but she takes pity on the young slave Emmeline, who faces the same fate that Cassy has endured.

Minor Characters

A multitude of minor characters, black and white, appear in the novel. These characters serve a variety of purposes. Many of the black characters, including old Prue, Mammy, Rosa, and Adolph, reveal the range of conditions under which slaves function and the various strategies they develop to get by. For the women, such as old Prue, Mammy, and Aunt Hagar, separation from their children or the inability to prevent the death of a child creates a pain almost too great to bear. Some, like old Prue, die from the consequences of the vicious punishments they suffer. The white characters reflect a range of attitudes toward slavery and the corruption that slavery causes. Stowe creates a continuum, from the Quakers like Aunt Dorcas, who oppose slavery and treat all as equals, to the slave trader Haley and his associates, who profit from the sale of slaves and justify slavery by insisting on a racial hierarchy. Many of the white characters fall between these two extremes, but Stowe suggests that those who do not actively oppose slavery bear responsibility for its continuation.

Themes

Clearly the dominant theme of Stowe's novel is the immorality of slavery and its detrimental effects. She explores how slavery functions as a dehumanizing institution, generating internalized ideas of inferiority in those who live as slaves and perpetuating artificial ideas of superiority in those who are slave holders or who benefit from the system. She demonstrates how individuals conditioned by the slave system rationalize their cruelties by claiming that they have no choice, that forces outside themselves dictate their options. Stowe also sees slavery as a force undermining democratic ideals. While she attributes her belief in the value of the individual to her evangelical background, she also incorporates Romantic ideas about the uniqueness of each person to critique a system that denies those trapped within it the possibility of engaging in self-realization.

Another theme at work in *Uncle Tom's Cabin* is the need for family and community, the defining ties that provide an individual with a sense of identity and place. For many of the slaves in Stowe's novel, the loss of family ties proves to be the greatest hardship. Stowe sees the forced separation of husbands and wives, parents and children, as psychologically destructive and calls upon readers to recognize that family ties for slaves have as much meaning as they do for the free. For Stowe, family ties are also the foundation for an individual's connections to a wider community. In contrast to Emerson's emphasis on self-reliance, Stowe argues that all are part of a social fabric and that individual choices have ramifications for others as well as the self.

Stowe also critiques other forces in America that help to perpetuate slavery. She reprimands those, especially ministers, who use the Bible and religious rhetoric to justify slavery, suggesting that they preach a false Christianity. She also challenges the values of the marketplace that emphasize profit and competition, juxtaposing them with the values of the domestic sphere that emphasize nurturing and compassion. For Stowe, the desire for wealth and power regardless of the human cost ultimately creates a figure like Simon Legree, who is willing to sacrifice his soul and the lives of others for material gain.

8

Henry David Thoreau
Walden or, Life in the Woods
1854

In the 1840s, groups of idealistic Americans chose to remove themselves from what they thought were the misdirected aims and actions of their culture, especially those fostered by industrialization and the emphasis placed on the values of the marketplace. They attempted to create utopian communities based upon alternative ideologies and expectations. Among the Transcendentalists, enthusiasm for such a project led to the founding of Brook Farm in 1841. A rural settlement that was intended to combine agriculture with artistic and creative endeavors, Brook Farm promoted cultivation of the earth and cultivation of the self. Although there was great hope that such a project would be a model for others to imitate, Brook Farm, like most other utopian projects, lasted only a short time and disbanded in 1847. Henry David Thoreau did not join the Brook Farm project, but he engaged in his own experiment to test whether he could step outside the familiar patterns of social and economic life in the 1840s. This change in perspective would also allow him to critique what he saw as failings in the dominant culture. When he moved to Walden Pond on July 4, 1845, Thoreau embarked upon a two-year sojourn that gave him the opportunity to engage in the close observation of nature, a process of introspection, and an analysis of the life that many of his neighbors accepted without question.

While Thoreau lived at Walden he worked on the manuscript of *A Week on the Concord and Merrimack Rivers* (1849), a record of the boat trip he took with his brother John in 1839. He also kept a journal and began the first draft of what eventually became *Walden or, Life in the Woods* (1854). In *Walden*, Thoreau said that he went to "the woods" in order "to live deliberately" (394), but this phrase, "to live deliberately" might describe his entire adult life. The verb *deliberate* means "to think about or discuss issues and decisions carefully," while the adjective *deliberate* denotes "careful and thorough consideration," an "awareness of consequences," and a process "slow, unhurried, and steady as though allowing time for decision on each individual action involved" (*Webster's Ninth New Collegiate Dictionary*). Not only during his time at Walden, but in all that he did, Thoreau wished to be conscious of and fully engaged by the process of living. He wanted to be aware of the choices he made and the consequences of those choices, to claim his own life and attempt to achieve the self-reliance that his friend Emerson had praised. In *Walden,* Thoreau considered the life choices that faced him and his contemporaries and offered his arguments for choosing one path of life over another.

BIOGRAPHICAL CONTEXT

Many people think of Thoreau as a loner, but he was surrounded by a network of family and friends throughout his life. Born in Concord, Massachusetts, on July 12, 1817, he was the third child of John and Cynthia (Dunbar) Thoreau, whom they named David Henry (he changed the order in 1837). John Thoreau farmed and managed a store in Concord, but at the time of his son's birth was experiencing financial difficulties. In attempts to find more profitable ventures, John Thoreau moved his family to various locations but returned to Concord in 1823, when he joined his brother-in-law's pencil-making business. This move allowed the Thoreau family to attain a level of financial stability and returned Henry to the town where he would reside, except for brief intervals, for the rest of his life.

In Concord, Thoreau attended the public grammar school. Although he enjoyed learning, he preferred spending time outdoors. He chaffed at the confining situation of the classroom, where he was expected to engage in rote memorization of passages from the Bible and classic works of literature. He enjoyed his extended family in Concord, which included a number of aunts as well as his brother and two sisters. In 1828, Henry and his older brother John entered Concord Academy, where the curriculum was more broad and demanding. When the Thoreau family decided it could afford to send only one son to college, they chose Henry, who was considered more studious, and he entered Harvard in 1833. At Harvard, Thoreau continued to study Greek, Latin, and mathematics, and added modern languages to his curriculum. He completed his degree in 1837, finishing 19th in a class of about 50.

When he returned to Concord, Thoreau took a job teaching in the town grammar school that he had attended, but he quit after being ordered to flog his students. Unable to find another teaching position, Thoreau went to work for his father at the pencil factory. While looking for a teaching post, Thoreau became better acquainted with Ralph Waldo Emerson, who had moved to Concord while Thoreau was a student at Harvard. This friendship was one of the most influential in Thoreau's life, not only from personal interaction and intellectual stimulation, but also because Emerson gave Thoreau access to his extensive personal library. Thoreau became part of the Hedge Club that met periodically at Emerson's house, and the principles discussed at its meetings became important to Thoreau's philosophy and personal code. Interested in personal growth and the inner life, Thoreau began keeping a detailed journal, a habit he maintained until his death. Looking for a wider forum in which to share his ideas, Thoreau delivered his first lecture, "Society," to the Concord Lyceum in 1838, a venue that was to remain his sounding board for various concepts, including early versions of the *Walden* manuscript.

In 1838, Thoreau and his brother John, who had also worked as a teacher, took over Concord Academy. They ran the school according to their own ideas, which included no corporal punishment, inquiry rather than rote learning, and field trips. The Thoreau brothers kept the school until 1841, counting among their pupils Louisa May Alcott. In late summer of 1839, the brothers took a two-week boat trip on the Concord and Merrimack Rivers, using their homemade craft, *Musketaquid*. This trip later became the basis for Thoreau's first book, *A Week on the Concord and Merrimack Rivers*. In 1839, the brothers also fell in love with the same woman, Ellen Sewall, but she eventually rejected them both as suitors. During this period, Thoreau was also writing poetry, essays, and translations and publishing work in *The Dial*, a journal of the Transcendentalist circle. When he closed the Concord Academy because of John's ill health, Thoreau became part of Emerson's household, working as a handyman and gardener, but spending much time reading in Emerson's library. The winter of 1842 brought deep sorrow to Thoreau's life when his beloved brother John died on January 11.

In the summer of 1842, Thoreau became friends with Nathaniel Hawthorne, who had moved to Concord with his bride Sophia. Hawthorne admired Thoreau's writing and attempted to help him with publication. Thoreau continued to write and lecture, and in 1843 filled in as editor of *The Dial* while Emerson was away. During the spring of 1845, Thoreau began building his cabin on the shores of Walden Pond on land owned by Emerson. He retired to the pond to work on his manuscript for what became *A Week*. While there he was arrested for failing to pay the poll tax in protest against the government's perpetuation of slavery. His tax was paid anonymously (probably by a family member), and he was released after being jailed for one night. Thoreau later wrote his best known essay, "Civil Disobedience," in defense of his action. He left Walden Pond in 1847 and moved back into the Emerson house to assist the family while Emerson was traveling in Europe. He finished his revisions and published *A Week* in May 1849; the book received mixed reviews and did not sell. Thoreau continued to work on his manuscript of *Walden* and worked as a surveyor to earn income.

Thoreau's opposition to slavery intensified with the passage of the Fugitive Slave Act in 1850, and, while he continued to study and write about the natural world, he also became an active supporter of the Underground Railroad, assisting runaway slaves to find the freedom that he prized so highly. In 1852, he published extracts from *Walden* in *Union Magazine*, but they drew little notice and he earned no money for them. The 1854 arrest of Anthony Burns in Boston under the provisions of the Fugitive Slave Law prompted Thoreau to write "Slavery in Massachusetts," which he read at an abolitionist rally and published in *The Liberator*, an abolitionist newspaper. That same year, *Walden* was published, and it received a number of positive reviews and sold well. Thoreau's popularity as a lecturer was also on the rise. He delivered "Getting a Living" (posthumously published as "Life without Principle") in Providence, Rhode Island, near the end of the year. Although not well received by its initial audience, the lecture came to be one of Thoreau's most successful and significant.

Thoreau continued to work as a surveyor and to travel, visiting Bronson Alcott in 1856 in New York, where they called on Walt Whitman, whose *Leaves of Grass* had appeared in 1855. Thoreau had some objections to Whitman's work, but he admitted to Alcott that Whitman was "a great man" (Harding 374). In 1857 Thoreau met another individual he came to consider a great man for acting on his principles, the abolitionist John Brown. When Brown was captured and sentenced to death for leading a raid on the federal arsenal at Harpers Ferry, Thoreau wrote "A Plea for Captain John Brown." In 1859, Thoreau's father died, leaving Thoreau with the responsibility of supporting his mother and sister. Thoreau continued his study of natural history, reading and defending Darwin's *Origin of the Species*. He also devoted more time to his study of the American Indians, a subject that had interested him since boyhood. Hoping to improve his precarious health, Thoreau traveled to Minnesota in 1861, where he gathered specimens for his botanical collection and observed the Sioux tribe in ceremonial dance. His health did not improve, and Thoreau returned to Concord, where he began to make arrangements for the publication of remaining works, including *The Maine Woods* (1864) and *Cape Cod* (1865). He died on May 9, 1862, and lies in Sleepy Hollow Cemetery in his native Concord.

THOREAU AS POET AND ESSAYIST

During his career, Thoreau experimented with both poetry and essays to express his insights and observations. His serious interest in poetry developed in 1837 and grew in tandem with his friendship with Emerson, who encouraged Thoreau's early efforts. Although Thoreau wrote a substantial number of poems, most before 1844, critics agree that few succeed as stand-alone pieces apart from the journal passages or prose sections of the works in which they are incorporated. The prose passages often provide additional commentary on the subject of the poem or provide a context from which the poem arises. Fourteen of Thoreau's poems appeared in *The Dial*, including two that appeal to modern readers, "Smoke" and "Haze." By 1845, Thoreau's poetic output diminished; he turned his energies toward prose, which he found a more effective vehicle for his ideas.

Thoreau's activity as a lecturer and his writing of essays are closely intertwined, for many of the essays that appeared during his lifetime or shortly after he died were originally delivered as lectures before the Concord Lyceum or other audiences. Thoreau's essays cover a range of topics, from literary and philosophical appraisals ("Thomas Carlyle and His Works"), to natural history ("The Succession of Forest Trees"), to individual reform ("Life without Principle"), to anti-slavery ("Slavery in Massachusetts"). In many essays that were published prior to *Walden*, Thoreau began to articulate insights and principles that he explores more fully in his most famous work. These topics include the human relationship to nature and the way that nature serves as a source of deeper truths for those who engage in intimate study of the natural world.

In "Civil Disobedience," Thoreau articulates his concerns about the relationship between the individual and the state, particularly the individual who finds himself in disagreement with the state's policies. He believes that under ideal conditions people will no longer need the structures of government because they will be truly self-governing, but, until that day arrives, he asks for a "better government" (204). Thoreau questions the integrity of the state, suggesting that the self-interests of a few can direct the policies of the government against the will of the people, in this particular case through the prosecution of the Mexican War, which Thoreau aligns with pro-slavery forces. He argues that people are too ready to surrender their consciences and moral judgment to the dictates of the state, rather than risk rejection for speaking out against what they see as wrongs perpetrated by the state. He admits that an individual may not be able to eliminate these wrongs, but argues that he or she may refuse to give the state practical (financial) support to continue them by withholding taxes. Thoreau further suggests that in the case of unjust laws, especially those that cause one to inflict injustice upon another, it is right to break them rather than wait for their gradual amendment or repeal. His arguments in "Civil Disobedience," particularly those pertaining to unjust laws and nonviolent resistance, had profound influence on Martin Luther King, Jr., and the Civil Rights movement of the 1950s and 1960s.

GENRE

When he began writing about natural history, Thoreau became part of a tradition in American letters that dates back to the earliest days of voyaging and discovery. The writings of early explorers depicted scenes of the "new world" they encountered, often blending realistic detail with idealized images as they attempted to record factual information while promoting further exploration and settlement. They saw in this new place a freshness, a pristine quality, that suggested the potential for new beginnings and rejuvenation (Lyon 17). Throughout the seventeenth and eighteenth centuries, as scientific interest in the natural world increased, various individuals carried out expeditions to collect specimens and describe in detail the flora and fauna of the eastern seaboard. Later works such as Thomas Jefferson's *Notes on the State of Virginia* (1784) and William Bartram's *Travels* (1791) reflect the continuing interest in documenting the landscape as well as animal and plant life through direct observation, a pursuit that shaped the Lewis and Clark Expedition in 1804 to 1806.

This positive interest in the natural environment contrasted with the attitudes of many settlers, especially those who had emigrated to New England. The Puritans in particular viewed the wilderness as a place of danger and moral chaos that needed to be subdued and regulated. Their attitude encouraged destructive practices and exploitation of the natural environment, behaviors continued and condoned by their descendents. Just as Thoreau wanted to reorient the individual's relationship to the state, he also wanted to change the way his contemporaries saw the natural world. He realized that many viewed nature solely in terms of resources that could be harvested to fuel technological advancement and the further development of an industrial economy. He attempted in his work to shift the emphasis away from what human beings could do with nature to what they could learn from nature. As early as 1842, in his essay "Natural History," Thoreau argued that nature, not society, is a source of health and well-being. He encouraged an intimate study of even the smallest elements of the natural world, stating, "Nature will bear the closest inspection; she invites us to lay our eye level with the smallest leaf, and take an insect view of its plain" (24). This close examination will lead to deeper levels of understanding, and he admonishes, "Let us not underrate the value of a fact; it will one day flower in a truth" (41).

Thoreau attempted to represent nature within his prose, not as it was defined by value-laden terms such as "wilderness" and "frontier," but as it presented itself in "wildness." He was attuned to nature's patterns and to the interconnections within the natural world and between the natural world and humans. He wanted individuals, who, by the 1840s, were becoming more distant from the natural world through urbanization and industrialization, to see themselves as part of something that had its own integrity. For Thoreau, looking at society from the perspective of his cabin in the woods allowed him to see differently, to offer a set of values and insights that challenged his contemporaries' assumptions about their lives, their culture, and their connection to the physical world. Thoreau's fusion of autobiography, philosophy, and observations of nature provided a model that influenced the work of many later writers, including Mary Austin, Aldo Leopold, Edward Abbey, and Annie Dillard.

WALDEN

In living at the pond and in writing *Walden*, Thoreau consciously placed himself outside the mainstream of his cultural moment in order to view the social world that surrounded him with a critical eye. He creates an "I" persona that narrates the text, but this persona is a construct that combines the voice of the autobiographer with that of a seer, one whose insight goes beyond the surface to reveal what is unobserved by others, to elucidate spiritual truths. He condenses his two years at the pond into one, using the seasonal cycle of birth, growth, death, and rebirth to create a metaphor for a process of observation and deliberation that supports the emergence of a more fully aware self. Likewise, the cycle of the day is used to suggest the continuing potential for newness in life, for refreshment and reawakening, that is always available to those who seek it. Thoreau encourages his audience to read nature for truths that can be discerned through close observation and to consider how the truths of the natural world speak to human conditions and experiences.

The book raises a number of issues and arguments, but Thoreau's central concern remains how people have become separated from nature and have allowed the weight of social customs, habits, and material gains to deprive them of the freedom to know themselves and to seek their spiritual and intellectual fulfillment. He worries that his contemporaries have become immersed in desires for material comfort, social status, and money so that these factors define their lives and obscure what Thoreau believes is the purpose of living. Throughout the book he emphasizes the value of simplicity as a means of eliminating that which is unnecessary to one's inner life, drawing upon images of molting and shedding to suggest the ways in which humans can also part with accumulated detritus in exchange for the opportunity to encounter their true selves and truths in nature. He does not advocate seeking a permanent escape in nature, but finds through his sojourn at the pond a deeper knowledge that he believes will allow people to live more fully.

These ideas were not unique to Thoreau; they find expression in the works of other Romantic writers, including the English poet Wordsworth, whose sonnet "The world is too much with us; late and soon" describes how people sacrifice imagination and insight for the emptiness of material gain. Wordsworth claimed that in "getting and spending, we lay waste our powers / Little we see in Nature that is ours," articulating the problem that Thoreau examines in detail. Thoreau draws on some of the precepts set forth by his friend Emerson, particularly ideas found in the essay "Self-Reliance," in which Emerson advocates the value of nonconformity and the need to trust one's insights and intuitions. Thoreau makes a symbolic claim to self-reliance when he chooses to move into the cabin at Walden Pond on Independence Day of 1845.

Some readers are put off by Thoreau's tone in the opening chapter, for he is critical and strident, rebuking his neighbors for their way of life and seeming to assert a personal superiority. This tone creates a distancing effect, so that the persona who narrates *Walden* can look objectively upon the world around him. Thoreau also wants readers to grasp the seriousness of the situation as he sees it, echoing the tradition of the New England jeremiad through which writers pointed out failings of the community to call people back to the true way. In the opening chapter, "Economy," Thoreau sets forth his critique of contemporary culture and the ways that culture works against individual fulfillment and freedom. He explores the concept of economy as a careful management of wealth and resources, but he defines wealth as something apart from the monetary connotations it carries for most people. He believes each individual is given great resources in him- or herself, but that most people squander these resources in the pursuit of social affirmation and material gain. He encourages readers to seek an economy that will provide the means to turn daily life into something noble and elevated. He argues that people have granted artificial importance to things that should make little difference, criticizing the preoccupations with fashion, news, elaborate cuisine, and overly decorated houses. Thoreau speaks of an "advantage to [living] a primitive and frontier life, though in the midst of an outward civilization, if only to learn what are the gross necessaries of life" (332).

In part, Thoreau's experiment at Walden Pond is an attempt to discover what those "gross necessaries" might be and to discover how to obtain them without expending all one's resources. He acknowledges that his view of what is adequate in the categories of food, clothing, and shelter probably seemed abstemious to his neighbors. His diet consisted primarily of "rye and Indian meal without yeast, potatoes, rice, a very little salt pork, molasses, and salt" as well as water (370), although he admits to dining out on occasion. Rejecting the idea that surface appearances offer the measure of an individual, he remarks on his neighbors' greater concern to "have fashionable, or at least clean and unpatched clothes, than to have a sound conscience" (340) and warns against pursuing activities that require new attire. Thoreau uses hyperbole to make his point about housing necessities, suggesting that a tool storage box measuring six feet by three (about the size of a coffin) located near the railroad is sufficient for shelter and would require little maintenance. His own cabin at Walden was a bit bigger, measuring 10 feet by 15, but it was plainly furnished and never inhibited his freedom to explore the natural setting around him.

"Economy" also contains a critique of industrial production and the factory system that had begun to supplant farming as the principal source of economic livelihood for many New Englanders. Thoreau sees the factory system as one that crushes individuality, for those who work in factories have their days regulated by clocks and bells and their work governed by the machines they tend. He claims that the purpose of the factories that produce textiles is "not that mankind may be well and honestly clad, but unquestionably that the corporations may be enriched" (44). He looks for ways to liberate people from unnecessary work and claims that by working about six weeks a year, he can meet his expenses. His ability to limit the amount of time he works for pay reflects the benefit of simplicity, for he argues that he does not wish to spend his time "earning rich carpets" (378) when he values his freedom more. Thoreau gives an account of his resources and how he has used them wisely to make his life at Walden possible. By including what appear to be ledgers measuring his income and outgo, Thoreau turns a tool used by both householders and corporations to his own purposes, measuring profit not in terms of monetary gain but in terms of free time. However, he fails to include in his accounts all the services provided to him by the women in his family.

If he had paid for these services, he might have had to work more to make ends meet.

The tone of the book changes as Thoreau shifts from his overt critique and begins to explore what his two years at the pond have revealed to him. The text at times becomes playful, revealing a wry humor and a love of puns and wordplay. The breadth of Thoreau's personality becomes evident, so that instead of the dour curmudgeon that he is sometimes thought to be, a Thoreau emerges who can enjoy a joke and even turn humor toward himself. The second chapter, "Where I Lived, and What I Lived For," begins the narrative of the year at the pond. Here is Thoreau's statement of purpose: "I went to the woods because I wished to live deliberately, to front only the essential facts of life, and to see if I could not learn what it had to teach, and not, when I came to die, discover, that I had not lived" (394). Thoreau places himself in the role of student who seeks a knowledge not found in books, although he does not reject books entirely. He also returns to critique as he considers how people surrender control of their lives to things outside themselves, whether it be the railroad, the factory, or the news. Thoreau wants to redirect readers' perceptions, to get them to penetrate appearances in search of those "essential" facts or truths that are life-giving and sustaining. The chapter closes with a metaphor of mining to reinforce the idea of searching for the rich vein of truth beneath the surface of life, a vein that runs through subsequent chapters.

Thoreau's account of his experiences at Walden Pond does not employ a simple chronology. Instead, while he progresses through the seasons of the year and presents some factual detail, he also pairs chapters to address particular themes. In the first pairing, "Reading" and "Sounds," Thoreau examines two ways in which individuals acquire knowledge and an understanding of the world. In "Reading," Thoreau considers the study of written texts. To him, reading is a rigorous activity, one that demands commitment and discipline, both in the act of reading itself and in the choice of material to be read. He praises the classics as "the noblest recorded thoughts of man" (403), while he questions the value of popular literature and newspapers with which most readers pass the time. He suggests that most readers settle for the mundane and the easy rather than challenging themselves through encounters with life-changing texts. By limiting their exposure to great thoughts and classic arguments, people cultivate a provincialism that narrows their understanding, instead of achieving what Thoreau sees as the liberality that comes with wisdom. He challenges readers and the townsfolk of Concord to invest not in modern conveniences but in resources that will enrich the life of the mind.

Conversely, in "Sounds" Thoreau writes of the encounter with the natural world, that other source of wisdom and understanding that his contemporaries usually neglect. He praises quiet contemplation and observation, mentioning the sounds in the natural environment—some as blatant as the calls of birds or the croaking of bullfrogs, others as subtle as the fall of a fan of sumac leaves. He contrasts these sounds to the intrusive sounds of the train—both its whistle and its rumble—that for Thoreau signify how industry and commerce regulate most lives. When it is present, the noise of the train drowns out the sounds of nature, just as the preoccupation with business and the market distracts most people from contemplation of the world around them.

"Sounds" ends with the comment that the cabin had "no gate—no front-yard—and no path to the civilized world" (424). The chapter that follows this remark, entitled "Solitude," praises the privacy of Thoreau's cabin and the opportunity to enjoy his own company and that of nature. This chapter again considers the practice of contemplation, suggesting that when one is not distracted by the company of others, one can perceive the fine threads of connection between self and the natural world. He explains that in solitude one moves through the natural world as a part of it, sensing "the presence of something kindred" (427) and the presence of "the workman whose work we are" (429). Here Thoreau suggests the profound spiritual essence that he finds in the natural world, so that when his acquaintances ask him whether he is lonely, he feels he has enjoyed the most perfect company. He claims that encounters with "an old settler and original proprietor" (the Creator) and "an elderly dame" (Mother Nature) during his sojourn at the pond have provided all the company he needs.

In contrast to the contemplative musings of "Solitude," Thoreau presents the bustle and activity of "Visitors." He enjoys company and kept "three chairs in my house; one for solitude, two for friendship, three for society" (435). But he asserts that even in close quarters like those of his cabin, individuals seldom hear each other. He describes some of his visitors in general, and he describes a Canadian wood-chopper at length. Thoreau sees in this wood-chopper a primitive innocence that intrigues him. The wood-chopper is content with his life and is unencumbered by ambitions or material desires; neither is he perplexed by the philosophical questions that intrigue Thoreau. The wood-chopper has a child-like sensibility and evaluates any situation by how it relates to his own experience rather than adhering to the opinions of others. His simple self-reliance and honesty allow him to enjoy life and cause Thoreau to identify in him a "certain positive originality" (442). Thoreau claimed he also welcomed children and young women, pilgrims who came to the cabin to enjoy freedom and leave the village behind. Those who called with their own agendas, however, including snooping housekeepers and earnest reformers, he was happy to avoid.

The contrasts between the chapters "The Bean-Field" and "The Village" raise questions about the purpose of labor and the use of creative energy. "The Bean-Field" explores aspects of cultivation and self-cultivation. Thoreau examines the relationship between the farmer and the natural world, in which the activity of farming binds the farmer to the land and increases awareness of the natural world and its rhythms. As he describes his activities of planting, hoeing, and weeding, Thoreau records the appearance of a number of birds and other woodland creatures, all of which reaffirm his ties to the natural world. His discovery of arrowheads while he is hoeing also links him to the activity of earlier inhabitants (447). Throughout this chapter, Thoreau's knowledge of classical texts informs his writing, especially Virgil's *Georgics*, which addresses the work of the farmer or cultivator of land. *Georgics* emphasizes the productive use of energy in meaningful toil, and Thoreau takes pains to emphasize his productivity as a bean-farmer, incorporating another accounting chart to underscore his success. In *Georgics*, Virgil presents a contrast between the farmer and the city-dweller, treating the city-dweller as a figure who lacks discipline and fails to engage in productive work. Thoreau's chapter "The Village" presents a similar picture as he describes the love of gossip and the idle speculations of those who live in town. He also draws a distinction between his own reflective thought process and the superficial concerns of those who spend their days congregating in the village center. Here Thoreau also briefly mentions his arrest for failure to pay tax, the catalyzing event for his essay "Civil Disobedience."

While Thoreau continues to develop this pattern of "dialogic pairings" of chapters (Schneider, "Walden" 96), he also creates a shift in emphasis with "The Ponds," a chapter at the center of the book. This chapter focuses specifically on Walden and Thoreau's new relationship to it. He admits that he used to visit it "adventurously" in the company of a friend (462), but that now, making his home by its shore, he has come to see it in a different light. The depths of Walden Pond offer a metaphor for the depths of Thoreau's interior journey. He considers how his activities on the pond, such as fishing, provide him with a tangible link to the natural world as hoeing beans did in "The Bean-Field."

Thoreau, however, goes beyond the concrete and tangible in his consideration of the pond, for its mirrored surface that reflects the sky offers him an image to convey the "double vision" of the seer, who, by going deep within, also reaches new heights of understanding. About the pond he claims, "It is the earth's eye; looking into which the beholder measures the depth of his own nature" (471). Thoreau juxtaposes the physical details of Walden's surroundings and the precise identification of fish and birds with allusions to Walden's spiritual value, emphasizing its purity, transparency, and longevity. He speculates that Walden may have existed in its pure state when Adam and Eve were driven out of Eden, suggesting the enduring integrity of the pond in contrast to the corruption wrought by humans, an idea repeated at the close of the chapter.

As the chronology moves through autumn and into winter, Thoreau addresses a variety of topics. In "Baker Farm," he considers the life of Irish immigrant John Field, who struggles to provide for his family and lives in squalor. Thoreau believes that Field has come to see as necessities things that Thoreau lives without, and so Field can never free himself from his condition. The issue of appetites influences "Higher Laws," in which Thoreau considers the animal nature in humans. He discusses his choice to avoid eating "animal food" and to limit his intake of food in general to preserve "his higher or poetic faculties in the best condition" (493). Likewise, he advocates temperance in drink, claiming water to be the only pure beverage.

He claims that "we are conscious of an animal in us, which awakens in proportion as our higher nature slumbers" (497), as he addresses the relationship between chastity or continence and the creative impulse that brings forth genius. Unlike Whitman, who celebrates the link between sexuality and creativity, Thoreau suggests that by restraining sexual impulses, one can redirect energy into creative endeavors. Ultimately, Thoreau believes that living by higher laws demands discipline and commitment, but that to do so offers liberation from the mundane. The chapter "Brute Neighbors," on the other hand, which describes the wildlife that inhabit the woods around the cabin, prompts Thoreau's consideration of the ways in which wild creatures interact with their environment. He does not paint nature as entirely peaceful and benevolent; the battle of the ants, which he records in detail, is likened to "the ferocity and carnage of a human battle before my door" (507).

As the season turns toward winter, Thoreau begins to think of his need for heated shelter and in "House-warming" describes his effort to construct a hearth and chimney. He also admits his satisfaction with his cabin and its snug simplicity. He dreams of a larger house—basically his cabin on a grander scale—that would be a model of openness and hospitality, in contrast to large houses in which guests are relegated to distant quarters and all work and activity is removed from view. To Thoreau, the homes of his contemporaries reflect the artificiality in American culture, where appearance matters more than substance and artificial refinement is valued above sincerity. He comes to regret his decision to use a cook-stove during his second winter, even though it uses wood more efficiently, for it robs him of the companionship and meditative inspiration of the open fire.

Once he has moved "indoors" for the winter and the weather keeps most visitors away, Thoreau reflects on the "Former Inhabitants" of the area around Walden. He mentions Cato Ingraham, a slave who had a small house in the woods; Zilpha, a colored woman, who also lived in a little house closer to town and spun linen for villagers; and Brister Freeman, another slave, and his wife Fenda. He also mentions others who lived near the pond, all who existed at the margins of Concord life. In doing so, Thoreau marks his place as someone looking at the village from the margins, from the point of view of an outsider. Thoreau remarks that "now only a dent in the earth marks the site of these dwellings" (531), suggesting the process by which nature reclaims any space that is not maintained by human endeavor.

"House-Warming" mentions the first ice to appear on Walden Pond and describes how it becomes like a lens through which Thoreau can examine the pond. In "Pond in Winter," Thoreau takes advantage of the ice cover to survey Walden with "compass and chain and sounding line" (549). His precise measurements question the assumptions individuals have made about Walden, showing that it is not bottomless, nor does it contain passages to "Infernal Regions" (549). In this chapter, Thoreau looks at contrasting aspects of Walden: its physical properties and its symbolic value.

After he describes his own process of taking Walden's measure, Thoreau describes the ice-cutting industry that operates on Walden in the winter. He recounts the activity of the cutters and includes a bit of humor when he says they invited him to help saw ice pit fashion, with him underneath (below the ice). He emphasizes the purity of Walden's water that is evident in the quality of its ice. He also speculates about where the waters of Walden end up, since the ice is shipped great distances. He suggests that the waters of Walden have mingled with the Ganges, the sacred river of India. Thus, Thoreau moves from the concrete to the abstract, inviting readers to imagine this commingling of spiritual waters. Thoreau returns to the notion of Walden as symbol—that its unusual depth invites deeper reflection and introspection than if it were a shallow pond, corresponding to a shallow self. He considers that humans do not yet know the many laws of nature and that what we perceive as irregularities in nature are only evidence that we do not yet know enough to perceive nature's full harmony.

The chapter "Spring" evokes the culmination of the year's cycle. The season is embraced as a symbol of renewal and rebirth, beginning with the ice's gradual disappearance from the pond. He describes the booming sounds of the cracking ice. He describes in detail the flow of sand on days of thaw, seeing in it evidence that the earth is a kind of "living poetry" (568). For Thoreau, this flow is evidence that creation is ongoing, that earth is not fixed but ever changing, reinforcing Thoreau's belief that humans and human culture can change as well. He then recounts the various signs of spring as they occur, including the greening of the grass, which he takes as a "symbol of perpetual youth" (570). Like Whitman, Thoreau sees the grass as a manifestation of the life force that sustains nature, that reawakens each spring after winter dormancy. Thoreau likens the return of spring to the "creation of Cosmos" (572), emphasizing the order and harmony in the natural world.

Thoreau then turns from the changes apparent in nature to the changes possible for people. He suggests that the potential for transformation exists in each individual who takes the time to engage in the introspection or personal "soundings" in which Thoreau has engaged at the pond. He emphasizes the importance of living in the present moment, rather than dwelling on the past. As he approaches the end of his sojourn at Walden, Thoreau claims that we "need the tonic of wildness" (575) to keep from stagnating and becoming complacent. His choice of the word *tonic* is significant, for it refers not only to a medicine that makes an individual feel more energetic, but something that provides the basis for harmony.

Thoreau left Walden on September 6, 1847, having spent two years, two months, and two days engaged in his experiment to confront the essentials of life. In the last chapter, "Conclusion," Thoreau summarizes what the experience at Walden has meant for him. The chapter might as easily have been titled "Commencement," because Thoreau suggests the possibilities for new beginnings as well as a sense of closure, much like the end of Whitman's "Song of Myself." Thoreau returns to precepts that were established in opening chapters, encouraging readers not to accept the routine habits of daily life as barriers to exploring the true self. Quoting lines from William Habington, a seventeenth-century English poet, Thoreau wants readers to explore "a thousand regions in your mind / Yet undiscovered" (577), embracing the potential to think, to imagine, to create. He makes references to explorers such as Columbus, Lewis and Clark, and Frobisher, yet he argues that their ventures revealed no more exciting discoveries than one may find within the self. He reasserts the value of self-reliance and independence of thought as articulated by Emerson, the importance of an individual obeying the "laws of his being" (579) rather than the rules and codes of society.

Thoreau admits that his sojourn at the pond was only one segment of his life, that he will take from it what he has learned, but that he has new explorations awaiting him. He closes his argument with an urge to action, encouraging readers to embrace simplicity, to go beyond the ordinary and commonplace, to find meaning in the particular and individual. He wants readers to embrace life and to shun the material trappings and preoccupation with money that inhibit self-cultivation and a deeper understanding of truth. He also calls for the freedom to engage in such pursuits, exclaiming "If a man does not keep pace with his companions, perhaps it is because he hears a different drummer. Let him step to the music which he hears, however measured or far away" (581).

9

Walt Whitman
"Song of Myself"
1855

When Walt Whitman published the first edition of *Leaves of Grass* in 1855, the collection of poems was met with widely different responses. Emerson praised Whitman's originality, Edward Everett Hale his simplicity, and Fanny Fern his freshness. Some reviewers, however, called the book lawless, indecent, and even obscene. Many reviewers were unsure what to make of Whitman's verse, finding that its lack of conventional meter and rhyme made it more like "excited prose broken into lines" (Norton in *Critical Essays* 19) than anything they considered poetry. Others objected to Whitman's language, which they found too casual, coarse, and impolite, suggesting that the book, with its open references to the human body and sexuality, should not be read aloud in mixed company. Undaunted by the negative reactions to his work, Whitman continued to publish editions of *Leaves of Grass* throughout his lifetime, adding new poems, revising those that had appeared earlier, and sometimes removing entire groups of poems. He believed that literature, especially poetry, could be a unifying force for the nation, celebrating America's democratic impulse and the value of each individual.

His long poem "Song of Myself," which appeared as the opening poem of the collection in 1855, was included in each edition. Like the other poems in the first edition, it was untitled. Whitman labeled it "Poem of Walt Whitman—American" in the 1856 edition; simply "Walt Whitman" in the 1860 edition; and, finally, "Song of Myself" in the 1881 edition, a title he retained in the final edition of *Leaves* in 1891–1892. Over time, he revised the poem, altering phrases and punctuation, and, in 1867, he numbered the individual sections, 52 in all. The poem wove together Whitman's ideas on the self, the body, the spirit, democracy, and language, creating an epic that suggests a new way of understanding both individual and national consciousness. In the preface to the first edition of *Leaves*, Whitman articulated the ideals of America that in his view made the United States "the greatest poem" (5). In "Song of Myself," he created a persona, a seer and singer, who perceived opportunities for realizing those ideals and gave voice to them in the language of ordinary people.

BIOGRAPHICAL CONTEXT

The only nineteenth-century American poet besides Henry Wadsworth Longfellow to gain a significant literary reputation in England, Walt Whitman was as forthright and brash as Longfellow was reserved and genteel. The second son of Walter and Louisa (Van Velsor) Whitman, Walt Whitman was born on Long Island, New York, in 1819. The family moved to Brooklyn in 1823, where Walt lived until 1835, although he often spent time on Long Island. Whitman's father was a house-builder, and the Whitman family struggled financially in Brooklyn, as Walter Whitman's hopes for profit from the building trade failed to materialize. Walt attended public school in Brooklyn until the age of 11, when family finances forced him to go to work. His first job was as an office boy for a law firm. In 1831 he was apprenticed at the *Patriot* and later the *Star*, newspapers published in Brooklyn. These apprenticeships marked the beginning of Whitman's long association with journalism and printing. As was the case for other nineteenth-century authors who had limited formal education, including Mark Twain and William Dean Howells, Whitman learned about politics, prose style, and popular literature while working in newspaper offices. An avid reader, Whitman supplemented his education through close attention to the works of Homer and Shakespeare, as well as the Bible and plays of ancient Greece.

When his family returned to Long Island in 1833, Whitman remained in Brooklyn and found work as a printer in Manhattan, but his job disappeared after a fire in 1835 destroyed much of the printing district. Unable to find employment in the city, Whitman joined his family on Long Island, where he worked as a country school teacher from 1836 to 1841. Like Henry Thoreau, Whitman objected to the use of corporal punishment and the methods of instruction then in common practice in public schools, especially rote memorization and forced recitation. Although he returned to journalism in 1841, Whitman's experiences as a teacher continued to influence his work, for he wrote many editorials on education reform and later, in his poetry, often used the teacher-student relationship to shape the speaker-reader relationship.

In 1841, Whitman also campaigned for Martin van Buren, who was running for president on the Democratic ticket. Influenced by his father's liberal political views, Whitman's involvement with politics had begun during his days as a printer's apprentice, since almost all newspapers were affiliated with political parties. He remained actively engaged by politics and the political issues of the times for most of his adult life.

Finding work as a compositor for a New York newspaper, Whitman returned to the city, where he also began to publish short fiction, including "Death in the School Room," a piece that combined his interest in education reform with the sensationalism that was practiced in much newspaper writing. While he continued to work for several newspapers, Whitman published his only novel, *Franklin Evans* (1842), a reform-oriented narrative that focused on the evils of alcohol and the benefits of temperance. Like many of his short stories, it combined sensational elements with moral lessons. In 1845, Whitman moved to Brooklyn, where his family had relocated, working first for the *Evening Star,* then becoming editor of the *Daily Eagle.* As editor, he wrote many of the paper's articles, including those that treated political issues, especially the rising tensions in the debate over slavery and its expansion into the territories.

In 1848, Whitman moved to New Orleans to take over editorship of the *Daily Crescent.* His employment there lasted only four months, but his time in New Orleans and his trip back to New York—which entailed travel up the Mississippi River, across the Great Lakes region, and through upstate New York—was a significant experience. His exposure to Southern sensibilities and his observations of geographic and cultural differences came into play as he later crafted the preface and poems that appeared in *Leaves of Grass.* Returning to Brooklyn, Whitman founded a newspaper, which he printed until 1849. From 1849 to 1854, he undertook a number of ventures, including running a printing office, operating a bookstore, working in carpentry, and freelancing. During this time, he began to publish poems and worked on the material that would shape his first collection of verse.

The publication of *Leaves of Grass* in 1855 marked Whitman's emergence as a new poetic voice in America. Although he published the volume anonymously, he wanted it to be noticed and to reach a wide public. When initially it did not receive the attention he desired, Whitman sent copies to many established poets and authors, including Longfellow, Whittier, and Emerson. Supposedly a disgusted Whittier threw his copy into a fire, but Emerson reacted favorably. He wrote a laudatory letter to Whitman, stating "I greet you at the beginning of a great career" (quoted in J. Miller, 12). As the volume preface explains, Whitman perceived his role as poet to be that of someone who spoke both to and for the American people, expressing American ideals and values in language that was true to the American experience, including the use of slang and colloquialisms. Emerson's endorsement of his work so pleased Whitman that he used the letter in the 1856 edition of *Leaves*. Although later in life Whitman often claimed that his work was ignored when it first appeared, the first and second editions sold moderately well, and by 1860 he was at work preparing a third.

Within days of the publication of the first edition of *Leaves*, Whitman's father died, and Whitman assumed more responsibility for his family. He continued to write prose pieces and from 1857 to 1859 edited the Brooklyn *Times*. In 1860, he traveled to Boston to oversee production of the third edition of *Leaves*, which contained new groupings of poems, including "Children of Adam" focusing on heterosexual love and "Calamus," on homosexual love. Whitman met Emerson while in Boston, and Emerson encouraged him to edit the "Children of Adam" poems, finding them too explicit. Whitman refused, seeing in such action acceptance of the genteel circumlocution he wished to challenge. While promoting his new edition, Whitman, always interested in the political scene, watched as the election of Abraham Lincoln brought the crisis over slavery and the preservation of the Union to a head.

The Civil War became a defining event in Whitman's life. During the first two years of the war, he continued to work as a journalist in Brooklyn, but when his brother George was wounded in 1862, Whitman went to Washington, D.C., in search of him. Whitman ended up staying in Washington for 10 years. During the war, he secured an appointment to a government clerkship that also allowed him to visit the hospitals to care for wounded and dying soldiers. He also became a great admirer of President Lincoln, whom he saw as an honest man and a great leader. From his experiences and observations came *Drum-Taps* (1865), Whitman's moving collection of poems about the Civil War that contained his elegy for Lincoln, "When Lilacs Last in the Dooryard Bloom'd." After the war, Whitman remained in the city, continuing to hold government jobs and working on a fourth edition of *Leaves*, which appeared in 1867, and a fifth edition, published in 1870, each of which contained new poems and revisions of earlier pieces. He also published essays, some of which were collected in *Democratic Vistas* (1870), and saw his poems included in anthologies edited by others, a sign of the acceptance he had been seeking.

A great believer in health reforms that attracted followers in the antebellum period, Whitman began to suffer from health problems during the war, and these grew worse in the 1870s. In 1873, he had a major stroke and, unable to care for himself, left Washington to join his brother George's household in Camden, New Jersey. The 1870s were a challenging decade for Whitman. A number of deaths in his family, including that of his mother in 1873, distressed him. He also wrestled with complications in his personal life, including tensions in his long-term romantic friendship with Peter Doyle. Whitman continued to write and in 1877 began to deliver public lectures. His program on Lincoln, during which Whitman recited "O Captain, My Captain," became a favorite with audiences. In 1881, he supervised preparation of a new edition of *Leaves of Grass* (1881–1882). In 1882, he published *Specimen Days,* a collection of autobiographical sketches, commentary on other authors and thinkers, and personal observations of America, many drawn from his travels as far west as the Rocky Mountains.

During the last decade of his life, Whitman continued to suffer health problems, but participated in the preparation of a biography, *Walt Whitman,* by friend and admirer, Richard Bucke. When his brother George decided to move, Whitman remained in Camden, buying a house on Mickle Street, where he spent his remaining years. Concerned throughout his life about his public image and the legacy that would be attributed to him, Whitman worked on the last edition of *Leaves* (1891–1892) and organized *Complete Prose Works* (1892). While he worked on the final edition of *Leaves,* Whitman's health failed rapidly, and he died on March 26, 1892, in his house in Camden. His funeral drew hundreds who paid their last respects and lined the streets when his coffin was taken to the Harleigh Cemetery, a sign that Whitman had found an audience that admired and valued his contributions to American poetry.

GENRE

When *Leaves of Grass* first appeared, the free-flowing lines of the poems surprised and puzzled many readers, whose concepts of poetry were based on the acceptance of traditional verse forms and meter. Now labeled free verse, a translation of the late nineteenth-century French term *vers libre,* Whitman's poetic line developed its cadence through phrasing, repetition of words, and use of parallel syntactic structures, rather than the syllable count and patterns of stress that readers expected. Whitman was not the first nineteenth-century American poet to attempt innovations in verse, but his was the most sustained and successful effort (Dickinson's unique work was not published as she had written it until the twentieth century). His first experiments in this style appear in his notebooks in the late 1840s, as he sought an "organic" form that would capture the rhythms of ordinary speech. For Whitman, everyday speech had a musicality about it, inflected by the presence of colloquialisms, slang, and contractions. Whitman also detected musicality in place names and in the names and actions of occupations, something he attempted to capture in the many catalogs that appear in his poems.

To some readers the term free verse suggests poetry that has no structure, that reflects no artistry or control on the part of the poet. Whitman, however, drew on many techniques and devices to shape his lines and to create unity and coherence in their progression. He often relied upon anaphora, the repetition of a word or words at the beginning of two or more successive lines, to establish relationships between images or ideas. His lines frequently contain parallelism, the repetition of phrase or sentence structure, to suggest equality among images, ideas, or individuals. His diction relied heavily on verbs, especially present participles, which invest his verse with action and energy (Greenspan 99). Although he seldom used end rhyme, Whitman often incorporated alliteration and assonance, using the repetition of initial consonants or of vowel sounds to sustain cadence and create musicality. Through these techniques and his innovation in line length, Whitman captured the natural flow of human speech.

Whitman's embrace of free verse and his success in using it had a profound impact on poetry in the twentieth century, opening the way for further experimentation in form and style. Many early twentieth-century poets, such as Carl Sandburg and William Carlos Williams, identified with the Whitman tradition, and Whitman continued to influence later writers, including Alan Ginsberg and Adrienne Rich. Even poets who rejected free verse, such as Robert Frost and W. H. Auden, in effect were responding to Whitman as they upheld the value and discipline of traditional poetic form.

"PREFACE" TO LEAVES OF GRASS (1855)

To appreciate many of the themes and issues that Whitman explores in "Song of Myself," one must begin with the 1855 "Preface" to Leaves of Grass. In it, Whitman articulates what he views as the uniqueness of America, the role of the poet, the essential qualities of poetry, and the value of simplicity and candor. Whitman also asserts, as did many of his contemporaries, the need for new literary forms that reflect the values and understanding of the present, rather than relying on traditional forms forged in the mindset of the past. He uses the preface to claim space for his literary work, arguing that it answers the need for an American voice that celebrates the nation's optimistic and future-oriented sensibility.

Whitman characterizes the United States as a fruitful land, rich both in natural resources and in its people, in whom reside what Whitman calls America's genius, anchored in the love of freedom and the belief in equality. According to Whitman, ordinary Americans do not look to public officials or institutions to represent their ideals, but are themselves the living embodiment of those ideals, representing them through their daily actions and interactions. Whitman sees in the self-esteem of common people, in their own recognition of individual worth, a force that undermines the concept of hierarchy that had defined social and personal relations in the past. He supports equality between men and women. He celebrates the notion of comradeship, seeing in it bonds of solidarity that reinforce equality. For Whitman, the relationship between the individual states that make up the nation mirrors the comradeship embraced by individuals, suggesting an important connection between the personal and the political. He also believes that the freedom Americans enjoy includes liberation from the burden of the past and the opportunity to embrace change and the future.

As he considers the nature of America, Whitman claims that its poets must also be liberated from the past and must be able to recognize what is poetical and worthy of celebration in the present. The poet should not lose sight of what is valuable from the past, but must not imitate the voices that have come before. Instead, the poet must be receptive to that which is new, especially that which is part of the common experience. Like Emerson, Whitman argues that the poet can elevate the common or low to be the fit subject of poetry by seeing it from a new perspective. Whitman claims that the poet absorbs the elements that define the country and then "incarnates" the country in verse, taking inspiration from the life around him or her and then embodying it through language so that its value and implications can be recognized by others. Whitman links this to the poet's role as seer—one who perceives that which is true and makes it plain for others, one who looks to the future and can envision that which does not yet exist. Whitman also defines the poet as someone who must be complete in him- or herself, fully individual and self-reliant, yet immersed in the common life. This defines one of the major creative tensions within Whitman's poetry as he attempts to find that balance between the individual and what he terms the "en-masse."

Whitman champions American English as a suitable language for poetry, seeing in its assimilation of words from other languages a reflection of the way that the United States can absorb individuals from all backgrounds, making Americans the "race of races" (7). He sees in the language of the streets the energy and inventiveness of the people, who speak directly about their experience. Whitman argues that the poet must do the same, avoiding the artificial and euphemistic expressions that characterize genteel discourse, for this violates honesty and denies the integrity of both daily life and the human body. Whitman also considers the form of poetry, arguing, as did Emerson, that it is not the rhyme or the meter that ultimately makes a poem but the ideas and understanding that inform it. He claims that "nothing is finer than the silent defiance advancing from new free forms" (14). In closing, Whitman states, "The poems distilled from other poems will probably pass away" (26), underscoring the value of the original and new, what he sees as the value of his own work.

"SONG OF MYSELF"

As the opening poem of the 1855 edition of *Leaves of Grass,* "Song of Myself," as it came to be titled, gives voice to Whitman's understanding of the self and the creative process. In addition, it weaves together thematic elements and motifs, including the relationship between body, mind, and spirit; the continuous and repeating cycle of life and of nature; the worth of ordinary individuals and their work; and the ultimate equality found in death. Whitman also tests the boundaries of American equality and inclusiveness by naming in his poem those who have been excluded in the past. This process of naming, evident especially in his many catalogues of persons, occupations, and places, manifests his belief that the American poet metonymically calls the nation into being in verse. He also questions what it means to be an individual, to be simultaneously part of and separate from the whole.

At the outset of the poem, Whitman raises the possibility of idleness that frees the mind to contemplate things beyond its usual preoccupations. He pairs this notion with the motif of the journey or quest, suggesting that the poem will reveal insights that cannot be had by traditional methods of study and work. Instead, these insights come through discovery of the truths found in nature and within the self, apprehended through intuition. Whitman invites readers to approach life in a new way, to see differently as he has come to see differently. He encourages readers to embrace the creative potential that exists within the self and unites the individual with the creative energy of the universe. He uses impressions from all five senses to suggest how the body is integral to knowledge and argues that no one sense is superior to the others. He emphasizes process throughout the poem; that things (including the self) are not fixed and static, but always changing and evolving. This concept of a changing self appealed especially to Whitman, who made and remade his own image over the course of his career and used photographs to project alternative identities. Such flux and change makes room for contradiction and the creative tension that emerges from it, as Emerson had also argued.

The length of the poem and its multiplicity of themes and topics have challenged readers who have attempted to discern an underlying structure or pattern of organization. Over the years, critics have offered readings of the poem that divide its sections into groupings to trace the development of what they consider its central precept. Many focus on the process of spiritual illumination or enlightenment, while others emphasize the nature of creativity and coming into self-knowledge. They agree that such groupings reveal a narrative pattern within the poem and that Whitman's arrangement of sections is not arbitrary. They disagree, however, about the number of groupings and where to mark the divisions. Recent critics have argued that such divisions are problematic and distort the interweaving of themes and motifs that generates the poem's overall unity. Whitman's only clue to the pattern of organization appears in his decision to enumerate the 52 sections of the poem, a number that recalls the 52 weeks of the year, one means by which he hints at the importance of cycles and repetition or circularity within the poem as a whole.

Through its title "Song of Myself" and the poem's opening line, "I celebrate myself," (27) Whitman evokes the concept of autobiography, an account of one's life often written to provide instruction or example. The relationship between speaker and reader is central to the poem, for the second line states, "And what I assume you shall assume," inviting a bond of sympathetic understanding and shared insight, based in the transcendent idea that "every atom belonging to me as good belongs to you" (27). At various points within the poem, the speaker promises that all that he has come to know can be known to the reader as well, suggesting the possibility of a mutual journey toward insight and truth. The relationship that unfolds between speaker and reader often resembles that of teacher and student. However, the speaker does not recommend the perusal of books, but rather close attention to life and nature. At times the "you" recedes in the poem, as the speaker describes what he has seen or done or thought or perceived, but "you" remains an understood, albeit silent, presence throughout. Toward the end of the poem, the speaker, as all teachers must, sends readers forth on their own journey, admonishing "Not I, nor anyone else can travel that road for you, / You must travel it for yourself" (82).

The journey moves both outward and inward as the poem progresses. What become the first seven sections of the poem lay the groundwork for the journey and introduce some of the major recurring ideas. Drawing on

Romantic and Transcendentalist attitudes, Whitman suggests that the more fully one is immersed in nature, the more fully one can know and understand the self. For Whitman, this immersion is not just metaphorical but physical, and his speaker delights in the contact with the natural world that his senses convey. The speaker chooses to step out of doors, to inhale the "atmosphere," to seek what is natural rather than remain in the realm of the artificial, no matter how pleasing it may be (27). He invites readers to leave the school room and the library to find another path toward understanding. Whitman also invites readers to experience a degree of intimacy with the speaker. At the end of section 19, the speaker states, "This hour I tell things in confidence, / I might not tell everybody, but I will tell you" (45). This singling out treats the reader as one privileged to hear truth, to know that which the universe has to reveal, but which only the true poet perceives.

The earliest sections of the poem discuss the body and various bodily functions, claiming for them a rightful place as part of nature. Whitman challenges the false modesty of Victorian America that relies upon euphemism when speaking of the body. He states "Welcome is every organ and attribute of me, and of any man hearty and clean, / Not an inch nor a particle of an inch is vile, and none shall be less familiar than the rest" (29). Rather than accept the practice of denying the body or mortifying the flesh to attain wisdom or spiritual insight, Whitman argues that the body provides yet another avenue toward that insight. He rejects notions of the mind-body or flesh-spirit dichotomy and instead sees body, mind, and spirit as inextricably linked, as a single whole. In section 21 he chants, "I am the poet of the body, /And I am the poet of the soul" using parallelism to stress the equality between the two (46). If one aim of the journey is to attain wholeness, then, in Whitman's view, the body must be a part of that process.

Whitman also draws links between human sexuality and the creative energy within the universe. He refers to the "procreant urge" in section 3 and compares sexual desire to the drive to create. For Whitman, intercourse also provides a tangible image to convey the infusion of spirit into body that allows for creativity. Whitman attempts to convey the mystical experience that has given the speaker a new way of seeing the world and encountering life, the first instance of which occurs in section 5. In addressing sexuality, Whitman believes that the poet can transcend gender difference, can see from a female as well as male point of view. In section 11, Whitman speaks of female sexual desire, as a woman gazes at 28 young men bathing, imaginatively joining in their frolic and caressing their bodies. He does not condemn her desire or her imagined encounter. (Many readers see in this section an expression of Whitman's homoerotic desire as well.) The speaker proclaims in section 21, "I am the poet of the woman the same as the man, /And I say it is as great to be a woman as to be a man" (46).

Like Thoreau, Whitman sees the danger in being caught up in the debate over the news or in the exchange of gossip, because in focusing on such trivialities, one risks losing sight of the larger questions. For Whitman these larger questions are shaped by apprehension of the continuities in human experience and the continuities expressed in the repeated cycles of nature. In section 6, Whitman turns his attention to the grass and considers what it may signify and represent. He suggests the many ways one can read nature as an outward sign of underlying truths. One of the central truths he addresses is death, but he treats death not as an ending, but as the ultimate source of equality and unity. As a natural part of the cycle of life, in death the body becomes part of nature in a different way and the soul reintegrates with the larger spirit that energizes creation. Thus, according to the speaker, humans enjoy a type of immortality, although they do not recognize it as such.

Having established some of the principles that will inform the journey, Whitman begins to move outward, beginning in section 8, as the speaker describes some of the activities that occur within the city and "what living and buried speech is always vibrating here" (34). From the city, the speaker moves to the farm, then to the woodland wilderness and the ocean shore, indicating how far and wide the journey will reach. He also captures through two vignettes the historical moment, as he describes the marriage of a trapper and the appearance of a runaway slave. In the 1855 text, the marriage of the trapper acknowledges America's continuing settlement of the West, but hints that such settlement depends upon force. The description of the trapper notes, "One hand rested on his rifle . . . the other hand held firmly the wrist of the red girl" (35). By the 1881 edition, Whitman had softened this image, so that the rifle has disappeared and the trapper "held his bride by the hand" (196). The runaway slave draws the issue of slavery and abolition into the poem, as the speaker provides comfort to the runaway, treats him as an equal, and offers protection from those who might be in pursuit in the form of the "fire-lock lean'd in the corner" (197).

Sections 12 and 13 describe the work and actions of common laborers, capturing the poetry of their movements and gestures. Whitman reiterates one of his central themes—inclusiveness—when he states "not a person or object is missing, /Absorbing all to myself and for this song" (199). To underscore this concept, he creates in section 15 one of his trademark catalogues of individuals and their actions, claiming at the end in the 1881 version that, "And of these one and all I weave the song of myself" (203). Section 16 suggests that Whitman's song takes in all points of North America, regardless of regional differences, that he is comrade of Northerner and Southerner alike, that his poetry can unite that which may seem divided or different. The picture of inclusiveness continues in sections 18 and 19, when Whitman claims that his song is also for the defeated, the failed, and the dead. He embraces nature, fully and physically, in sections 21 and 22, while section 23 welcomes the work of science and the facts it generates, incorporating that, too, into his storehouse of material for the song that continues to unfold.

The ever-increasing circles of inclusiveness culminate in section 24, when Whitman identifies himself as "Walt Whitman, an American, one of the roughs, a kosmos" (50), the term *kosmos*, taken from the Greek, meaning world or universe. In addition to proclaiming that he embodies worlds, Whitman places himself at the center of the circles of inclusiveness. He merges himself with what he had earlier termed "the kelson [a central support] of the creation" (31), which he labels love. Welcoming the unrefined, Whitman reiterates his ability to absorb all in his embrace of democracy, in his desire to be the voice of those who have not been heard in poetry before. (Interestingly, he later revises the line to read "Walt Whitman, a kosmos, of Manhattan the son" [210], distancing himself from the coarser elements of city life.)

Claiming the poet's transforming power that Emerson also described, Whitman's speaker declares himself to be divine and states that, through him, "forbidden voices" (50) will speak, "transfigured" (50) by the light that the poet sheds upon them. These voices, through the speaker, chant praise and acceptance of the human body in its entirety, celebrating sexuality and the physical presence of the self. Fully embodied in this physical self, the speaker then offers one of the mystical visions that appears in the poem, as he observes that "My voice goes after what my eyes cannot reach, / With the twirl of my tongue I encompass worlds and volumes of worlds" (52). In the sections that follow, Whitman continues to explore the ways in which the self takes in that which is external to it, through listening and touching, moved by various stimuli that contribute to the song. He lists sounds from daily life and describes the power of music, first instrumental, but even more so vocal, that carries the speaker out of himself to a different plain of consciousness. Touch becomes a means of connection to others and, like music, heightens awareness. It also stimulates erotic arousal and release, suggesting parallels between sexual ecstasy and enhanced states of consciousness. Through what his senses absorb, Whitman looks for ways to describe the mystical experience, to suggest how the self transcends its own physical boundaries to experience oneness with the world or kosmos.

As he had after the opening sections of the poem, Whitman turns outward from the mystical experience of oneness to consider the various parts that create that whole. Section 31 begins with a statement of awe at the perfection of nature and the miracle of life, present in the most ordinary of things, like a blade of grass or an ant or a mouse. The speaker has absorbed both the animate and the inanimate, the past as well as the present. He claims, "I think I could turn and live awhile with the animals . . . they are so placid and self-contained (58). He considers how they are free from the dissatisfactions Whitman senses in his contemporaries, their whining and acquisitive impulses, their worship of hierarchy and ambition. The speaker's contemplation of the animals returns him to the meditative state he enjoyed when he first "loafed on the grass" (59), and he again sets forth on an imagined journey, explaining "I am afoot with my vision" (59) as he creates another catalogue of places and actions that suggest how all-encompassing both his journey and his embrace can be.

After listing myriad possibilities, the speaker imagines himself as at one with specific others. He considers the nature of the heroic heart that endures great pain: the courageous skipper, the "hounded slave," the "mash'd fireman," the "old artillerist" (64–66), claiming a sympathetic bond with each. "I am the man. . . . I suffered. . . . I was there" (64). The speaker again reiterates his ability to absorb the nation and all it contains, that "All these I feel or am" (65). As he continues with his consideration of the inter-mingled nature of heroism and suffering, Whitman develops two vignettes from U.S. history. In the first (section 34), he re-imagines a massacre during the Mexican War, not the well-known story of the Alamo, but a bloodier carnage, a "murder in cold blood" (66) that took place a few weeks later. After being held briefly as prisoners, 412 young men, "the glory of the race of rangers" (67), were executed by their Mexican captors. For Whitman, their heroism emerges when "none obeyed the command to kneel," and to the end they refused to recognize the superiority of another or the system of social hierarchy their captors represent. The second vignette, which spans sections 35 and 36, recounts the tale of John Paul Jones's taking of the British ship *Serapis* during the Revolutionary War. American forces are out-gunned, but Jones, tenacious in the fight, holds out until the British surrender, despite the fact that his own ship is sinking. In the aftermath of the encounter, Whitman details the cost of battle, the dead and dying, the wounded and maimed. He feels the loss as much as the victory, but he sees valor in the sacrifices made for higher purpose.

This awareness of suffering leads to a section in which the speaker identifies himself with prisoners, the dying, and beggars—those usually labeled outcasts. He then identifies himself with Christ, a figure who also embraced outcasts, suffering a crucifixion and experiencing a resurrection, rising with a new sense of his power. He greets his followers with the French term for students, *eleves*, as he speaks of his connections to them. In the 1855 version, he exclaims, "I see you understand yourselves and me" (71). In later versions, Whitman modified the lines to read "Eleves, I salute you! Come forward!/ Continue your annotations, continue your questionings" (231), shifting the emphasis to one of continued inquiry, impelling readers forward within the poem. In the lines that become sections 39 to 42, the speaker explores this empowered self, its magnetism, how it attracts men and women who "desire he should like them and touch them and speak to them and stay with them" (72). He revels in his capacity to take in all and to inspire, claiming as his lineage the gods and prophets of ages past, but correcting the misapprehensions of those who had failed to see divinity present within humans as well. While he again celebrates the connection between procreative potential and creative powers, he also acknowledges, "I know perfectly well my own egotism" (76), an aspect of the persona that some readers found, and still find, troubling.

Throughout the poem, Whitman raises questions about spirituality, about the relationship between the spirit and the body, and how traditions of the past have shaped the ways in which his contemporaries define this relationship. In the 1850s, religion played a significant role in American life, both within the home and in the public sphere. In the poem, Whitman suggests alternatives to the predominant religious views of his day, seeing in them elements that limit or constrict an appreciation of human potential. In section 43, the speaker announces that his faith has encompassed all traditions and that he can embrace both believers and doubters. He encourages readers to join him in this new understanding, that what is "untried and afterward is for you and me and all" (78). He returns to consideration of the purpose of the journey, announcing in section 44 that it is to "launch all men and women forward into the unknown" (79). He invites readers to stand up, referring to the opening sections of the poem, which spoke of lounging on the grass, suggesting that a different part of the journey is about to begin, one that moves toward the future. He recounts the factors and forces that have shaped him and made him ready to step forward, to celebrate as yet unknown potentials present in the ever expanding realm of space and time.

As he moves toward closure, the speaker announces that he is on a "perpetual journey" and returns to the relationship between speaker and reader, claiming that he leads each reader to a prospect from which to view the road that lies ahead. He offers encouragement, writing that the road "is not far . . . it is within reach" (82), but that the reader must follow his or her own journey, an admonition that echoes Thoreau's advice in the closing chapters of *Walden*. The speaker promises companionship on the journey, but emphasizes that the journey never ends, that the process of the journey is more important than knowing the destination. The speaker acknowledges the metaphor of the journey or quest and what its outcome should be: to be conscious or aware of "every moment of your life" (83). As if to remind readers of the guideposts for this journey, the speaker recaps the central tenets of his understanding, repeating the importance of sympathy for others and of recognizing the divinity present within the self. He again places death as a part of the cycle of life and that which connects humans to the natural world. He reasserts the concept of kosmos, a harmonious order, stating, "It is not chaos or death . . . it is form and union and plan . . . it is eternal life . . . it is happiness" (87).

The lines that comprise the last two sections of the poem contain references to the speaker's ability to absorb past and present, as Whitman proclaims the poet's ability to be for all time as well as his own time. They emphasize the value of process and change, as the speaker asks, "Do I contradict myself?" and then accepts contradictions because he contains "multitudes" (87), an echo of Emerson's argument in "Self-Reliance." These lines reiterate the invitation to readers to join in the journey, to begin the process of self-discovery. They also bid farewell, because in closing the speaker offers himself to the cycle of life and the continuity of nature, stating, "I bequeath myself to the dirt to grow from the grass I love" (88), a final dissolution of the boundaries of self into the realm of the mystical and transcendent.

10

Emily Dickinson
Selected Poems

In contrast to Walt Whitman, who declared himself the poet of the American people and claimed a public role, Emily Dickinson remained a poet of private experience, publishing only a few poems during her lifetime. For some readers, the mystery of Emily Dickinson and the biographical puzzles in her life shape the way they read her poems, as though they are looking for clues to solve a riddle. The absence of public activity in her adult life led many early biographers to speculate about a secret love or early heartbreak as the reason she chose to forego the expected path of marriage and motherhood that defined women's lives in her day. Others popularized an image of Dickinson as a recluse cut off from human contact—an image that persists in the minds of some today. Although she did not have a conventional social life and, like her younger sister, did not marry, Dickinson read widely and corresponded regularly with many friends and colleagues. She was very much attuned to the literary and intellectual trends of her day. What her poems do reveal is a woman and a poet interested not only in the domestic world around her, but also in nature and science, religion and spirituality, art and music, literature and the imagination. They also reveal a poet whose work ranges from the serious and intense to the light and playful.

Despite the differences in their personalities and in the style and form of their poetry, Dickinson, like Whitman, responded to the ideas and arguments being advanced by Emerson, particularly those related to originality, genius, the nature of poetry, and the attributes of the poet. Dickinson, too, wished to "speak of the general condition and for all men and women" (Wolff 142), drawing from deep thought and careful observation those truths

that transcend individual experience. Dickinson acknowledged that she saw
"New Englandly," that her frames of reference, understanding, and inner
conflicts were shaped by the culture in which she lived. A significant part
of that culture perpetuated the legacy of Calvinism that had shaped New
England from its founding. In a religious and social climate that still experienced periods of revival enthusiasm or "awakenings," Emily Dickinson's
rejection of orthodoxy, in her spiritual life and in her poetry, placed her at
odds with the world around her. Her poems and her poetic voice may have
puzzled her contemporaries, but since the publication of her complete poems
in 1955, she has been reappraised as a major voice in American poetry.

BIOGRAPHICAL CONTEXT

The child of a dominant father and a retiring mother, Emily Dickinson
was born on December 10, 1830, to Edward and Emily (Norcross) Dickinson.
Their second child and first daughter, Emily grew up in a household shaped
by her father's Calvinist legacy as well as his forceful personality and commitment to duty. A reserved and emotionally distant man, Edward Dickinson
had a profound impact on all three of his children, influencing their life decisions and outlooks. He also played a significant role in the civic and cultural
life of Amherst, Massachusetts, the town where Emily spent all but a small
portion of her life. The Dickinsons believed in educating their daughters as
well as their son, seeing a young woman's store of knowledge as something
that would later be beneficial to her husband and children. After receiving
early training in reading and religion at home, Emily attended Amherst
Academy. There she studied languages, history, botany, geology, and moral
philosophy. She was a good student and an avid learner. During her childhood and school years, she developed lasting friendships with a number of
young women, including the future author Helen Hunt Jackson. When she
completed her studies at Amherst Academy, she attended Mount Holyoke
Female Seminary for a year.

During much of Dickinson's adolescence and young adulthood, she grappled with issues of religious faith, specifically with experiencing a conversion
and making a public profession of her belief in and acceptance of Christ as her
savior. Such a conversion experience was necessary in the Calvinist tradition
for full church membership and was expected of young women in Dickinson's
circle. To support those who hoped for such a conversion, prayer meetings
and other revival activities were scheduled, and Dickinson attended some
of these in Amherst as well as required sessions at Mount Holyoke. As she
watched family members and friends undergo conversions, Dickinson realized

that she was not sharing in this experience; she did not recognize a change within herself and in her relationship to God. Instead, Dickinson began to question the orthodox interpretations of the nature of God and his relationship to and conduct toward human beings. Such questions would shape many of the poems she wrote throughout her adult life as she explored the tensions between faith and doubt, between submission and self-assertion, between immortality and death.

While wrestling with these matters of profound importance, Dickinson was involved in the social life of Amherst in the company of her brother and sister. In the early 1850s, she interacted with a number of young men who appreciated her intelligence and her facility with words. She also watched with mixed emotions as her brother, Austin, courted and married Susan Gilbert, who had become one of Dickinson's closest friends. During this time, Dickinson was thinking about the direction of her own life, finding the conventional roles for women in Amherst to be limited and uninspiring, not convinced that the marriage relationship as it was defined in the nineteenth century was right for her. She often explored her questions and doubts in letters to close friends, including Susan Gilbert, in the nineteenth-century language of romantic friendship that has led some biographers to raise questions about Dickinson's sexual orientation. Throughout the 1850s, Dickinson continued to make visits to friends and family and joined in some of the social events at Evergreens, the home of Austin and Susan Dickinson that was next door to the Dickinson home.

Upon returning home from Mount Holyoke, Dickinson embarked on a lifelong course of reading that included Shakespeare, Milton, and Keats as well as the Brontë sisters, George Eliot, and Elizabeth Barrett Browning. Dickinson also knew the work of many of her American contemporaries, among them Hawthorne, Longfellow, Emerson, and later Thoreau, who became a favorite. She read many newspapers and magazines and was aware throughout the 1850s and 1860s of the significant political and social issues of her day. She, like many of her contemporaries, clipped items and illustrations from the newspapers, sometimes using these bits and pieces as inspiration or decoration for her poems. During this time she also began experimenting in verse, gradually developing the unique voice and form that characterizes her mature poetry. By 1858 she had begun sewing together packets of her poems, known as fascicles, which numbered 40 by the time of her death.

Dickinson's retreat from the world occurred slowly, as she declined invitations and preferred to spend increasing amounts of time in her family home. Biographers and readers have speculated over the cause of this withdrawal, some suggesting that a significant emotional crisis precipitated it, others arguing that

Dickinson chose to invest her time and energies in her creative work. In 1858, Dickinson drafted the first of what are often called the "Master" letters, three romantic and passionate missives to an unknown recipient. Biographers have identified two men, Samuel Bowles and Charles Wadsworth, both married when Dickinson knew them, as the most likely recipients of the letters, but the question remains unresolved. These letters have fueled the debate over what was happening in her personal life and how it affected her poetry.

In 1861, her poem "I taste a liquor never brewed" (#214) appeared in the *Springfield Republican*, a newspaper edited by Bowles, followed in 1862 by "Safe in their Alabaster Chambers" (#216). In 1862, she also began her correspondence with Thomas Wentworth Higginson, an influential editor and critic, whom she approached with questions about publishing her work after his essay "Letter to a Young Contributor" had appeared in the *Atlantic Monthly*. Along with her letter, Dickinson enclosed copies of four of her poems. Higginson responded to Dickinson's letter, asking questions and offering comment on her work, but in further correspondence advised her not to seek publication. Despite this advice, Dickinson continued to correspond with him for the rest of her life.

In the early 1860s, Dickinson suffered problems with her eyes that she feared would lead to blindness. She sought treatment for her condition in Cambridge and lived away from home for a few months in 1864 and in 1865 with her Norcross cousins. Some biographers believe that this threat to her sight rather than a romantic disappointment or emotional breakdown was the crisis that led to her further withdrawal from the world when she returned to Amherst. While she struggled with this condition, she published a handful of poems, including some that were anonymous contributions to *Drum Beat*, a fundraising vehicle for the U.S. Sanitary Commission during the Civil War (Dandurand 17–18). These included "Blazing in gold, and quenching in purple" (#228), later reprinted in the *Springfield Republican;* "Flowers—Well—if anybody" (#137), also reprinted in the *Republican;* and "These are the days when Birds come back" (#130). Her poem "Success is counted sweetest" (#67) appeared in the Brooklyn *Daily Union*, possibly without her consent, and "Some keep the Sabbath going to Church" (#324) appeared in *Round Table*. In 1866 "A narrow fellow in the grass" (#986) also appeared in the *Republican*. After this burst of activity, nothing more is known to have appeared until 1878, when "Success" was reprinted anonymously in *A Masque of Poets*.

In the last two decades of her life, Dickinson continued to write poems and to correspond with friends, but she also dealt with a number of personal losses. In 1874, Edward Dickinson died unexpectedly in Boston. The following year

Dickinson's mother suffered a stroke that left her paralyzed, and Dickinson assumed responsibility for her mother's care. She sought consolation and support in a romantic relationship with Judge Otis P. Lord, a recent widower she had known for many years. Although this relationship provided Dickinson emotional sustenance, she continued to grieve the loss of friends and family, including Samuel Bowles who died in 1878 and Charles Wadsworth in 1882. Late in 1882, Dickinson's mother died, but a worse shock came in 1883 when Dickinson's young nephew, Gilbert, a personal favorite, died from typhoid. In 1884 Judge Lord died, as did Dickinson's lifelong friend Helen Hunt Jackson in 1885. Dickinson herself was beginning to suffer from the illness that took her life, Bright's disease, a form of kidney failure. Emily Dickinson died on May 15, 1886. In sorting through Dickinson's papers to carry out instructions to burn them, her sister Lavinia (Vinnie) found the fascicles as well as loose sheets of poems. She saved them and invited Mabel Loomis Todd, a neighbor of the Dickinson family (and Austin's lover), to prepare a collection of poems for publication. Enlisting the help of Thomas Wentworth Higginson, Todd edited the first volume of selections from Dickinson's verse, *Poems by Emily Dickinson*, which appeared in 1890.

GENRE

Emerging from or representing a personal vision or insight, the lyric poem often expresses a mood or feeling. Usually written in the first person, the poem reflects a specific point of view, but the "I" speaker or persona of the poem is not necessarily the poet. The opportunity to employ speakers other than the autobiographical self allows the poet greater freedom of imagination and subject matter. By constructing alternate identities within poems, poets can transcend the boundaries of age, gender, and experience. Whether the speaker of the poem is the poet or a constructed persona, the verse in a traditional lyric has a musical quality, created by both meter and rhyme scheme. The term *lyric* derived from classical Greek origins, when it was used to identify songs meant to be sung to the accompaniment of a lyre.

Dickinson was conscious of the musical element associated with the lyric and had a strong musical sense, having studied piano when she was young. In shaping her poems, Dickinson drew on the metrical pattern of English hymnody, frequently using a "fourteener" or verse composed of 14 syllables. Usually written in iambic feet, the fourteener is often divided into a line of four feet (eight syllables) followed by a line of three feet (six syllables) and arranged in four-line stanzas or quatrains. This form is called the ballad stanza or common meter, the latter term used in *Christian Psalmody*, a collection of hymns by Isaac Watt that was commonly found in most nineteenth-century New England households. This hymnal, and others like it, was used in church services for congregational singing and at home for family worship. Growing up in the traditions of New England church practice, Dickinson would have heard these hymns from the time she was a child. The usual rhyme scheme for the ballad stanza is *abcb,* or sometimes *abab,* a pattern that emphasizes regularity and makes the stanzas or verses easy to memorize. Dickinson also made use of other stanza forms derived from familiar hymns.

Dickinson's innovations in common meter and rhyme were challenging for her friend T. W. Higginson. She uses this familiar form (and others like it) as a starting point, but then intentionally breaks the form by using phrasing and punctuation that runs across the expected stopping point of the line or end of the stanza. She also at times adds additional unstressed syllables to a line, disrupting the traditional metrical count. This forces readers to read again more slowly to determine the relationship between words, lines, and meaning. Although she uses true rhyme, Dickinson also incorporates slant rhyme (words with similar but not identical sound), consonant rhyme (the repetition of end consonants), eye rhyme (words that look alike but are pronounced differently), and no rhyme at all. The variations in rhyme have the effect of disrupting reader expectations, drawing greater attention to the specific word choices Dickinson makes.

Like Emerson, Dickinson wanted readers to participate in the thought process, to gain a sense of the creative mind at work. In addition to her variations in stanza form, her frequent use of the dash forces readers to engage in the process of association, of "filling in the blanks" to begin to understand the idea behind the poem or to understand the implied comparison in a metaphor. She often employs diction that would have resonated with meaning for her contemporaries, but she also chooses words and allusions to express meanings that were unique and personal. She follows her own pattern of capitalization, at times using it for emphasis, but not always doing so consistently. All of these techniques anticipate the continuing innovations in poetry that occur throughout the twentieth century. Dickinson's influence can be seen in the work of later poets, including Adrienne Rich, as well as in the many poems that refer to her, from Hart Crane's "To Emily Dickinson" (1927) to Lucy Brock-Broido's *The Master Letters* (1995).

SELECTED POEMS

Emily Dickinson composed more than 1,770 poems whose subjects reflect her awareness of the natural world, her appreciation for the work of other writers, and her ability to read beneath the surfaces of daily life. She also explored the tensions between religious practice and spirituality, between her own calling as a poet and the expected roles for women in her day, and between desire and renunciation. Dickinson confronts the pain of depression and the mystery of death. Many of her poems reflect her love of irony and word play as well as her ability to undercut the assumptions, both religious and social, that shaped her culture. The arrangement and compilation of the poems in her fascicles remains a point of discussion among Dickinson scholars who have tried to determine whether she had a specific logic for the groupings. This debate intensified in the 1980s following R. W. Franklin's publication of *The Manuscript Books of Emily Dickinson*, which reproduced the fascicles and sheets as they appeared in manuscript form. Although her early editors were at times criticized for ordering her poems under conventional subject headings, for ease of reading the poems discussed here are arranged in groups of the topical areas she addressed. They represent only a small number of Dickinson's total output but offer an opportunity to look closely at some of her subjects and techniques. The poems' numbers are those found in Thomas Johnson's *The Complete Poems of Emily Dickinson*, because they have served as common shorthand to identify her poems in anthologies and critical articles.

Nature

Dickinson, like Henry Thoreau, studied the natural world, seeing beauty in its common features and truth in its functions. Her poems reveal her habit of close observation and her wide-ranging knowledge that encompasses not only the familiar landscape, but bird and animal behavior, the cycle of the seasons, and atmospheric events. Dickinson incorporated specific details to create images and metaphors, details of which casual observers are unaware. Not all of Dickinson's poems present speakers who find comfort or solace in nature. At times nature is portrayed as an additional source of despondency or it reinforces, through its indifference to human emotion, a sense of loneliness or isolation rather than connection.

In one of her most frequently anthologized poems, "A Bird came down the Walk—" (#328), Dickinson considers the movement and behavior of a common bird on the ground and then in the air. She conveys the speaker's interaction with the bird, first as a distant observer, "He did not know I saw—," then as one who attempts contact, "I offered him a Crumb" (156). She begins in the first two stanzas by describing the bird's typical feeding and drinking behavior; her word choice accentuates the violence of the food chain as the bird bites the worm in two and eats it "raw." Dickinson uses verbs with strong consonant sounds—"ate," "drank," "hopped," "let," "glanced," and "stirred" (156)—all of which suggest finite and separated actions. In stanza three, she suggests the bird's agitation at being too long on the ground, for its eyes "hurried all around," reminding the speaker of "frightened Beads" (156).

As the speaker attempts to interact with the bird, the bird takes wing, and the tone of the poem changes. In stanza four and throughout stanza five, the change in diction emphasizes the change in motion—the words "unrolled," "rowed," "softer," "home," "oars," and "Ocean" emphasize vowels sounds, especially the long o that creates a feeling of continuity and ease. Dickinson continues to build that impression in the last stanza through images of oars that move seamlessly through the water and butterflies that make no visible ripple as they flutter in the midday air. Dickinson suggests that the bird truly is more at home when in flight; when it is in its element, it moves fluidly without fear or hesitation.

Dickinson uses a creature's movement to different effect in "A narrow Fellow in the Grass" (#986). In this poem, Dickinson creates a male persona remembering childhood encounters with snakes and their lingering effect. She plays with the fear of snakes experienced by most people, one rooted in the snake's archetypal connection to Satan (and sometimes to sexuality) that strikes at something deep within the human psyche. The poem is constructed in the form of a riddle, never specifically naming the creature. Instead, she describes its motion and movement, assuming that readers, like the speaker of the poem, will experience the shock of recognition that creates "Zero at the Bone—" (460).

The speaker begins by describing the movement of the snake, who "rides" through the grass as though on a conveyance, its locomotion barely perceptible. Likewise, its appearance is unexpected and brief, "The Grass divides" and "then it closes at your feet" (460), suggesting surprise, at both the appearance of the snake and its proximity. The speaker also invites readers to share in a common recollection of experience with the phrase "did you not" in the first stanza. The long middle stanza of the poem describes the creature's habitat and then recounts the speaker's encounter with it when a barefoot boy. He describes passing what he thought was a "Whip lash / Unbraiding in the Sun" (460), only to have it wrinkle and disappear upon his approach. The reference to a whip lash provides the central clue to the creature's identity, because coach whip was the nickname given to the black racer, a sleek and fast snake common to western Massachusetts. The last two stanzas present the contrast in feeling that the speaker experiences between other creatures and the snake. For most, the speaker feels "a transport / Of cordiality" or sincere affection, but toward the snake he admits to a different response, one that causes "tighter breathing" (a word play on the racer as a constrictor), and a shiver of fear.

The speaker in Dickinson's "These are the days when Birds come back—" (#130) directly states her desire to be one with nature, to enjoy a "Communion." This, like many of Dickinson's nature poems, reveals the way in which Dickinson sees nature and spirit intertwined. The first three stanzas create an image of a warm autumn day in New England, one that makes the speaker think of the beginning of June with the promise of summer still ahead, rather than the winter that looms. The speaker wishes that such a return of summer might be possible, that the few birds signal incoming spring migration rather than the departure that characterizes fall. She admits, however, that this is a "fraud that cannot cheat the bee," for flowers have gone to seed, there is no nectar to gather, and leaves are falling.

Yet the speaker is willing to suspend disbelief, to succumb to the "old—old sophistries of June" (61) during this temporary respite. The word "sophistries" refers to deceptive arguments, and here the speaker alludes not only to the deceptive autumn day, but to the deceptive quality of early summer, which seems as though it could last forever. The last two stanzas introduce the spiritual element of the poem, for the speaker sees those mild summer days as a blessing and refers to them as a "sacrament," an outward sign of an inward grace. She links them to a "Last Communion in the Haze," a last gathering of all the elements that had made up summer and the feeling it inspires, and pleads "Permit a child to join" (61). The use of the word "child" suggests innocence and one who believes without question. That the speaker wishes to join in this communion suggests her desire to hold on to the hope associated with early summer, even though she knows that summer has passed. A similar sentiment influences #131, in which the speaker asks to have a "sunny mind / Thy winter will to bear" (62).

In contrast to the desire to hold on to summer and what it represents expressed in #130, Dickinson conveys the feeling of anticipation that accompanies the first signs of newness and renewal in "A Light exists in Spring" (#812). The speaker notices the quality of light in March when the first signs of the change in season occur in New England, a light "Not present on the Year / At any other period—" (395). She speaks of the color that emerges in this light that cannot be verified by science, but is something that "Human Nature feels" (395). This light illuminates what it touches so that the speaker perceives her surroundings anew and feels an awakening, as if the light "almost speaks to you" (395). Unfortunately, this light and its effects are only temporary, and, as the season moves forward, it "passes and we stay—" (395), the sense of newness and renewal fading back into the commonplace. The speaker captures this feeling in the closing stanza, when she compares the "loss" of this first light and the quickening it brings to "Trade" encroaching "Upon a sacrament" (395). This analogy suggests the effect of the commercial and mundane intruding upon the holy, a type of sacrilege that has a diminishing effect.

For Dickinson, nature provides opportunities to explore connections to the spiritual, and, in "Some keep the Sabbath going to Church—" (#324), she does so with a touch of humor as well. She creates a contrast between those who follow conventional religious practice and her own unorthodox view that leads her to find spiritual connection and signs of God's presence in nature. The speaker admits to keeping the Sabbath at home, but not in an indoor space, for she stands within an orchard, in the company of birds. Specifically, her companion is the bobolink, a bird with a distinctive song whose colorings resemble those that might be seen on choir robes. The speaker then claims that instead of traditional church vestments, such as the surplice (a white garment with long, flowing sleeves), she just wears her "Wings." This feature, associated with angels as well as birds, implies that the speaker can be transported spiritually by her experience in nature. The final stanza refers to God as the preacher, "a noted Clergyman" whose sermons are "never long," (153) compared to the lengthy and sometimes dull homilies delivered at church services. He speaks directly through his creation, and in absorbing the lessons evident in nature, the speaker does not have to wait to get to heaven as do those who follow orthodox thinking; instead, she is "going all along" (154), finding signs of heaven in the world around her.

Nature does not always provide comfort or inspire feelings of communion in Dickinson's work. In "I dreaded that first Robin, so," (#348), the speaker has suffered an anguish, possibly the death of a loved one, that has made the return of spring a painful experience. In the sixth stanza, she refers to herself as the "Queen of Calvary," alluding to the scene of the Crucifixion and the suffering associated with it. The speaker does not want to see signs of renewal and rebirth, because she does not feel these to be possible within herself. The first five stanzas contain words that refer to what happened at Calvary, including "pierced" and "mangled," to suggest the effects that the signs of spring have upon her, intensifying her pain. She has steeled herself against this effect, and claims to have "mastered" the first robin, to have found some way to cope; she admits that "He hurts a little, though" (165). All the signs of returning spring arrive on time, none showing deference to her and her feelings. The speaker knows that she cannot stop the cycle of nature, even if she wishes she could step outside it. In the last stanza, she mentions "Plumes," a reference to Victorian funerary decoration, again suggesting an experience of loss. The final sound of drums suggests both a procession of the signs of spring and a funeral march, reinforcing the sense that this return of spring brings suffering instead of relief.

Loss, Defeat, and Pain

Many of Dickenson's poems address situations of loss or defeat. Sometimes these arise out of personal failures, the death of loved ones, or the struggle with depression. Some poems treat the feeling of loss experienced in the change of seasons, particularly the approach of winter, a time associated with death and dormancy. Other poems use loss to explore the speaker's relationship to a God who seems distant and unknowable or a God who withholds love. Some of the poems that deal with loss explore the pain associated with it. Others explore the nature of pain without tying it to specific causes.

The early "Success is counted sweetest" (#67) addresses the experience of defeat. This three-stanza poem suggests that those who have lost perceive more clearly the full meaning of victory. The speaker begins by situating the poem as sympathetic to those who have failed, whose hunger for success makes them more attuned to it. They are able to "comprehend the nectar," referring to a sweet beverage often considered the drink of the gods, which alludes to the privileged status of those who consume it. In the second stanza, the speaker draws on martial imagery—"the purple Host" and taking "the Flag"—to convey the idea of a contest, one in which there must be winners and losers. The situation established in the second stanza continues without the intrusion of punctuation until partway through the opening line of the third stanza, "As he defeated—dying—" (35), which creates the effect of pausing in the position of the downed contestant and seeing from his point of view. In that position, one hears the "strains of triumph," the martial music of success, but they fall on the "forbidden ear" of one who will not hear the music played for him. Dickinson's word choice here links the poem to religious experience, particularly that of conversion, that identified one as a member of the elect who would gain the victory of salvation. For one who failed to have such an experience, the feeling of defeat was indeed intense.

Loss and the feeling of defeat and betrayal shape "If I'm lost—now" (#256). This poem begins by inverting the line from John Newton's popular eighteenth-century hymn "Amazing Grace." Newton's line reads, "I once was lost, but now am found," whereas Dickinson's speaker begins, "If I'm lost—now / That I was found—" (117). The speaker goes on to describe the experience of being admitted into heaven, its "Jasper Gates" opening for her. Once there, the speaker encounters angels who "softly peered" into her face and touch her, "Almost as if they cared" (117). The phrase "Almost as if" plays a key role in this line, for it suggests that things are not what they seem. The speaker finds herself "banished—now" as though she had been admitted by mistake. Instead of experiencing the Savior's welcome as a member of the elect, the speaker recounts the loss that occurs "when the Savior's face / Turns so—away from you—" (117). This turning away, a pointed rejection, suggests one way that God, here in the person of the Son, withholds love or approval.

A similar sense of separation and defeat informs "Those—dying then" (#1551), a much later poem. Its brief two stanzas contrast past and present and belief and disbelief. The speaker begins by explaining how those who died in the past, and presumably in the faith, "Knew where they went— They went to God's Right Hand—" (646). This position, according to church tradition, is one of authority and exaltation, awarded to those who have gained God's favor, one of the rewards of faith anticipated by those who have had conversion experiences. The remainder of this first stanza, however, suggests that this is no longer possible because "That Hand is amputated now / And God cannot be found—" (646). This complex statement suggests both a diminishing of God's power in the present and his retreat, even from those who seek him.

The second stanza adds to the complexity, for it refers to "The abdication of Belief." The word "abdication" suggests ambiguity, because it means to relinquish something once held (in this case faith or belief), but is also associated with renouncing a throne or high office, as God appears to have done in his retreat. The next line, "Makes the Behavior small—" (646) seems again to refer to this retreat, the word "small" identifying something mean or petty. The speaker then claims "Better an ignis fatuus / Than no illume at all—" (646), asserting that a false light or a false hope is preferable to none. In making this claim, the speaker seems to mourn the realization that a powerful God is an illusion, sensing that the illusion is better than nothing.

In addition to expressing feelings of loss that relate to the human relationship to God, Dickinson also expresses feelings of loss related to the sense of self, especially when that self is beset by depression. "Crumbling is not an instant's Act" (#997) examines the gradual process of decline that marks the slide into despair. The first word of the poem, "crumbling," suggests the process of disintegration, the coming apart of what was once an integrated whole. The speaker claims that this does not happen in a single moment, but occurs over time as a succession of small and often unnoticed episodes culminate in the final collapse. The second stanza describes the minor incidents through metaphors, comparing them to a "Cobweb" and a "Cuticle," implying almost imperceptible alterations or incidents. The speaker then refers to a "Borer" and "Elemental Rust" (463), something eating away from the inside that may not be perceived until the damage is done. All these small events result in "Ruin," which the speaker label's "Devil's work / Consecutive and slow" (463), suggesting that it occurs in the fine details and not through a single major event. Thus "slipping," connoting a smooth and quiet slide, better describes the process than the usual sense of "crash," which implies something sudden and violent.

Some of Dickinson's poems avoid connecting pain to a specific cause, making the sensation of pain the focus of the poem. In #650, "Pain—has an Element of Blank—," Dickinson suggests how pain can be all consuming, that it forms a constrictive circle around those who suffer, for it "cannot recollect / When it begun—" and "has no Future—but itself" (323). This enclosure appears unbreakable. Even though the last two lines of the poem include the phrase "enlightened to perceive / New Periods" (324), which initially raises the hope of some alleviation or change, the last line in full reads "New Periods—of Pain" (324), closing off the possibility.

Similarly, in #536, "The Heart asks Pleasure—first—" (262), the speaker moves from pleasure through a progression of painful feeling and a closing down of emotion toward a final dissolution. The extensive use of dashes slows the pace of reading, separating each stage of the decline. Initially, the heart seeks "Excuse from Pain—" then resorts to "little Anodynes" or drugs that allay pain, and then seeks sleep as an escape, each stage suggesting the need for increasing levels of unconsciousness. Ultimately, the final escape from pain seems possible only in death, but the sufferer is powerless to effect this. Instead, this release comes only at the hands of the Inquisitor, a figure associated with torture used to break the will of one who held heretical or contrarian beliefs. The Inquisitor determined who was sent to death, which, for someone who had suffered great pain, might seem a "privilege" offering release.

Love and Passion

Given the complex relationships she experienced, it is no surprise that Dickinson wrote many poems that explore love and passion as well as desire and its frustration. Few of her poems offer a simple view of love. Many capture a sense of longing, wished-for possibilities, or fulfillment denied. Others explore the willing sacrifice or renunciation of a love relationship deemed impossible in the present in hope of consummation at some point in the hereafter. In contrast to Whitman's overt references to the body, sexuality, and sexual pleasure, Dickinson often employs metaphor, allusion, and allegory to convey sexual knowledge or the undercurrents of sexual tension.

"If you were coming in the Fall" (#511) sets up a progression of possible moments of reunion for a pair of lovers, each stage in the progression entailing a longer period of time. The poem appears to begin in spring, as the speaker claims she would "brush the Summer by" if her beloved were expected in the fall, a significant choice given Dickinson's preference for the season. As the length of time before reunion expands to a year and then to centuries, the speaker expresses the paradox of her willingness to wait, but also her desire to hurry the passage of time through various gestures. If the reunion cannot occur until the afterlife, the speaker offers to cast off her current life "like a Rind," a useless crust or peel, in exchange for the pleasure anticipated in "Eternity" (249). The last stanza, however, turns from possibility to uncertainty, the condition of not knowing how long she must wait becoming a "goad," a thorn or spur that induces pain, much like the bee's sting. Fulfillment or consummation becomes something indefinite, leaving the speaker suspended in a state of longing.

Another of Dickinson's frequently anthologized poems, "Wild Nights—Wild Nights!" (#249) presents the possibility of union and sexual satisfaction, but again, it is to be hoped for in the future, not enjoyed in the present. The speaker sees the situation in the conditional, using the phrases "Were I with thee" and "Might I but moor" (114), indicating that these are hoped for but not realized situations. The middle stanza compares the heart to a sailor, who in the security of "port" is freed from the demands of the journey or the quest, who is safe from the buffeting winds that can drive the sailor off course. For the speaker, to be so anchored in the company of her beloved would be paradise, would allow the "luxury" of wild nights that would prompt the sexually contented exclamation "Ah, the Sea!" (114).

At times Dickinson's persona speaks from the point of view of a married woman, as does the speaker in "I'm 'wife'—I've finished that—" (199). Here the speaker contrasts her new situation with the girlhood that preceded it, suggesting that new knowledge and understanding, including sexual knowledge, shape her frame of reference. Her status as a married woman has granted her an authority that she identifies with an absolute ruler like the czar. She also places the word "Woman" in quotations, implying that through marriage she has been transformed and has claimed her adult identity. Now her earlier life looks "odd" in its innocence. The second stanza compares the mystery of marriage and sexual union to the mystery of heaven, claiming that once one has passed over to the other side, one marvels at the naiveté of the unknowing. The last stanza, however, creates ambiguity in the poem, for the speaker claims that if marriage provides "comfort" then maidenhood must have been a source of pain. But the speaker stops herself from continuing the comparison, asserting the claim "I'm 'Wife'!" (94) as if the comparison may bring to light realizations she does not wish to acknowledge.

Death

Many people consider Emily Dickinson a poet of death, and two of her most famous poems, "Because I could not stop for Death—" (#712) and "I heard a Fly buzz—when I died—" (#465) address this subject. In both poems, Dickinson's speaker narrates an experience from beyond the grave, much like the speaker in #256.

In "Because I could not stop for Death—" Dickinson personifies death as a courtly gentleman caller, who "kindly stops" for the speaker when she is still in the midst of life. This treatment makes death seem less threatening, and the poem lacks allusions to pain or betrayal that appear in other poems on death. His arrival, unexpected as it is, causes the speaker to "put away / My labor and my leisure too," (350) in response to his politeness or "Civility." She joins him in his carriage, which may well be a hearse, and they "slowly drive" onward, since death knows "no haste," and literally has all the time in the world. The speaker acknowledges her own haste, however, in departing with him, unprepared for the journey, "For only Gossamer was my gown— / My Tippett—only Tulle—" (350), delicate and sheer fabrics worn for ornament, not warmth or protection. The speaker rides with death as they pass familiar scenes of life and then cross over to an unknown realm as they pass the "Setting Sun." Death brings his passenger to a new abode, the grave; its "Roof was scarcely visible—" and its "Cornice—in the Ground—" (350). In the last stanza, the speaker reflects on the passage of time since her suitor came for her, how quickly ages pass when one enters "Eternity." The poem, like many by Dickinson, ends with a dash, suggesting open-ended possibility rather than the finality usually associated with death.

In "I heard a Fly buzz," Dickinson presents an ironic situation that undercuts the speaker's (and possibly some of Dickinson's orthodox contemporaries') expectations surrounding death. The poem opens with the speaker acknowledging the presence of a fly and describing the atmosphere within the room as the speaker waits for death. The depiction of that atmosphere as "like the Stillness" that occurs "Between the Heaves of Storm—" (223) suggests both relief and anticipation. Those who will mourn the speaker's passing have assembled in the room, their "Breaths . . . gathering firm" also conveying a sense of anticipation. Both the speaker and her companions await the final death throes, when "the King / Be witnessed—in the Room—" (224). As orthodox believers, they expect that if the individual about to die is one of the elect, then her last vision will be of Christ welcoming her into his kingdom.

Many descriptions of the deaths of those termed "saints" in the New England tradition report such visions, with witnesses recording the final words of the dying that attest to such moments. Thus the speaker in this poem and her companions watch for this to happen. The speaker relishes being the center of attention. In light of her imminent departure, the speaker has willed away her earthly possessions, those things that no longer have meaning to her as she awaits the welcome into paradise. And "then it was / There interposed a Fly" (224). With great irony, Dickinson interposes this common insect which distracts the speaker and comes "Between the light" and the speaker, blocking her vision. In what was to be her moment of glory, the speaker "could not see to see—" and is left in a state of uncertainty. The final dash again creates open-ended possibility, but this time it undermines the assurance that the speaker has hoped for in death.

Creativity and the Imagination

For Dickinson, one source of compensation for the uncertainties in the human condition is the power of the imagination and the potential for creativity. Many of her poems celebrate the capacity of the human mind, as in #632 "The Brain—is wider than the Sky" or the power of reverie that shapes #1755, "To make a prairie it takes a clover and one bee." In others she honors the work of fellow poets and authors, as in #148, "All overgrown by cunning moss" about Charlotte Brontë, or #449, "I died for Beauty—but was scarce" that implies a connection to the sensibility of John Keats.

Perhaps the most appropriate poem to close a discussion of American Romantic literature is #657, "I dwell in possibility—" in which Dickinson gives voice to Romantic and Transcendentalist sensibilities. The speaker begins by claiming that possibility, which she considers a "fairer House than Prose," is a preferable space to occupy. She aligns prose with the known and expected, engaging in word play in which prose implies prosaic. For the speaker, "possibility" represents potential, including creative potential. It also reflects the optimism that was characteristic of much Transcendentalist thinking. The "house" of possibility is ideal, its plentiful windows and doors admitting light, while its fair visitors, possibly inspiration and insight, provide the poet with material for her poems. By dwelling here the speaker explains that she can "gather Paradise" (327), that through the work of creativity, she can reach for that which lies beyond the ordinary grasp. By dwelling in the House of Possibility, the speaker can fulfill her calling as a poet.

Bibliography

PRIMARY SOURCES

Cooper, James Fenimore. *The Leatherstocking Tales*. Vol. I. New York: Library of America, 1985.

Dickinson, Emily. *The Complete Poems of Emily Dickinson*. Ed. Thomas H. Johnson. Boston: Little, Brown, 1955.

Emerson, Ralph Waldo. *Collected Poems and Translations*. New York: Library of America, 1994.

Emerson, Ralph Waldo. *Essays and Lectures*. New York: Library of America, 1983.

Hawthorne, Nathaniel. *Novels*. New York: Library of America, 1983.

Longfellow, Henry Wadsworth. *Poems and Other Writings*. New York: Library of America, 2000.

Melville, Herman. *Redburn, White-Jacket, Moby-Dick*. New York: Library of America, 1983.

Poe, Edgar Allan. *Essays and Reviews*. New York: Library of America, 1984.

Poe, Edgar Allan. *Poetry and Tales*. New York: Library of America, 1984.

Stowe, Harriet Beecher. *Uncle Tom's Cabin, The Minister's Wooing, Oldtown Folks*. New York: Library of America, 1982.

Thoreau, Henry David. *Collected Essays and Poems*. New York: Library of America, 2001.

Thoreau, Henry David. *A Week on the Concord and Merrimack Rivers, Walden; or, Life in the Woods, The Maine Woods, Cape Cod*. New York: Library of America, 1985.

Whitman, Walt. *Complete Poetry and Collected Prose*. New York: Library of America, 1982.

SECONDARY SOURCES

General

Abrams, Robert E. *Landscape and Ideology in American Renaissance Literature: Topographies of Skepticism.* Cambridge, Eng.: Cambridge University Press, 2004.

Andrews, William. *Literary Romanticism in America.* Baton Rouge: Louisiana State University Press, 1981.

Boswell, Jeanetta, ed. *The American Renaissance and the Critics: The Best of a Century in Criticism.* Wakefield, NH: Longwood Academic, 1990.

Buell, Lawrence. *Literary Transcendentalism: Style and Vision in the American Renaissance.* Ithaca, NY: Cornell University Press, 1973.

Cameron, Kenneth Walter, ed. *Concord Literary Renaissance.* Hartford, CT: Transcendental Books, 1988.

Chai, Leon. *The Romantic Foundations of the American Renaissance.* Ithaca, NY: Cornell University Press, 1987.

Dekker, George. *The American Historical Romance.* Cambridge, Eng.: Cambridge University Press, 1987.

Elliott, Emory, ed. *The Columbia History of the American Novel.* New York: Columbia University Press, 1991.

Elliott, Emory, ed. *The Columbia Literary History of the United States.* New York: Columbia University Press, 1988.

Fielder, Leslie. *Love and Death in the American Novel.* New York: Stein and Day, 1975.

Gilmore, Michael T. *American Romanticism and the Marketplace.* Chicago: University of Chicago Press, 1985.

Kolodny, Annette. *The Land Before Her.* Chapel Hill: University of North Carolina Press, 1984.

Levernz, David. *Manhood in the American Renaissance.* Ithaca, NY: Cornell University Press, 1989.

Lewis, R.W.B. *The American Adam.* Chicago: University of Chicago Press, 1955.

Loving, Jerome. *Lost in the Customhouse: Authorship in the American Renaissance.* Iowa City: University of Iowa Press, 1993.

Matthiessen, F.O. *The American Renaissance.* London and New York: Oxford University Press, 1941.

Myerson, Joel. *Transcendentalism: A Reader.* London and New York: Oxford University Press, 2000.

Pease, Donald E. *Visionary Compacts: American Renaissance Writings in Cultural Context.* Madison: University of Wisconsin Press, 1987.

Powell, Timothy B. *Ruthless Democracy: A Multicultural Interpretation of the American Renaissance.* Princeton, NJ: Princeton University Press, 2000.

Reynolds, David S. *Beneath the American Renaissance: The Subversive Imagination in the Age of Emerson and Melville.* Cambridge, MA: Harvard University Press, 1988.

Reynolds, Larry J. *European Revolutions and the American Literary Renaissance.* New Haven, CT: Yale University Press, 1988.

Samuels, Shirley, ed. *The Culture of Sentiment: Race, Gender and Sentimentality in Nineteenth-Century America*. Oxford, Eng.: Oxford University Press, 1992.

Shucard, Alan. *American Poetry: The Puritans through Walt Whitman*. Boston: Twayne, 1988.

Smith, Henry Nash. *Virgin Land: The American West as Symbol and Myth*. Cambridge, MA: Harvard University Press, 1950.

Tompkins, Jane. *Sensational Designs: The Cultural Work of American Fiction, 1790–1860*. New York: Oxford University Press, 1985.

Cooper

Dekker, George. *James Fenimore Cooper: The Novelist*. London: Routledge & Kegan Paul, 1967.

Dekker, George, and Jon P. McWilliams, eds. *Fenimore Cooper: The Critical Heritage*. London: Routledge & Kegan Paul, 1973.

Gardner, Jared. *Master Plots: Race and the Founding of an American Literature, 1787–1845*. Baltimore: Johns Hopkins University Press, 1998.

Mayer, Magdalen. "Racial Perceptions in James Fenimore Cooper's *The Last of the Mohicans*." *Blurred Boundaries: Critical Essays on American Literature, Language and Culture*. Eds. Klaus Schmidt and David Sawyer. Frankfurt am Main, Germany: Peter Lang, 1996, 41–54.

Peck, H. Daniel, ed. *New Essays on* The Last of the Mohicans. Cambridge, Eng.: Cambridge University Press, 1992.

Peck, H. Daniel. *A World By Itself: The Pastoral Moment in Cooper's Fiction*. New Haven, CT: Yale University Press, 1977.

Raillton, Stephen. *James Fenimore Cooper: A Study of His Life and Imagination*. Princeton, NJ: Princeton University Press, 1978.

Ringe, Donald A. *James Fenimore Cooper*. Updated Edition. Boston: Twayne, 1988.

Romero, Laura. "Vanishing Americans: Gender, Empire and New Historicism." *American Literary Studies*. Eds. Michael A. Elliott and Claudia Stokes. New York: New York University Press, 2003, 41–62.

Slotkin, Richard. *Regeneration through Violence: The Mythology of the American Frontier, 1600–1860*. Middletown, CT: Wesleyan University Press, 1973.

Wallace, James D. *Early Cooper and His Audience*. New York: Columbia University Press, 1986.

Dickinson

Bennett, Paula. *Emily Dickinson: Woman Poet*. Iowa City: University of Iowa Press, 1990.

Bloom, Harold, ed. *Emily Dickinson*. New York: Chelsea, 1985.

Cady, Edwin H, and Louis J. Budd, eds. *On Dickinson: The Best from American Literature* Durham, NC: Duke University Press, 1990.

Crumbley, Paul. *Inflections of the Pen: Dash and Voice in Emily Dickinson*. Lexington: University Press of Kentucky, 1997.

Dandurand, Karen. "New Dickinson Civil War Publications." *American Literature* 56.1 (1984): 17–27.

Dobson, Joanne. *Dickinson and the Strategies of Reticence: The Woman Writer in Nineteenth Century America.* Bloomington: Indiana University Press, 1989.

Doriani, Beth Maclay. *Emily Dickinson, Daughter of Prophecy.* Amherst: University of Massachusetts Press, 1996.

Duchac, Joseph. *The Poems of Emily Dickinson: An Annotated Guide to Commentary Published in English, 1978–1989.* New York: Hall, 1993.

Duchac, Joseph. *The Poems of Emily Dickinson: An Annotated Guide to Commentary Published in English, 1890–1977.* Boston: Hall, 1979.

Eberwein, Jane Donahue. *Dickinson: Strategies of Limitation.* Amherst: University of Massachusetts Press, 1985.

Farr, Judith. *The Passion of Emily Dickinson.* Cambridge, MA: Harvard University Press, 1992.

Ferlazzo, Paul J. *Emily Dickinson.* Boston: Twayne, 1976.

Guthrie, James R. *Emily Dickinson's Vision: Illness and Identity in Her Poetry.* Gainesville: University Press of Florida, 1998.

Heginbotham, Eleanor Elson. *Reading the Fascicles of Emily Dickinson: Dwelling in Possibilities.* Columbus: Ohio State University Press, 2003.

Jackson, Virginia. *Dickinson's Misery: A Theory of Lyric Reading.* Princeton, NJ: Princeton University Press, 2005.

Keller, Karl. *The Only Kangaroo among the Beauty: Emily Dickinson and America.* Baltimore: Johns Hopkins University Press, 1979.

Kirk, Connie Ann. *Emily Dickinson: A Biography.* Westport, CT: Greenwood, 2004.

Knapp, Bettina L. *Emily Dickinson.* New York: Continuum, 1989.

Miller, Cristanne. *Emily Dickinson: A Poet's Grammar.* Cambridge, MA: Harvard University Press, 1987.

Mitchell, Domhnall. *Emily Dickinson: Monarch of Perception.* Amherst: University of Massachusetts Press, 2000.

Oberhaus, Dorothy Huff. *Emily Dickinson's Fascicles: Method & Meaning.* University Park: Pennsylvania State University Press, 1995.

Petrino, Elizabeth A. *Emily Dickinson and Her Contemporaries: Women's Verse in America, 1820–1885.* Hanover, NH: University Press of New England, 1998.

Phillips, Elizabeth. *Emily Dickinson: Personae and Performance.* University Park: Pennsylvania State University Press, 1996.

Pollak, Vivian R. *Dickinson: The Anxiety of Gender.* Ithaca, NY: Cornell University Press, 1984.

Porter, David. *Dickinson: The Modern Idiom.* Cambridge, MA: Harvard University Press, 1981.

St. Armand, Barton Levi. *Emily Dickinson and Her Culture.* Cambridge, Eng.: Cambridge University Press, 1984.

Small, Judy Jo. *Positive as Sound: Emily Dickinson's Rhyme.* Athens: University of Georgia Press, 1990.

Smith, Martha Nell. *Rowing in Eden: Rereading Emily Dickinson.* Austin: University of Texas Press, 1992.

Wardrop, Daneen. *Emily Dickinson's Gothic: Goblin with a Gauge*. Iowa City: University of Iowa Press, 1996.

Wolff, Cynthia Griffin. *Emily Dickinson*. Reading, MA: Addison-Wesley, 1988.

Emerson

Allen, Gay Wilson. *Waldo Emerson: A Biography*. New York: Viking, 1981.

Bosco, Ronald A., and Joel Myerson, eds. *Emerson in His Own Time: A Biographical Chronicle of His Life, Drawn from Recollections, Interviews, and Memoirs by Family, Friends, and Associates*. Iowa City: University of Iowa Press, 2003.

Buell, Lawrence. *Emerson*. Cambridge, MA: Belknap, 2003.

Burkholder, Robert E., and Joel Myerson, eds. *Critical Essays on Ralph Waldo Emerson*. Boston: Hall, 1983.

Cady, Edwin H., and Louis J. Budd, eds. *On Emerson: The Best from American Literature*. Durham, NC: Duke University Press, 1988.

Cayton, Mary Kupiec. *Emerson's Emergence: Self and Society in the Transformation of New England, 1800–1845*. Chapel Hill: University of North Carolina Press, 1989.

Ellison, Julie. *Emerson's Romantic Style*. Princeton, NJ: Princeton University Press, 1984.

Goodman, Russell B. *American Philosophy and the Romantic Tradition*. Cambridge, Eng.: Cambridge University Press, 1990.

Greenberg, Robert M. *Splintered Worlds: Fragmentation and the Ideal of Diversity in the Work of Emerson, Melville, Whitman, and Dickinson*. Boston: Northeastern University Press, 1993.

Grossman, Jay. *Reconstituting the American Renaissance: Emerson, Whitman, and the Politics of Representation*. Durham, NC: Duke University Press, 2003.

Irey, Eugene F., ed. *A Concordance to Five Essays of Ralph Waldo Emerson*. New York: Garland, 1981.

Larson, Kerry. "Individualism and the Place of Understanding in Emerson's Essays." *ELH* 68.4 (2001): 991–1021.

Leary, Lewis. *Ralph Waldo Emerson: An Interpretive Essay*. Boston: Twayne, 1980.

McAleer, John. *Ralph Waldo Emerson: Days of Encounter*. Boston: Little, Brown, 1984.

Mitchell, Charles E. *Individualism and Its Discontents: Appropriations of Emerson, 1880–1950*. Amherst: University of Massachusetts Press, 1997.

Porte, Joel. *Emerson in His Journals*. Cambridge, MA: Harvard University Press, 1982.

Porte, Joel. *Ralph Waldo Emerson*. New York: Chelsea, 1980.

Porte, Joel, and Saundra Morris, eds. *The Cambridge Companion to Ralph Waldo Emerson*. Cambridge, Eng.: Cambridge University Press, 1999.

Richardson, Robert D., Jr. *Emerson: A Mind on Fire*. Berkeley: University of California Press, 1995.

Rowe, John Carlos. *At Emerson's Tomb: The Politics of Classic American Literature*. New York: Columbia University Press, 1997.

Sacks, Kenneth S. *Understanding Emerson: "The American Scholar" and His Struggle for Self-Reliance.* Princeton, NJ: Princeton University Press, 2003.

Wider, Sarah Ann. *The Critical Reception of Emerson: Unsettling All Things.* Rochester, NY: Camden House, 2000.

Worley, Sam McGuire. *Emerson, Thoreau, and the Role of the Cultural Critic.* Albany: State University of New York Press, 2001.

Yannella, Donald. *Ralph Waldo Emerson.* Boston: Twayne, 1982.

Hawthorne

Baym, Nina. The Scarlet Letter:*A Reading.* Boston: Hall, 1986.

Bell, Michael Davitt. *Hawthorne and the Historical Romance of New England.* Princeton, NJ: Princeton University Press, 1971.

Bensick, Carol M. "Dimmesdale and His Bachelorhood: 'Priestly Celibacy' in *The Scarlet Letter.*" *Studies in American Fiction* 21 (1993): 103–10.

Bercovitch, Sacvan. *The Office of the Scarlet Letter.* Baltimore: Johns Hopkins University Press, 1991.

Bercovitch, Sacvan. "*The Scarlet Letter*: A Twice-told Tale." *Nathaniel Hawthorne Review* 22.2 (Fall 1996): 1–20.

Brodhead, Richard. *The School of Hawthorne.* New York: Oxford University Press, 1986.

Budick, Emily Miller. *Engendering Romance: Women Writers and the Hawthorne Tradition, 1850–1990.* New Haven, CT: Yale University Press, 1994.

Clark, Michael. "Another Look at the Scaffold Scenes in Hawthorne's *The Scarlet Letter.*" *ATQ* 1 (1987): 135–44.

Colacurcio, Michael J. *New Essays on* The Scarlet Letter. Cambridge, Eng.: Cambridge University Press, 1985.

Egan, Ken, Jr. "The Adulteress in the Market-Place: Hawthorne and *The Scarlet Letter.*" *Studies in the Novel* 27 (1995): 26–42.

Elbert, Monika. "Hester's Maternity: Stigma or Weapon?" *ESQ: A Journal of the American Renaissance* 36 (1990): 175–207.

Gale, Robert L. *A Nathaniel Hawthorne Encyclopedia.* Westport, CT: Greenwood, 1991.

Herbert, Walter T. *Dearest Beloved: The Hawthornes and the Making of the Middle-Class Family.* Berkeley: University of California Press, 1993.

Hoffman, Elizabeth Aycock. "Political Power in *The Scarlet Letter.*" *ATQ* 4 (1990): 12–39.

Hutner, Gordon. *Secrets and Sympathy: Forms of Disclosure in Hawthorne's Novels.* Athens: University of Georgia Press, 1988.

Johnson, Claudia Durst. *Understanding* The Scarlet Letter. Westport, CT: Greenwood, 1995.

Kesterson, David B. *Critical Essays on Hawthorne's* The Scarlet Letter. Boston: Hall, 1988.

Mellow, James R. *Nathaniel Hawthorne in His Times.* Boston: Houghton Mifflin, 1980.

Miller, Edwin Haviland. *Salem Is My Dwelling Place: A Life of Nathaniel Hawthorne.* Iowa City: University of Iowa Press, 1991.

Pennell, Melissa McFarland. *Student Companion to Nathaniel Hawthorne.* Westport, CT: Greenwood, 1999.

Pimple, Kenneth D. "'Subtle but Remorseful Hypocrite': Dimmesdale's Moral Character." *Studies in the Novel* 25 (1993): 257–71.

Scharnhorst, Gary. *The Critical Responses to Nathaniel Hawthorne's* The Scarlet Letter. Westport, CT: Greenwood, 1992.

Wineapple, Brenda. *Hawthorne: A Life.* New York: Knopf, 2003.

Longfellow

Anderson, Jill. "'Be Up and Doing': Henry Wadsworth Longfellow and Poetic Labor." *Journal of American Studies* 37.1 (2003): 1–15.

Arvin, Newton. *Longfellow: His Life and Work.* Boston: Little, Brown, 1963.

Calhoun, Charles C. *Longfellow: A Rediscovered Life.* Boston: Beacon, 2004.

Derbyshire, John. "Longfellow and the Fate of Modern Poetry." *New Criterion* (Dec. 2000): 12–20.

Eberwein, Jane Donahue. "'The Wind's Will': Another View of Frost and Longfellow." *Colby Library Quarterly* 16 (1980): 177–81.

Evans, James Allan. "Longfellow's Evangeline and the Cult of Acadia." *Contemporary Review* (Feb. 2002): 104–12.

Fletcher, Angus. "Whitman and Longfellow: Two Types of the American Poet." *Raritan* 10.4 (1991): 131–45.

Gartner, Matthew. "Becoming Longfellow: Work, Manhood, and Poetry." *American Literature* 72.1 (2000): 59–86.

Gartner, Matthew. "Longfellow's Place: The Poet and Poetry of Craigie House." *New England Quarterly* 73.1 (2000): 32–57.

Gioia, Dana. "Longfellow in the Aftermath of Modernism." *The Columbia History of American Poetry.* Eds. Jay Parini and Brett C. Millier. New York: Columbia University Press: 1993, 64–96.

Gruesz, Kirsten Silva. "Feeling for the Fireside: Longfellow, Lynch, and the Topography of Poetic Power." *Sentimental Men: Masculinity and the Politics of Affect in American Culture.* Eds. Mary Chapman and Glenn Hendler. Berkeley: University of California Press, 1999, 43–63.

Haralson, Eric L. "Mars in Petticoats: Longfellow and Sentimental Masculinity." *Nineteenth-Century Literature* 51.3 (1996): 327–56.

Irmscher, Christoph. "Longfellow Redux." *Raritan* 21.3 (2002):100–29.

Jackson, Virginia. "Longfellow's Tradition: Or, Picture-Writing a Nation." *Modern Language Quarterly* 59.4 (1998): 471–96.

Link, Eric Carl. "American Nationalism and the Defense of Poetry." *Southern Quarterly* 41.2 (2003): 48–59.

McFarland, Ron. "Dramatic Transformations of Evangeline." *American Drama* 8.1 (1998): 26–49.

Rechel-White, Julie A. "Longfellow's Influence on Whitman's 'Rise' from Manhattan Island." *American Transcendental Quarterly* 6.2 (1992): 121–29.

Seelye, John. "Attic Shape: Dusting Off *Evangeline.*" *Virginia Quarterly Review* 60.1 (1984): 21–44.

Wagenknecht, Edward. *Henry Wadsworth Longfellow: His Poetry and Prose.* New York: Ungar, 1986.

Melville

Arvin, Newton. *Herman Melville.* Westport, CT: Greenwood, 1972.

Bender, Bert. *Sea-Brothers: The Tradition of American Sea Fiction from* Moby-Dick *to the Present.* Philadelphia: University of Pennsylvania Press, 1987.

Bickman, Martin, ed. *Approaches to Teaching Melville's* Moby-Dick. New York: Modern Language Association of America, 1985.

Bloom, Harold, ed. *Herman Melville's* Moby-Dick. New York: Chelsea, 1986.

Bloom, Harold, ed. *Ahab.* New York: Chelsea, 1991.

Brodhead, Richard H., ed. *New Essays on* Moby-Dick. London: Cambridge University Press, 1986.

Bryant, John, ed. *A Companion to Melville Studies.* Westport, CT: Greenwood, 1986.

Cesarino, Cesare. *Modernity at Sea: Melville, Marx, Conrad in Crisis.* Minneapolis: University of Minnesota Press, 2002.

Gilmore, Michael T. *Twentieth Century Interpretations of* Moby-Dick: *A Collection of Critical Essays.* Englewood Cliffs, NJ: Prentice-Hall, 1977.

Gretchko, John M. J. *Melvillean Loomings: Essays on* Moby-Dick. Cleveland: Falk & Bright, 1992.

Grobman, Neil R. "The Tall Tale: Telling Events in Melville's *Moby-Dick.*" *Journal of the Folklore Institute* 12 (1975): 19–27.

Gunn, Giles, ed. *A Historical Guide to Herman Melville.* New York: Oxford University Press, 2005.

Herbert, T. Walter, Jr. *Moby-Dick and Calvinism: A World Dismantled.* New Brunswick, NJ: Rutgers University Press, 1977.

Higgins, Brian, and Hershel Parker, eds. *Critical Essays on Herman Melville's* Moby-Dick. New York: Hall, 1992.

Irey, Eugene F. ed. *A Concordance to Herman Melville's* Moby-Dick. New York: Garland, 1982.

McSweeney, Kerry. *Moby-Dick: Ishmael's Book.* Boston: Twayne, 1986.

Miller, Edward Haviland. *Melville: A Biography.* New York: Braziller, 1975.

Parker, Hershel, et al. *Moby-Dick as Doubloon: Essays and Extracts (1851–1970).* New York: Norton, 1970.

Peretz, Eyal. *Literature, Disaster & the Enigma of Power: A Reading of 'Moby Dick'.* Stanford, CA: Stanford University Press, 2003.

Robertson-Lorant, Laurie. *Melville: A Biography.* New York: Clarkson Potter, 1996.

Selby, Nick, ed. *Herman Melville: Moby-Dick.* New York: Columbia University Press, 1998.

Sten, Christopher. *Sounding the Whale: Moby Dick as Epic Novel*. Kent, OH: Kent State University Press, 1996.

Van Cromphout, Gustaaf. "*Moby-Dick:* The Transformation of the Faustian Ethos." *American Literature* 51.1 (1979): 17–32.

Weiner, Susan. "Melville at the Movies: New Images of *Moby-Dick*." *Journal of American Culture* 16.2 (1993): 85–90.

Poe

Allison, John. "Coleridgean Self-Development: Entrapment and Incest in 'The Fall of the House of Usher.'" *South Central Review* 5.1 (1988): 40–47.

Benton, Richard P. "Poe's 'The Cask' and the 'White Webwork Which Gleams.'" *Studies in Short Fiction* 28.2 (1991): 183–94.

Burduck, Michael L. *Grim Phantasms: Fear in Poe's Short Fiction*. New York: Garland, 1992.

Cassuto, Leonard. "The Coy Reaper: Unmasque-ing the Red Death." *Studies in Short Fiction* 25.3 (1988): 317–20.

Dayan, Joan. "From Romance to Modernity: Poe and the Work of Poetry." *Studies in Romanticism* 29.3 (1990): 413–37.

Dudley, David R. "Dead or Alive: The Booby-Trapped Narrator of Poe's 'Masque of the Red Death.'" *Studies in Short Fiction* 30.2 (1993): 169–73.

Evans, Walter. "'The Fall of the House of Usher' and Poe's Theory of the Tale." *Studies in Short Fiction* 14 (1977): 137–44.

Fisher, Benjamin Franklin, IV, ed. *Poe and His Times: The Artist and His Milieu*. Baltimore: Edgar Allan Poe Society, 1990.

Freedman, William. *The Porous Sanctuary: Art and Anxiety in Poe's Short Fiction*. New York: Peter Lang, 2002.

Gargano, James W. "The Theme of Time in 'The Tell-Tale Heart.'" *Studies in Short Fiction* 5 (1968): 378–82.

Gargano, James W. "'The Cask of Amontillado': A Masquerade of Motive and Identity." *Studies in Short Fiction* 4 (1967): 119–26.

Gruesser, John C. "Madmen and Moonbeams: The Narrator in 'The Fall of the House of Usher.'" *Edgar Allan Poe Review* 5.1 (2004): 80–90.

Hayes, Kevin J., ed. *The Cambridge Companion to Edgar Allan Poe*. Cambridge, Eng.: Cambridge University Press, 2002.

Hoffman, Daniel. *Poe Poe Poe Poe Poe Poe Poe*. New York: Paragon House, 1972.

Johnson, Christy Price. "Sublime Terror in Edgar Allan Poe's 'The Raven.'" *Tennessee Philological Bulletin* 34 (1997): 43–52.

Kennedy, J. Gerald, ed. *A Historical Guide to Edgar Allan Poe*. Oxford, Eng. Oxford University Press, 2001.

May, Charles E. *Edgar Allan Poe: A Study of the Short Fiction*. Boston: Twayne, 1991.

May, Leila S. "'Sympathies of a Scarcely Intelligible Nature': The Brother-Sister Bond in Poe's 'Fall of the House of Usher.'" *Studies in Short Fiction* 30.3 (1993): 387–96.

Obuchowski, Peter. "Unity of Effect in Poe's 'The Fall of the House of Usher.'" *Studies in Short Fiction* 12 (1975): 407–12.

Peeples, Scott. *Edgar Allan Poe Revisited.* New York: Twayne, 1998.

Person, Leland S., Jr. "Poe's Composition of Philosophy: Reading and Writing 'The Raven.'" *Arizona Quarterly* 46.3 (1990): 1–15.

Rosenheim, Shawn, and Stephen Rachman, eds. *The American Face of Edgar Allan Poe.* Baltimore: Johns Hopkins University Press, 1995.

Silverman, Kenneth, ed. *New Essays on Poe's Major Tales.* Cambridge, Eng.: Cambridge University Press, 1993.

Smith, Dave. "Edgar Allan Poe and the Nightmare Ode." *Southern Humanities Review* 29.1 (1995): 1–10.

St. Armand, Barton Levi. "Poe's Emblematic Raven: A Pictorial Approach." *ESQ: A Journal of the American Renaissance* 22 (1976): 191–210.

Stepp, Walter. "The Ironic Double in Poe's 'The Cask of Amontillado.'" *Studies in Short Fiction* 13 (1976): 447–53.

Timmerman, John H. "House of Mirrors: Edgar Allan Poe's 'The Fall of the House of Usher.'" *Papers on Language and Literature* 39.3 (2003): 227–44.

Tombleson, Gary E. "Poe's 'The Fall of the House of Usher' as Archetypal Gothic: Literary and Architectural Analogs of Cosmic Unity." *Nineteenth-Century Contexts* 12.2 (1988): 83–106.

Voloshin, Beverly R. "Explanation in 'The Fall of the House of Usher.'" *Studies in Short Fiction* 23.4 (1986): 419–428.

White, Patrick. "'The Cask of Amontillado': A Case for the Defense." *Studies in Short Fiction* 26.4 (1989): 550–55.

Stowe

Ammons, Elizabeth, and Susan Belasco, eds. *Approaches to Teaching Stowe's Uncle Tom's Cabin.* New York: Modern Language Association of America, 2000.

Duvall, John N. "Authentic Ghost Stories: *Uncle Tom's Cabin, Absalom, Absalom!,* and *Beloved.*" *Faulkner Journal* 4.1–2 (1988–1989): 83–97.

Fick, Thomas H. "Authentic Ghosts and Real Bodies: Negotiating Power in Nineteenth-Century Women's Ghost Stories." *South Atlantic Review* 64.2 (1999): 81–97.

Fluck, Winfried. "The Power and Failure of Representation in Harriet Beecher Stowe's *Uncle Tom's Cabin.*" *New Literary History* 23.2 (1992): 319–38.

Gallagher, Noelle. "The Bagging Factory and the Breakfast Factory: Industrial Labor and Sentimentality in Harriet Beecher Stowe's *Uncle Tom's Cabin.*" *Nineteenth-Century Contexts* 27.2 (2005): 167–87.

Hedrick, Joan. *Harriet Beecher Stowe: A Life.* New York: Oxford University Press, 1994.

Lewis, Gladys Sherman. *Message, Messenger, and Response: Puritan Forms and Cultural Reformation in Harriet Beecher Stowe's Uncle Tom's Cabin.* Lanham, MD: University Press of America, 1994.

Lowance, Mason I., Jr. et al., eds. *The Stowe Debate: Rhetorical Strategies in Uncle Tom's Cabin*. Amherst: University of Massachusetts Press, 1994.

Rugoff, Milton. *The Beechers*. New York: Harper and Row, 1981.

Ryan, Susan M. *The Grammar of Good Intentions: Race & the Antebellum Culture of Benevolence*. Ithaca, NY: Cornell University Press, 2003.

Sundquist, Eric J., ed. *New Essays on Uncle Tom's Cabin*. Cambridge, Eng.: Cambridge University Press, 1986.

Wallace, Michelle. "The Celluloid Cabin: Satirical Distortions of Uncle Tom in Animated Cartoon Shorts, 1932–1947." *Studies in Popular Culture* 23.3 (2001): 1–10.

Watson, Reginald. "The Mulatto as Race Leader in Stowe's Uncle Tom's Cabin." *MAWA Review* 18.1–2 (2003): 57–71.

Thoreau

Ackland, Michael. "Thoreau's *Walden*: In Praise of Mental Perception." *American Transcendental Quarterly* 49 (1981): 35–71.

Allen, Thomas. "Clockwork Nation: Modern Time, Moral Perfectionism and American Identity in Catharine Beecher and Henry Thoreau." *Journal of American Studies* 39.1 (2005): 63–86.

Bloom, Harold, ed. *Henry David Thoreau's Walden*. New York: Chelsea, 1987.

Boone, Joseph Allen. "Delving and Diving for Truth: Breaking through to Bottom in Thoreau's *Walden*." *ESQ: A Journal of the American Renaissance* 27.3 (1981): 135–146.

Buell, Lawrence. *The Environmental Imagination: Thoreau, Nature Writing and the Formation of American Culture*. Cambridge, MA: Harvard University Press, 1995.

Dolis, John. "Thoreau's *Walden*: Intimate Space and the Economy of Being." *Consumable Goods*. Ed. David K. Vaughn. Orono: University of Maine Press, 1987, 185–193.

Harding, Walter. *The Days of Henry Thoreau*. Princeton: Princeton University Press, 1992.

Lyon, Thomas J., ed. *This Incomperable Lande: A Book of American Nature Writing*. Boston: Houghton Mifflin, 1989.

Marshall, Ian. "Thoreau's *Walden* Odyssey." *American Transcendental Quarterly* 59 (1986): 53–62.

McIlroy, Gary. "Pilgrim at Tinker Creek and the Social Legacy of *Walden*." *Earthly Words: Essays on Contemporary American Nature and Environmental Writers*. Ed. John Cooley. Ann Arbor: University of Michigan Press, 1994, 87–104.

Melley, Timothy. "Performing Experiments: Materiality and Rhetoric in Thoreau's *Walden*." *ESQ: A Journal of the American Renaissance* 39.4 (1993): 253–77.

Myerson, Joel, ed. *The Cambridge Companion to Henry David Thoreau*. Cambridge, Eng.: Cambridge University Press, 1995.

Myerson, Joel, ed. *Critical Essays on Henry David Thoreau's Walden*. Boston: Hall, 1988.

Packer, Barbara. "Turning to Emerson." *Common Knowledge* 5.2 (1996): 51–60.

Schneider, Richard J., ed. *Approaches to Teaching Thoreau's* Walden *and Other Works*. New York: Modern Language Association of America, 1996.

Schneider, Richard J. *Henry David Thoreau*. Boston: Twayne, 1987.

Schneider, Richard J. "Walden." *The Cambridge Companion to Henry David Thoreau*. Ed. Joel Myerson. Cambridge, Eng.: Cambridge University Press, 92–106.

Schueller, Malini. "Carnival Rhetoric and Extra-Vagance in Thoreau's *Walden*." *American Literature* 58.1 (1986): 33–45.

Shwartz, Ronald B. "Private Discourse in Thoreau's *Walden*." *South Carolina Review* 13.1 (1980): 63–70.

Strong, David. "The Significance of the Loss of Things: Walden Pond as 'Thing.'" *Soundings: An Interdisciplinary Journal* 75.1 (1992): 147–74.

Wider, Sarah Ann. "'And What Became of Your Philosophy Then?': Women Reading *Walden*." *Nineteenth-Century Prose* 31.2 (2004): 152–71, 266–67.

Whitman

Allen, Gay Wilson. *The New Walt Whitman Handbook*. New York: New York University Press, 1975.

Allen, Gay Wilson, and Ed Folsom, eds. *Walt Whitman and the World*. Iowa City: University of Iowa Press, 1995.

Aspiz, Harold. *So Long! Walt Whitman's Poetry of Death*. Tuscaloosa: University of Alabama Press, 2004.

Asselineau, Roger. *The Evolution of Walt Whitman*. Iowa City: University of Iowa Press, 1999.

Asselineau, Roger. *The Transcendentalist Constant in American Literature*. New York: New York University Press, 1980.

Beach, Christopher. *The Politics of Distinction: Whitman and the Discourses of Nineteenth-Century America*. Athens: University of Georgia Press, 1996.

Bellis, Peter J. *Writing Revolution: Aesthetics and Politics in Hawthorne, Whitman, and Thoreau*. Athens: University of Georgia Press, 2003.

Birmingham, William. "Whitman's Song of the Possible American Self." *Cross Currents* 43.3 (1993): 341–57.

Bloom, Harold, ed. *Walt Whitman*. New York: Chelsea, 1985.

DeLancey, Mark. "Texts, Interpretations, and Whitman's 'Song of Myself.'" *American Literature* 61.3 (1989): 359–81.

Erkkila, Betsy. *Whitman the Political Poet*. Oxford, Eng.: Oxford University Press, 1989.

Erkkila, Betsy, and Jay Grossman, eds. *Breaking Bounds: Whitman and American Cultural Studies*. New York: Oxford University Press, 1996.

Gardner, Thomas. *Discovering Ourselves in Whitman: The Contemporary American Long Poem*. Urbana: University of Illinois Press, 1989.

Greenspan, Ezra. "Some Remarks on the Poetics of 'Participle-Loving' Whitman." In *The Cambridge Companion to Walt Whitman*. Ed. Ezra Greenspan. Cambridge, Eng.: Cambridge University Press, 1995, 92–109.

Killingsworth, M. Jimmie. The *Growth of Leaves of Grass: The Organic Tradition in Whitman Studies*. Columbia, SC: Camden House, 1993.

LeMaster, J. R., and Donald D. Kummings, eds. *Walt Whitman: An Encyclopedia*. New York: Garland, 1998.

Loving, Jerome. *Walt Whitman: The Song of Himself*. Berkeley: University of California Press, 1999.

Mack, Stephen John. *The Pragmatic Whitman: Reimagining American Democracy*. Iowa City: University of Iowa Press, 2002.

Maslan, Mark. *Whitman Possessed: Poetry, Sexuality, and Popular Authority*. Baltimore: Johns Hopkins University Press, 2001.

Miller, Edwin Haviland. *Walt Whitman's "Song of Myself": A Mosaic of Interpretations*. Iowa City: University of Iowa Press, 1989.

Miller, James E., Jr. *Walt Whitman*. Boston: Twayne, 1990.

Nathanson, Tenney. *Whitman's Presence: Body, Voice, and Writing in* Leaves of Grass. New York: New York University Press, 1992.

Pannapacker, William. *Revised Lives: Walt Whitman and Nineteenth-Century Authorship*. New York: Routledge, 2004.

Price, Kenneth M., ed. *Walt Whitman: The Contemporary Reviews*. Cambridge, Eng.: Cambridge University Press, 1996.

Price, Kenneth M. *Whitman and Tradition: The Poet in His Century*. New Haven, CT: Yale University Press, 1990.

Reynolds, David S. *Walt Whitman's America: A Cultural Biography*. New York: Knopf, 1995.

Reynolds, David S., ed. *A Historical Guide to Walt Whitman*. New York: Oxford University Press, 2000.

Salska, Agnieszka. *Walt Whitman and Emily Dickinson: Poetry of the Central Consciousness*. Philadelphia: University of Pennsylvania Press, 1985.

Schwiebert, John E. *The Frailest Leaves: Whitman's Poetic Technique and Style in the Short Poem*. New York: Peter Lang, 1992.

Vendler, Helen. *Poets Thinking: Pope, Whitman, Dickinson, Yeats*. Cambridge, MA: Harvard University Press, 2004.

Warren, James Perrin. "'The Free Growth of Metrical Laws': Syntactic Parallelism in 'Song of Myself.'" *Style* 18.1 (1984): 27–42.

Woodress, James, ed. *Critical Essays on Walt Whitman*. Boston: Hall, 1983.

Index

About the Author

MELISSA McFARLAND PENNELL is Professor of English at University of
Massachusetts, Lowell.